Praise for *Listen*

"*Listening to the Heart* takes us on a liberating journey. Kittisaro and Thanissara inspire us with their personal stories of struggle and insight and share their deeply lived understanding of the Buddha's teaching. A beautiful book."

—JOSEPH GOLDSTEIN, author of *Mindfulness*

"Genuine and insightful, *Listening to the Heart* is both a memoir and a clear guide to authentic practice. Kittisaro and Thanissara unfold the layers of their experience to share their understanding, from deep inner processes to vital social and relational aspects of living a good life."

—SHARON SALZBERG, author of *Lovingkindness and Real Happiness*

"This is a wonderful and profound book, deeply researched, written with illuminated elegance; it challenges us all both to deepen our sacred practice and to act for compassion in the world."

—ANDREW HARVEY, founder of the Institute for Sacred Activism and author of *The Hope*

"This book is luminous in clarity and depth. Let these teachings turn you toward the jewel of your own awakening heart."

—TARA BRACH, PhD, author of *Radical Acceptance* and *True Refuge*

"From Oxford to Thailand to South Africa, from monastery to frontline work in the crying heart of Zulu country, Thanissara and Kittisaro share their amazing journey. Written with honesty, courage, and deep wisdom, *Listening to the Heart* shows how to free the mind and open the heart. Even more, the deep caring and love that permeate the pages inspire the reader to want to make a difference in the world—and the book provides the map to do it. Highly recommended."

—JAMES BARAZ, cofounder of Spirit Rock Insight Meditation Center and coauthor of *Awakening Joy*

"Thanissara and Kittisaro are the embodiment of Buddhist wisdom. Their teachings are clear, simple, elegant, and profound. They have a way of cutting through jargon and reaching the truth without resorting to dogma. We are blessed to have two such teachers among us."

—SATISH KUMAR, editor in chief of *Resurgence & Ecologist* magazine

"I'm not sure there is anyone who can strip away our naive illusions about the spiritual life as deftly and elegantly as Thanissara and Kittisaro. As we witness their sacred pilgrimage unfolding, we are awakened to the timeless noble truths of our precious human condition and set free."

—SHARDA ROGELL, guiding teacher at Spirit Rock Insight Meditation Center and author of *Pressing Out Pure Honey*

"*Listening to the Heart* is three books in one. It is a guide to deep understanding of Buddhist dharma, an explanation of psychological growth, and a love story.... It is a joy to read and filled with profound wisdom.""

—PHILLIP MOFFITT, author of *Emotional Chaos to Clarity* and *Dancing With Life*

Listening to the Heart

A Contemplative Journey to Engaged Buddhism

Kittisaro and Thanissara

North Atlantic Books
Berkeley, California

Published by
North Atlantic Books.
P.O. Box 12327
Berkeley, California 94712

Cover photo © iStockphoto.com/Shrekton
Cover and book design by Mary Ann Casler
Printed in the United States of America

Listening to the Heart: A Contemplative Journey to Engaged Buddhism is sponsored and published by the Society for the Study of Native Arts and Sciences (dba North Atlantic Books), an educational nonprofit based in Berkeley, California, that collaborates with partners to develop cross-cultural perspectives, nurture holistic views of art, science, the humanities, and healing, and seed personal and global transformation by publishing work on the relationship of body, spirit, and nature.

North Atlantic Books' publications are available through most bookstores. For further information, visit our website at www.northatlanticbooks.com or call 800-733-3000.

Library of Congress Cataloging-in-Publication Data
Kittisaro, author.
Listening to the heart : a contemplative journey to engaged Buddhism / Kittisaro and Thanissara.
pages cm
Includes bibliographical references.
ISBN 978-1-58394-839-2 (paperback) — ISBN 978-1-58394-840-8 (e-book)
1. Spiritual life—Buddhism. 2. Meditation—Buddhism. I. Thanissara, 1956– II. Title.
BQ5660.K58 2014
294.3'444--dc23 2014021828

2 3 4 5 6 7 8 9 SHERIDAN 19 18 17 16 15 14

Printed on recycled paper

To our parents,
for the precious gift of life

Contents

Preface

Enlightenment is intimacy with all things.

–Zen master Dogen

This book invites you to join us on a contemplative journey. Although it feels like we're going somewhere, in the paradoxical path of awakening we're learning to be more fully here, now. Though it sounds simple, this is not so easy to do. Lost in the dream of getting to the place we think we need to be, we generate all sorts of problems for ourselves and others. The poignant irony of our endless seeking is that what we are looking for is already here within the heart. When we stop, even for a moment, we taste peace. This is the taste of the Dharma.

The intention of this book is to share the paradoxical journey of being present. Sharing connects us with the mystery of life. Imagine sitting with a group of friends around a log fire under a night sky where a burst of stars shine like diamonds. As stories flow, the quality of listening deepens. Listening to the spoken words emerging from the silence connects us to the heart. The heart fathoms and meaning is found. Contemplation is the art of deep listening; it enables discovery.

Since 1992 we have lived, practiced, and taught the Dharma together. The layout of this book alternates our different voices, one chapter after another, in which we explore the awakening process as it threads through our lives. Similar to the Buddha and his teaching style, we return to core themes repeatedly, in order to deepen their meaning.

Through these pages, reflections, and stories, we meet as writer and reader. The deeper invitation of this book, however, is to stay with that inner quietness that listens, reflects, discerns, and distills insight. This contemplative process, what Ajahn Chah called "reading the book of the heart," is the way of peace, the road home. The words are simply an invitation to listen into the heart. As we listen, we hear the stillness and silence of the unmoving.

We also hear the world. These are uncertain times. So many structures and certainties are breaking apart. At any time a tsunami, hurricane, or earthquake can devastate, or the financial institutions of an entire country can collapse. Change is happening at such an immense pace, it's hard to have any idea of where we are headed. Our experience of time and distance is ever-shrinking as the Internet moves us into warp speed. Every day a flood of information makes "out there" more obviously "right here." As the consequences of actions rebound ever more quickly, it's as if there is no distance between thought and what it materializes. Everything is immediate. We live in increasingly virtual realities, and at the same time are confronted with the likelihood of no sustainable Earth for future generations. For many species, it is already too late.

Life has always been intensely challenging on planet Earth, but it's hard to imagine another time when the stakes were so high. We may feel anguished by what's happening, but what's happening is happening. None of this is outside the Dharma. The intensity of our times is pushing, squeezing, and pummeling us. The image that comes to mind is of a birth canal. It is as if we are being born into a different way of understanding everything. We are being called to be midwives of consciousness as it evolves out of a dualistic perspective.

We are awakening into an awareness that knows no ultimate separations. There is no *other* that is *out there.* We can talk about differences, such as national, geographical, and relational boundaries. However, consciousness, when it is aware of its own nature, knows itself as everything. It is reader and writer, the stars in the ink-black night and the one looking at those stars. As we realize this, we are drawn into intimacy with all life.

Yet we all experience a separate sense of self. The journey of the personal self is one of great struggle. At first, contemplative practice highlights the sense of self caught in its own fears, projections, and desires. We encounter the complex territories that are pertinent to awakening, the wounds that need to be healed. Finally, we see our true nature as both empty and yet interconnected with everything else, which is freeing and deeply nourishing. If we rush to this insight, and prematurely bypass our personal difficulties and negative emotions, we become split and disassociated rather than integrated and embodied.

The Dharma guides us through these territories. Aligning with the Dharma, we listen. We listen into the unmoving *suchness* here and now, and we listen into all that is unfolding, to every dimension of our being. We listen to the dying of a world we have known: every day new species gone forever, the terror and anguish of it. We listen to the crazy voices that advocate the extremes. We listen to our struggle at the cusp of scary and amazing times. We listen for an appropriate response. And we listen into the one who is listening. We hear it all. We hear our one true unfathomable, mysterious heart, and in doing so find an undying refuge. We find our way home.

Kittisaro and Thanissara
Chattanooga, Tennessee

CHAPTER ONE

An Invitation

Kittisaro

Buddhism is a religion of the heart. Only this. One who practices to develop the heart is one who practices Buddhism.

–Ajahn Chah

On any journey it is useful to have a map. If we have a good map, we won't get lost. We can orient ourselves as we traverse the territory. It is important, however, to distinguish between a map and the territory it depicts. A map lays out a landscape, but is not the actual ground, or the journey.

Essentially, Buddhism is a map. In this case, the journey is a pilgrimage to our true nature, to the place of safety and peace. Although it is nice to honor and appreciate the map, do we also use it to make our way to the destination? Or do we end up worshipping the map, longing to be somewhere else, or imagining that we have already arrived? While Buddhist teaching points to the way of awakening, it is not awakening itself. The goal of peace and freedom from suffering is not an external religious structure or a system of rituals and beliefs. It is a living realization within the heart, this heart that is aware here and now.

Not understanding this principle is the bane of religion. Religious doctrines, practices, and views are ultimately frameworks for helping people return to a state of true happiness. When we as spiritual practitioners lose sight of the essential purpose of religion, then the religious form itself becomes the main thing, and we end up falling short of our goal. It would be like bowing to the map and neglecting to utilize it for our journey home, or worshipping the key and forgetting to pick it up and unlock the door so we can free ourselves.

In a similar vein, the Buddha compared his teachings to a raft. If you're on the dangerous side of a river, where it's treacherous, and you want to go to the farther shore, where it's safe, you can gather some sticks and twigs to construct a raft, working with what is available around you. By applying effort, you can use that raft to cross over to safety. Having arrived, you don't need to carry it around on your head. You can use it, and then put it down for others. The Buddha, through this example and others, clarified that religious teachings are skillful means and not ends in themselves.

When the Buddha was asked what he taught, he often replied, "I teach just two things: suffering and the ending of suffering." The fruit of our efforts in spiritual practice is the arrival. We should regularly ask ourselves, "Does this activity take me where I want to go?" We might learn all the details of the map, but without application we are still no freer than when we started.

It's great if we become a super cool meditator, have a PhD in Buddhist philosophy, and get recognized as a famous teacher, or highly renowned monk or nun, but if the heart isn't free from suffering—or at least moving in that direction—we may have missed the point. In other words, we need to reflect on the results. What are the effects of spiritual practices in my life? Are wholesome qualities of the heart increasing—like generosity, kindness, and wisdom? Are unwholesome ones—greed, hatred, and delusion—decreasing? This is an important principle that the Buddha emphasized.

After his awakening, the Buddha was moved by compassion to share his insight for the welfare of others. He wondered, "Who will understand what I have realized?" He remembered the five ascetics, former colleagues in austere spiritual striving, who abandoned him when they thought he was giving up the true path. His failing, in their eyes, was eating a nourishing meal received from the hands of a young maiden. "They'll understand," he thought. The five ascetics became his first students. In his first discourse to them, he described four truths of existence that he called the Four Noble Truths.

The Buddha condensed his understanding into the simple and clear map of the Four Noble Truths: there is suffering; a cause of suffering; an end of suffering; and a path that leads to the end of suffering. Each of these truths is accompanied by a call to action. According to the Buddha, suffering needs to be "understood," the cause of suffering needs to be "abandoned," the ending of suffering is to be "realized," and the path leading to the cessation of suffering should be "cultivated." These truths are dynamic guidelines for skillful responses to the various circumstances of life. Perhaps it would be more accurate to call them the Four Ennobling Truths, for they guide us inward, to our truly wise and compassionate heart. They map the human journey from suffering to its cessation. They encompass a teaching that clearly reveals the way to the complete ending of distress. This is the ancient human pilgrimage from darkness to light, from being lost and endlessly wandering to finding our way home.

The essence of these teachings is the universal experience of suffering and the possibility of ending suffering. The Buddha realized that suffering arises from grasping, and non-suffering is revealed when there is letting go. Consciously allowing things to come and go as they are, we can recognize the true nature of every "thing," and see the impermanent characteristic of all that we take to be *me, mine,* and *the world.*

The first disciple who awakened during this teaching was Kondanna. It is said that at that moment Kondanna "entered the stream" and was irreversibly flowing toward full awakening, for he had tasted deep peace—nirvana or *nibbana*—and directly recognized in his own heart "that which never dies." He became known as Anna Kondanna, which means

"Kondanna Who Knows," or the one who has "profound knowing." The Buddha called this knowledge "opening the eye of Dharma."

What does Kondanna know and what is the nature of his realization? At the end of the discourse the Buddha declared, "Kondanna knows. He knows what arises, ceases." That might not sound spectacular. On an intellectual level we all know everything is impermanent. We know, for example, that it was morning and now it is evening; or that we were once a child and now we are older. We understand conceptually that everything is changing, even the stars and this great earth, but do we perceive impermanence in a profound and immediate way? Until we understand our false assumptions about reality, that we are attributing all sorts of solidity and stability where there isn't any, we won't experience the underlying peacefulness inherent in the heart. When we see clearly the ever-changing nature of all conditioned phenomena—including our thoughts, feelings, and perceptions of self and other—the futility of grasping for certainty becomes obvious. In letting go, we know freedom. Taking the insight of impermanence to heart will have a revolutionary impact on our life, just as it did on Kondanna.

The First Noble Truth states, "There is suffering." The experience of stress and limitation is central to our human condition. In Buddhist language this is called *dukkha*. It is an experience that everyone encounters. As the Buddha defined it, *dukkha* includes the pain of birth, old age, sickness, death, being with what we don't like, being parted from the loved, and not getting what we want. All these experiences are hard to bear. In summing up, he said, the focuses of the grasping mind are *dukkha*. This points to the suffering generated by our lack of understanding, the *dukkha* of ignorance.

Dukkha also means "not dependable" or "unsatisfactory." In this sense, we can see how pleasure is also *dukkha*, for it does not last. We can't rely on that which is inherently unstable and subject to the laws of impermanence. To do so generates anxiety, stress, and the wavering of heart that is called birth and death.[1] Even success, fame, praise, and happiness are transient experiences, and therefore unable to truly satisfy us. In brief, the mantra of *dukkha* is "It's not good enough."

In my youth I experienced a lot of *dukkha,* but I didn't know how to articulate it. Before I had any spiritual awakening my whole reality was focused on cultivating a successful self. I came from a very competitive family. We were all highly motivated to do the best we could. I grew up in Chattanooga, Tennessee, a city intensely interested in wrestling in those days. We even had a wrestling mat at home so I could practice every day, and my two brothers and I comprised a quarter of the wrestling team. For years I trained rigorously—running, climbing ropes, sometimes walking on my hands for fifty or a hundred yards, even doing five hundred push-ups a day before big tournaments. I had a lot of success. I was five-time Mid-South Champion, which might not be a big deal in the wider world, but it was for me as a high school student in Chattanooga. When I was seventeen, I won the National Invitational Tournament for Prep Schools. I was also first in my class academically for many years. I wanted to be a winner in everything I did.

I was aiming for success and afraid of failure. I believed that with all my hard work I could finally achieve "success," and arrive at a happiness that would last. When I flew up to Pennsylvania and won the National Prep Tournament, I had my first glimmer of insight into my distorted view. After I won the final match, the fulfillment of a childhood dream and years of hard work, the referee raised my hand up in victory. "Yes!!!" What an ecstatic moment, amid the cheers of our team. But how long does a hand stay up in victory? Within minutes of the awards ceremony, I found myself anxiously scanning the group of champions and wondering, "Who will I have to beat next year to defend my title?"

Already the next task was looming, and with it a disquieting anxiety. That incident gave me a glimpse of just how driven I was, and the elusive nature of my goal. What is success? Who am I really? Eventually I ended up getting hurt and had four screws put in my shoulder. I changed my wrestling style only to get the other shoulder hurt, effectively ending my sports career.

Academics, however, presented another forum for success. At Princeton University I was taking premedical courses, aiming to eventually become a doctor. I excelled in my studies, became Phi Beta Kappa, and won a Rhodes scholarship to Worcester College, Oxford. A big part of my mentality remained focused on trying to be the best, habitually comparing myself to others, and always striving to improve. I still felt that if I just kept going, I'd "make it." No matter how many successes I had, however, I never learned how to enjoy them. My perpetual aim for success was becoming highly problematic.

My loving mother and father were always looking for ways to enrich their children's lives. They offered us music lessons, sent us to good schools, encouraged us in our studies, and were totally supportive. They went to every single wrestling match we ever had; my mother took pictures and kept scrapbooks of all of our accomplishments. I'd open up my scrapbook and think, "Oh, yeah, that's pretty good. I'm a valedictorian, a National Champion. I'm a Rhodes Scholar." Then I would close the scrapbook, and the feeling would evaporate.

By the time I got to Oxford I was twenty-four, but I felt a hundred and four years old! I was exhausted. I could go home and look at the scrapbooks, see the trophies my parents kept on the shelves, or read about the accomplishments, but inside I was weary of nothing ever being quite enough, of being so dependent on external acknowledgement. I was suffering, but I had not yet heard of the Four Noble Truths.

Eventually the extreme imbalance of my world demanded attention. I felt a deep and urgent need to listen inwardly. I found myself leaving the halls of Oxford to sit in quiet places. I would slip out of the university and meditate in old stone churches in the English countryside, when no one else was there. I'd close my eyes and listen to the ringing silence, and tune into the ancient resonance echoing in the gray stones, of a search for something beyond this endlessly achieving world. Something was screaming within me, "Stop . . . and listen."

Around this time the porter at my Oxford college made a seemingly insignificant comment that ended up changing the course of my life. The porter's job is to let people in and out of the college gate and filter visitors. Oxford colleges are little worlds unto themselves, hidden behind imposing walls. Access to these hallowed domains is monitored by the porter, who directs people to where they need to go. The porter and I were friends and used to talk about all sorts of things. One evening he told me there were some Buddhist monks visiting nearby. Something in that snippet of information intrigued me. I went to visit the monks and heard them chanting. In the droning melody, I felt a long lost familiarity, like an old forgotten friend.

Pretty soon I found myself on my first ten-day meditation retreat. Basically, it was hell. I had never before stopped my life for any sustained length of time. I was asked to sit in periods of meditation from four in the morning until nine at night, and do nothing else for ten days. I constantly squirmed, trying to change my sitting posture. I was desperately uncomfortable. What's more, I couldn't speak or distract myself. The only instruction I actually understood (the Burmese monk couldn't speak English, and I certainly couldn't speak Burmese) was, "Watch your breath. Observe the sensations." Then one morning, on about day four, during a break, I experienced a moment where I was simply present, not looking ahead to the next important or interesting thing.

I was standing in front of an ordinary bush in the garden shrubbery. It was dawn and the rising sun reflected in the dewdrops on the leaves, making them look like a thousand jewels. I was timelessly content to just look and be. In that simple moment, I was filled with joy and a deep sense of fulfillment. I felt awe at the simple beauty of the shimmering dew as it reflected in the light. I was at ease, just standing, being awake and aware.

In those days as an Oxford student I was always going somewhere or getting something, and I certainly did not blissfully hang around bushes! Yet you could say this bush, this ordinary shrub, was my first spiritual teacher. The moments spent enjoying it seemed so long and precious. This was a wondrous revelation: inherent in the most ordinary moment was the possibility of beauty, peace, ease, and joy. The experience was delicious and filled me up. Although only a beginner at meditation, I could see that this training of attention was powerful. I was hooked.

Even though I had a taste of the power of presence on that first meditation retreat, it was relatively fleeting. Although I did feel I was developing some skill in meditation, I knew I needed to find a teacher, someone who knew the territory and could guide me so that I would be more able to access this place of calm and inner clarity. And right on cue, the mysterious synchronicity of the universe responded to my longing.

A travelling American psychiatrist named Dr. Douglas Burns was visiting the Buddhist center at the time of my retreat. He told the managers of the retreat he was looking for a place to stay in Oxford. Being a Buddhist scholar of sorts, he wanted to discuss his paper on the origin of thought with some Oxford professors. The managers knew I was a student at the university, so after the retreat they introduced us. He asked if he could stay with me for a few days, and I said, "Sure, no problem."

Back in my flat on Beaumont Street, Dr. Burns and I had the chance to talk for many hours. He lived in Thailand and told me about his different experiences there, and his many wide-ranging interests and adventures. He had dined with the king and queen of Thailand, and walked across the Arctic. He was a pilot, a scientist, a survivalist, and a great explorer. It seemed there was nothing he hadn't done. Dr. Burns was a strong, confident, no-nonsense, unflappable American. And he was very friendly. "Call me Doug," he said.

Doug was also doing research on the effects of meditation on the psyche. He had a passion for investigating Buddhist meditation monasteries and documenting the changes over time in the monks' personalities. He seemed to know about all the different monastic communities in Thailand and their teachers. Having just enthusiastically completed my first meditation retreat, I was all ears. At one point in our conversation, Doug looked at me, leaned forward, and his voice got very quiet. He said, "There's one really special monk, and he's enlightened. His name is Ajahn Chah." It was a powerful moment for me. I had never heard anyone speak with profound reverence like this. Coming from a confident man of the world, the striking change in his demeanor surprised me. He went on to say, "He has a few Westerners with him. There's a senior American monk there called Sumedho, and if he's not enlightened, he's pretty close!" The softly spoken words had a powerful impact on me. Did you ever see in the old movies where some bare-chested man strikes a massive brass gong? *Wonnnggg, wonnngggg.* Wow! That was it. Right then I knew I had to go and meet this wise teacher in the forests of Thailand.

I went to see Sir Edgar Williams, the warden of the Rhodes Trust, to tell him of my idea. I wanted to go to Thailand, study intensively with Ajahn Chah, and then return to Oxford to finish my thesis and complete the scholarship. Expecting disapproval, I was surprised when the warden said my idea sounded fascinating, and he hoped the experience would be enriching and meaningful.

Sir Edgar, however, was a shrewd judge of character. He had been an intelligence specialist in the Second World War and had helped track down Erwin Rommel in the desert. When I told him, "Look, I just want to explore this, I'll be back in a year or two," he disagreed firmly, "No, you won't." I insisted, "Yes, yes, I will." Sir Edgar then said warmly, "Look, Randy, you can come back, and we will keep your scholarship for you for two years. But I don't expect you to return. I can see you have found your vocation." His words were prophetic and kind. "Listen," he continued, "don't look back. You have learned a lot here these two years, have you not? You already have a degree from Princeton. You don't need another degree from Oxford, and it makes no difference to the Rhodes Trust whether you get it. It has always been the Rhodes philosophy that we emphasize the person, not the process." He knew me better than I knew myself, though I didn't understand this at the time.

After I got the leave of absence, I wrote my parents a letter and talked to them on the phone. They had been so thrilled I was at Oxford on a Rhodes scholarship, and upon hearing that I was going to Thailand they were horrified. Why was I throwing my scholarship away? My dad said, "Son, you'll get sick!" As it turned out, he was right.

In a few weeks I wrapped up my affairs at Oxford and was on a plane to Bangkok. When I arrived in Thailand, Doug Burns—my new American friend—agreed to take me to Ajahn Chah's monastery in the northeast and introduce me to the great teacher. I was secretly hoping Ajahn Chah would recognize me and say, "At last you've arrived!" Or perhaps he would tap me on the forehead and I would see blinding light, pass out, and wake up crying with relief, totally clear, happy, and at ease.

When I got to the monastery for the Westerners, I was shocked to meet the monks on alms round. Their shaven heads were like a line of skulls walking along. I felt queasy and uncomfortable. *Never mind,* I told myself, *I'll get used to it.* Doug then took me over to the main monastery to meet Ajahn Chah; as he could speak Thai, he offered to translate for me.

Ajahn Chah was sitting in a wicker chair receiving guests in the open shaded space below his *kuti,* the meditation hut where he lived, which was elevated on stilts to discourage the creepy crawlies. We approached and Dr. Burns bowed three times as a gesture of respect. I watched him and joined in as best I could. We sat on the polished concrete floor around Ajahn Chah, along with a few Thai monks attending to his needs and a group of visitors from the local villages. After a while Ajahn Chah looked at me and asked, "Why did you come?" I mumbled something about seeking enlightenment and balance in my life, but as I spoke my words felt tinny and weak. Doug translated my response.

Ajahn Chah asked me a few additional questions, and I told him I was doing a thesis on "Art, Science, and Mysticism in the Works of Aldous Huxley" at Oxford University. That seemed to amuse him. He asked me what I would do after that. I replied, "I'll go to medical school." He then asked, "And after that?" "I'll become a doctor." "And after that?" I gave a few more tentative answers, and with a twinkling smile he looked at me and picked up the spittoon next to him and ran his fingers round and round the circular rim. *What's he telling me?* I wondered.

He then asked me if I knew how to meditate. Ah, I felt on firmer ground here. After all, I had just completed a ten-day meditation retreat. In my calculations, having had a taste of what it was all about, via the "shimmering bush" experience, I thought I'd be able to crack open the whole enlightenment thing in a year or two. I was feeling pretty confident, and hoping he would notice that I was gifted at meditation and had a lot of potential. I described how I would systematically sweep the attention through different parts of my body, staying in touch with the sensations. Actually, although I didn't mention it to him, I was quite proud that I could sweep the mind down both sides of the body simultaneously. I was hoping he'd see that and be impressed.

Before I had finished, he got off his wicker chair and down onto the floor on all fours, and started sniffing around like a dog. I couldn't believe it. Meanwhile he was speaking in Thai, and everyone was laughing hysterically—the monks, the villagers, and Doug. With my renowned Piscean intuition, I could tell Ajahn Chah wasn't impressed with my meditation. Amid all the laughter, in which I participated because it was funny, I whispered to my friend, "Doug, what's he saying?" Finally, when the commotion died down, I got a translation: "Ajahn Chah says you don't need to sniff all over the place like a dog." Ajahn Chah got back on his chair and composed himself, wiping tears of laughter from his eyes. With a warm and loving smile he looked at me and said, "You don't need to look at so many things. One is enough." Pointing to his nose, he continued, "Observe your breathing here at the nostrils. When you know one thing well, you'll understand everything. If you try to look at everything and change the object of investigation all the time, you might end up not knowing anything thoroughly. Go and live with Sumedho and let him teach you how to be a monk."[2]

In my heart I felt warm, received, and accepted, curious as it might sound after that unorthodox introduction. How ironic to be pointed back to my nose. I'd spent my whole life ashamed of my nose, feeling I was ugly. One of my high school teachers used to kid me in class, "Son, you've got a nose like the keel of a ship." My nose was not my romantic idea of "the royal road to enlightenment"! Well, I had met the master and he'd certainly gotten my attention. His invitation to learn how to be a monk was very attractive. So that's what I did. Ajahn Chah sent me off to practice with Ajahn Sumedho, be with my breathing, and make friends with my nose! I quite gratefully complied.

In learning how to be with my breathing, I had to learn to be present. Everyone at the monastery was taught about the Four Noble Truths in a very practical and down-to-earth way. Ajahn Chah would frequently ask us to inquire, whatever we were doing, "Can you see *dukkha,* do you see the suffering?" In the daily life of a forest monk, I had plenty of opportunities to see *dukkha*. In the monastery for Westerners—Wat Nana Chat—we would get up at three a.m., go to morning chanting and meditation at four, walk for miles on alms round, and eat our one meal a day at about nine a.m. I cultivated patience with the sweltering heat, the ubiquitous mosquitoes, and painful feet that were cracked from walking barefoot.

During the day we would practice sitting and walking meditation, working in the monastery, sweeping the paths in the forest, or drawing water. In the evening there was more chanting and meditation, listening to talks from the Ajahn, and sitting up all night once a week. When that didn't seem to be tough enough, I took on extra practices for periods of time, like not lying down for three months to develop equanimity, patience, and vigor. I was sincere and worked hard. My old competitive pattern and judging mind, however, were still alive and well. I kept thinking I should be making more progress.

The Buddha pointed to an unavoidable reality, that of dissatisfaction, though it can take a while for us to hear the message. To use a wrestling analogy, we often get pinned by suffering, and rather than see it as a wakeup call, we squirm every which way to evade its impact. Many people think the Buddha taught that "life is suffering." That's not true. He said, "There is suffering and an ending of suffering." He realized that actually life is unfolding perfectly according to its own natural laws. At its core it is peaceful and luminous. Habitually wanting this moment to be other than it is, however, causes distress, and we lose sight of our true nature.

Ajahn Munindo,[3] a fellow monk with me in Thailand, tells the story of being in a hospital in Bangkok after having surgery on both his knees. Lying there in bed, looking at a cast on each leg, he was feeling miserable and utterly sorry for himself. How would he be able to sit cross-legged now? All the other monks would be sitting on the floor in neat rows, looking the part, and here he would be sitting in an armchair! It just wasn't fair, it wasn't right, and he desperately wanted it all to be different. When Ajahn Chah came to visit him, Munindo lamented, "It shouldn't be this way!" Ajahn Chah leaned over him and said, "If it shouldn't be this way, it wouldn't be this way!"

Here we begin to enter the contemplation of the Second Noble Truth. Suffering is something that is generated from the mind's inability to accept reality. In other words, *dukkha* is something *we* do. It is not being done to us. The Second Noble Truth states "there is a cause of suffering." The Buddha saw that the cause of suffering is desire, or craving—a thirsting that is born of ignorance. When there is ignorance, we are not clearly in touch with the reality of the moment. The Buddha called this ignorance *avijja,* which means not seeing, the absence of wisdom, or delusion. It is as if we are blind, stumbling along and bumping into things. We imagine that getting what we want and getting rid of what we don't want will end suffering, when actually that very resistance to life creates distress. Ajahn Chah put the cause of suffering very simply: the "wanting" and "not wanting" of the mind.

Our daily inner litany goes along these lines, *I want, I don't want, I've got to have, I've got to get rid of, I like, I don't like, too little, too big, too hot, too cold, I want to be with others, I want to be alone, it's not fair and what's more this isn't how any of it should be.* And so it goes on, day after day. When the Buddha pointed to freedom from suffering, he didn't mean that we would no longer feel pain or the poignancy of life. He was pointing to suffering as something we generate through ignorance. To feel pain is one thing. To suffer needlessly in reaction to the reality of that pain is quite another. This is a subtle but important point to understand.

Suffering is a choice we make; no one makes us suffer. We may feel pain of one sort or another, but our inability to respond with kindness, clarity, and mindfulness generates a sea of discontent. Actually, even our suffering has its perfection. It wakes us up. Or at least it offers us that opportunity. We can continue suffering unconsciously, on and on, or we can consciously engage the experience of *dukkha* and reflect, "What is going on here? Can I be with this, just as it is, for a moment?" When *dukkha* arises, rather than trying to change the ten thousand things to make us feel at ease, the practice of the ennobling truths directs us straight to the mind itself, to look at "wanting and not wanting."

I heard a story about a person on retreat who was suffering. Outside of the meditation hall was a small burbling stream. All the meditator could hear in the sound was the repetitive tune of "Stars and Stripes." It was driving him crazy. One day the teacher saw this guy in the stream moving the rocks around. When the teacher approached him and asked what he was doing, the student explained, "I'm trying to change the tune." One thing about meditation retreats is that you get to see how crazy the mind really is! We might smile at this story, but isn't that the same thing we're doing a lot of the time, endlessly moving the rocks around trying to get it right, exhausting ourselves? When will we realize we need to look somewhere else? The formation of the rocks is not the problem. It's our mind.

The Noble Truths of the Buddha are revealed when we start to look closer to home, at this very mind. Each of the truths has an accompanying practice. With the First Truth we are invited to "meet" suffering so that we can understand it. When stress, discontent, and suffering arise, we practice "turning to it" rather than running the other way. This practice is ennobling because we deepen our capacity to be with life as it is. To understand, we have to *stand under* and bear the experience of *dukkha.* In interrupting our habitual aversion to distress, we discover that we can actually contemplate this experience and recognize the cause of our agitation. Usually we think the cause of suffering is "out there." At some point we realize it is us out there in the stream, huffing and puffing, rearranging the circumstances of our lives. It's never-ending.

Rather than moving the rocks around endlessly, what happens if we let go and accept this moment as it is? The practice of the second truth is to "let go" of the chronic pathological "wanting and not wanting" of the mind. We learn to see how this seductive stream of desire is generating and perpetuating stress. We practice letting it go, or simply "letting be." To let be, and taste the peace of that, is the territory of the Third Noble Truth.

The Third Noble Truth states, "There is an end to suffering." There is freedom from this unnecessary cycle of pain. We don't have to blindly suffer. In letting go of the compulsive push and pull of the mind, we taste peace. We taste the peace that is inherent in the heart, always present, and inviting us to *come and see.* The practice of the third truth is not about attaining anything, but about recognizing a dimension of reality that is always here, but easily overlooked. This is the peace of *nibbana.*

Over the years, I've appreciated the beautiful simplicity of Ajahn Chah's first teaching to me. *Be with your breathing. When you know one thing well, you will understand everything.* "Breath" is a noun and sounds like a thing. But the word is misleading and cannot capture or fully describe the vibrant reality to which it refers. "Watch the breath" as a conceptual phrase can help direct attention, but when we actually meet "the breath," what do we notice? We see that the in-breath wells up and then disappears. Then the out-breath begins and ceases. The in and out breath arises and passes. Breathing is actually a dynamic, ever-changing process. The so-called "breath" is changing every instant. Even though I might call it "my breath" and say "my breath is calm" or "my breath is agitated," is it really "my breath" that is calm or agitated?

Can we truly call something that is changing every instant a "thing"? The words "my breath" assume ownership; but really it's just a way of talking. Breath is not actually mine; it's an aspect of nature. Upon investigation, we realize every "thing" is changing, ungraspable, and essentially not-mine or not-self. Sights, sounds, smells, flavors, and tactile experiences are all constantly changing. Is there any sight that we can keep? The daylight and scenery changes, even as we age and our eyes dim. Sounds are the same. What about feelings, moods, opinions, or accomplishments? We can't hold on to our possessions, friends, loved ones, or even to our body. So when we talk about *me* and *mine* what do these expressions really mean?

We take things that are impermanent to be stable and secure. Health, wealth, and success—how long do they last? If every sight, sound, feeling, and perception is impermanent, why do we hold on so tightly? Is that how we truly find security? Ajahn Chah would often say, *If you look for certainty in that which is actually uncertain, you are bound to suffer.* We do it all the time, of course, and so tend to feel let down a lot. We feel offended by other people or the things that happen, because we expected something else. "How can you let me down? How did this happen to me?" It's like shouting at the sun for setting: "Lovely sun, how can you desert me like that?" Ajahn Chah's classic example was going up to a duck and saying, "Why aren't you a chicken? How come you sit there and quack?" In the same way, we demand that the conditions of life give us something they never can. We want happiness and stability from that which is unreliable. We want fulfillment from something that is unable to fulfill us. If we aren't wise about this, we will experience a lot of stress, frustration, and disappointment.

After meeting Ajahn Chah, my attention, which had always been focused outwardly, was being directed inward, back to the heart itself. He pointed to what happens if we become aware of how conditions change and end. It sounds obvious, but for the first time I started to notice the ending of things. Ajahn Sumedho, the senior Western teacher, was very good at teaching this principle. I'd been so busy moving to the next achievement that I'd never waited around long enough to really notice things fading away. Looking with anticipation for the next wave to surf is one kind of experience, but it's altogether different when realize you can float in an entire ocean. Being aware of the changing nature of life, letting things pass without having to grasp them, I started to feel more peaceful. I began to get a feeling for what Ajahn Chah called "the one who knows," the inner listening. When a breath begins and ends, what remains unchanged? When a sound emerges and then subsides, there's still something. It isn't a thing, but a presence, a still, silent, and listening awareness. Conditions change but the "knowing" remains.

It is stressful to try and hold on when everything keeps changing. Wanting the changeable not to change, wanting praise never to turn to criticism, wanting energy never to fade into fatigue, wanting certainty never to collapse into doubt—it's all suffering. It's the same as hoping summer will never succumb to winter. It's as ridiculous as wanting the in-breath never to become an out-breath. Wanting life to be pleasant all the time is just like wanting one eternal in-breath. It simply can't happen. With practice, little by little, this sort of wise reflection leads to dispassion and a deeper refuge in awareness.

In an unexpected way, meditation revealed to me a whole new wonderful world I hadn't known before. At Princeton and Oxford, while writing my various papers and theses, I was always trying to produce a better idea, a more original thought; my professors exhorted me to demonstrate that my ideas were better than someone else's. You'd argue, "That interpretation is garbage," and proceed to annihilate it. In a way, it was academic warfare. When Ajahn Chah said it was possible to learn as much from stupid thoughts as wise ones, that was such a radically different approach. A wise thought arises and ceases. A stupid thought arises and ceases. A painful feeling arises and ceases. A pleasant feeling arises and ceases. I realized I didn't have to feel ashamed when there was confusion in the mind. Just let it be and know it for what it is. They are all just states of mind, coming and going. Rather than anxiously holding on to try to make sense of everything all the time, I got a feeling for letting go and letting be.

Skillful thinking is certainly useful, but if one is so preoccupied with the content of thought, one never notices the ground or source of thought, the womb of awareness where thoughts—and all other conditions—arise and cease. Before being introduced to the contemplative practices of the Buddha, I didn't have perspective on experience. I would immediately identify with it or reject it. By learning to mindfully witness and reflect on the changing nature of phenomena, I began to recognize a deeper part of my being I had never noticed. It was intriguing and revolutionary for me to explore the peaceful world of awareness.

I had discovered the power of the Dharma, and my faith in Ajahn Chah was deepening. Very soon my ambitions at Oxford seemed like a distant dream. I grew more excited about the activity of waking up. After my full ordination with Ajahn Chah, I really wanted to press on and get enlightened as quickly as possible. Eighteen months into my monastic life, I wanted to move monasteries to practice with one of the toughest Ajahns[4] around, Ajahn Jun—one of the early disciples of Ajahn Chah. I felt I wasn't working hard enough, even though the life was already rigorous. When I was with my fellow Westerners, I felt we would talk too much, and I had a yearning to go somewhere where I could focus more single-mindedly on the practice. At Ajahn Jun's I was the only Westerner, so I had no chattering *farangs* (foreigners) to distract my attention. When I arrived at Ajahn Jun's monastery, I intensified my efforts, cut back on eating, and did more meditation.

One day, five months into my stay, while I was working in the shed where we dyed our robes, I bent down to roll up a grass mat. As I picked up the mat an intensely sharp pain shot through my body. Instinctively, with lightning speed, my left hand pulled back, and there hanging from my ring finger was a huge centipede, six inches or more long. It had been hidden underneath the mat. A fellow monk quickly grabbed my arm and shook off the centipede and squeezed the blood and poison out of the two puncture marks. The next thing I knew my hand seemed to be on fire and an unbelievable burning pain filled my awareness. Centipedes were known to give one of the most painful and poisonous bites in the forest.

The monastery soon broke out into pandemonium. Monks were running around crying out, "The farang's been bitten by a centipede, the farang's been bitten." The Ajahn was informed. Old villagers came rushing up and started to recite healing mantras while spitting on my finger. A fire was lit to steam the bite, and various medicinal concoctions—including coconut milk—were applied. Everyone was extremely concerned. However, there was no doctor or hospital for miles. The burning pain was excruciating, and it was slowly working its way up my left arm. That night I sat up in the meditation hall rocking back and forth, moaning a lot of the time, trying to bear a seemingly unbearable pain. Being hypersensitive to a mere mosquito bite, I was fearful of what would happen when the poison hit my heart. Would it be curtains for me? What an inglorious ending to my enlightenment path!

I didn't die, but my hand stayed swollen for three weeks. Before the bite I was already unwell, having had diarrhea for six months. Not long after the bite, I started to urinate blood. Ajahn Jun got worried about me and sent me to the nearest hospital, back in Ubon. I was placed in the monk's ward. The monk on my right died the first night I was there, of cholera. The novice across the room had a huge sore on his leg, which the doctors thought they needed to amputate. His little brother was sleeping on the floor under his bed to keep him company. The monk on my left was afraid because he was having a kidney operation the next day. Moaning, pain, and suffering filled the room. I didn't want pain pills because I thought a good monk did not need them. In the middle of the night I heard screaming so loud it woke me up. Then I realized it was me, screaming in pain, so I asked for medicine.

After a day or two, Ajahn Chah came to visit. His arrival was like the rising sun. A lovely, glowing orange ball appeared on our horizon as he walked in. He went around to each person in the ward bestowing kindness and courage, even though I was the only monk he actually knew. When he came to me I said, "*Luang Por*[5] [Venerable Father], I want to get out of here." With a smile he replied, "If you run away I'm going to send the police after you." I laughed and said, "But what do I do about this unbearable pain?" *You need to know pain,* he replied. *Just that much. Know it as it is. You can do that.* And then he said, *When I die, I'll be at ease and okay. It's not going to be a problem.* His words on pain and death always stayed with me. Ajahn Chah had had a lot of sickness in his life; he had years of being with pain and discomfort, which culminated in a decade-long illness that left him unable to speak, paralyzed and bed-ridden. In the face of pain he encouraged patience and endurance. One of his gifts was to inspire the courage to be with suffering.

The exhortation of the First Noble Truth is to be interested in our suffering, and not afraid of it. When we do this, all the Four Truths are revealed. If you go deeply into suffering, you'll end up with non-suffering. As it turned out, I needed that encouragement, for soon afterward I fell into a deep depression. After I got out of hospital, I was sent back to the monastery for Westerners. The doctors couldn't figure out why I was urinating blood, and since I had lost a lot of weight, Ajahn Jun thought I should stay nearer the hospital.

Even though I had become very thin, I felt fat, greedy, and lustful. My mind was discouraged and I couldn't get any inspiration going. I'd been so used to being an individual of distinction, and now I was just another bald head lost in a row of monks. I'd look up the line—just bald heads. I'd look down the line—more bald heads. I was invisible, and what I saw of myself I hated. What's more, I really thought I'd never laugh again. The path seemed impossible, too difficult. I went to my Western abbot at the time, Ajahn Pabhakaro, and asked if he would take me to see Ajahn Chah. Pabhakaro could speak fluent Thai and Laotian. He was so good that if a Thai heard him speak on the telephone, they had no idea he was a Westerner.

Pabhakaro was a large, muscular, and radiant American. He was a helicopter pilot in Vietnam during the war, and his life took a radical turn when he came into contact with Buddhism while on R&R in Bangkok. In Vietnam every U.S. Army soldier received one five-day R&R—rest and relaxation military leave—during his one-year tour of duty. During his, Pabhakaro visited several Buddhist monasteries in Bangkok, and met some Western monks who were living there. Disheartened about the war, he eventually got an honorable discharge. A few years later he made his way back to Thailand and the forest monasteries of Ajahn Chah. As abbot he was very friendly and supportive of me. He could see I was in trouble, so he agreed to take me over to meet with Ajahn Chah.

When we arrived in the evening, Ajahn Chah was sitting as usual in his wicker chair in the space underneath his meditation hut. He was alone, since all the other monks were in the meditation hall chanting. I was grateful to have the chance to speak with him. It had always been a joy to sit nearby him as people came and went with their problems. Ajahn Chah exuded a great sense of freedom, and he loved to use humor. A few words here, a blessing there, consoling, fierce, gentle, challenging, he was liquid in his fluidity and mountain-like in his presence. He was masterful, and I was a wreck. He looked at me and grunted "What's up?" I looked up at him in his chair and said, "Luang Por, I'm a mess. My mind is full of desire and I feel depressed, miserable, and hopeless. This path seems impossible. It feels like I'm never going to laugh again." Pabhakaro dutifully translated.

"Hmmph," Ajahn Chah grunted back. He asked me to tell him about my life before I was a monk. He got me talking about wrestling, the tournaments, the constant competition, the judging mind. He listened.

"Neh!" he said. "You remind me of a baby squirrel." Pabhakaro whispered in my ear, "He says you remind him of a baby squirrel." *Oh, dear,* I thought, *I'm in trouble.* "One day," he continued, "that squirrel saw his mother leaping from branch to branch through the forest and he thought, 'That looks fantastic, I want to do the same.' So he went up a tree and leapt." Then Ajahn Chah paused. "*Dok!*[6] The squirrel fell down to the ground with a jolt and went to his mother crying. 'Son,' said the mother, 'You need to go to school.'"

Ajahn Chah told how the squirrel went to kindergarten, then on to first and second grade. Each time the squirrel would try his new moves, but soon, *Dok,* he would fall down again. Ajahn looked down at me, his eyes going round and round in circles with each *Dok!* Each time the young squirrel would cry, the mother sent him back to school. By the time the squirrel was in college, I was literally rolling around on the floor, laughing until I was crying. Ajahn Chah went on, Pabhakaro whispering in my ear the whole time. "He says the squirrel went to get a PhD." I was finished. Now I thought I'd never stop laughing. Finally I sat up in front of Ajahn Chah. Looking right at me with an ocean of kindness, he said, "And one day that squirrel could do everything its mother could do."

A beautiful feeling of happiness and relief filled my whole being, from the crown of my head down to the soles of my feet. I was delighted with that story. It gave me a sense of hope and confidence. But then Ajahn Chah started another story. "You know," he said, "you also remind me of a donkey."

Uh-oh, I thought. *What's he doing?* I was still enjoying the blissful afterglow of the squirrel story. Ajahn Chah told me about a donkey who loved to listen to the cicadas making music at dusk. He wanted to make music too. Being a very clever donkey, he decided to do some investigation. He watched the cicadas very carefully and saw that first thing at dawn they would eat dewdrops. So the industrious donkey got up extra early the next morning and went round licking thousands of dewdrops. After several hours of hard work, he thought, *That should do it.* Feeling confident and ready to enjoy the fruits of his labor, he opened his mouth wide to make beautiful music, and you know what happened? The donkey was so disappointed. Then Ajahn Chah just stopped. That was the end of the story.

Why did he tell me that? I wondered. For years I would only remember the squirrel story and its happy ending. *Just keep practicing, be patient, and everything will be all right,* I told myself. I didn't like the donkey story so much, and didn't want to think about it. But then slowly I began to realize its importance and have compassion for the donkey. I needed to learn how to accept and appreciate my own voice, my own limitations, and my own journey, and not try to be someone else. Self-aversion and wishful thinking are not the path to freedom. The beauty of awakening is inherent within our nature, within this very body and mind; it grows and flowers naturally. I can listen deeply and find my true sound when I am not so busy comparing myself to others. There it is again, learning to let go. Over the years these earthy teachings of Ajahn Chah have been good reminders, helping me start afresh when I find myself lost or struggling.

Sickness became a theme and a teacher for many, many years. Not long after the centipede bite and just weeks after seeing Ajahn Chah at his hut, I became so ill that I nearly died. I developed a high fever. The diarrhea continued to rage. I got severe headaches, and became extremely weak. Going in and out of consciousness, I started to hallucinate. The monks grew very worried about me, and Ajahn Chah decided to send me to Bangkok, where he had supporters who were good doctors. Lying on a stretcher at the train station, I remember a monk bending down over my face and telling me, "Ajahn Chah is sorry he cannot be here to see you now. He sent me to tell you not to worry, that he is thinking about you." Ajahn Pabhakaro rushed me down to Bangkok on the overnight train. I was delirious and remember very little of the journey. We were met by an ambulance and taken to what used to be the American military hospital, which probably saved my life. I had a severe case of typhoid fever. The doctor thought I was going to die.

Another dear friend, Ajahn Pasanno,[7] came down from the monastery to be with me in the hospital. He told me that when I was delirious, I spoke of being in the middle of a big battle, under the attack of an array of hostile forces. I don't remember. But at one point I do recall the doctor challenging me, being critical of my monastic lifestyle. In the end I got angry with him, which he said was the very reaction he was looking for. He felt anger was important—the kind of energy I needed to get my life force back. With massive doses of antibiotics, loving care from four of my dear fellow monks who took turns nursing me in the hospital, and skillful prodding from the doctor, I survived.

Around the same time my father had a major heart attack back in Tennessee, and I needed to go home to the United States. My life was at the cusp of another powerful change. I was returning as a different person. In my early years, one of my main identities was being healthy, strong, and a wrestler. In fact, when I was first a postulant in Thailand and wore white,[8] I had such well-developed pectoral muscles that the villagers used to laugh and say I looked like a nun. Now, after my bout with typhoid, I was very skinny and frail. I was entering a time of deep letting go.

When you try to let go, sometimes there is fear. *What will hold me? What will I lose? Who will I be then?* A memory helped me understand this principle. Near the end of my wrestling career I had a shoulder operation to protect the joint. Recuperating in the hospital bed, I had a bar above me that I could use to pull myself up. I would sit up in bed, holding the bar for support until I got tired of holding on. *But if I let go,* I would think, *what will happen? Will it hurt? How far back is the bed?* I knew the bed was back there somewhere. I was sitting on it, after all! But I was afraid to let go. Eventually I got so exhausted holding onto the bar that I had to let go. Of course, I didn't fall far. The bed held me and I was able to rest.

My experience in Thailand, and the subsequent years of debilitating illness, had brought me to a place where I had to *really* let go. I found out you land where you have always already been, fully here and now, held by the ground of pure awareness. Then you can rest. You don't have to hold on. It is peaceful. In our ordinary state of consciousness, we are clinging all the time. When I had typhoid and was really sick, even holding a thought was exhausting. Holding anything takes energy. In letting go, however, there is deep relief. There are still sensory impressions—sights, sounds, and sensations; we are still alive—but when we let go we trust something else. We let go of the struggle. We let go of looking outside for happiness and arrive in the ground of the heart. Non-grasping and non-rejecting is in itself *nibbana*. When we're so busy getting somewhere, or getting rid of things, we don't recognize the unshakable stability of where we always are.

Being with the breathing is a gateway to this understanding. The out-breath gives us a clue, for in itself it is a letting go. We can use the out-breath to practice letting be, and get a feeling for resting in awareness, the presence that always *is*. Conditions still arise and cease. Each sound still appears, but we notice it dissolves back into unmoving silence. Ajahn Chah encouraged us to patiently maintain this contemplation. He urged us to find that place where we're not desperately holding on. It is a place of true trustworthiness, a safe harbor, a place of peace. This is the end of suffering. We can rely on it. The Buddha called it a refuge that is *always here and now, inviting, to be experienced individually by each wise person.* When we follow these teachings, we're not rejecting the conditions of life but learning to find balance within them.

From this place of peace, connected to how things actually are, we can respond authentically to life. In our meditative work we continually realign ourselves in this place of inner listening. It's a big job, for we all have lots of unskillful habitual tendencies that perpetuate our suffering. The Fourth Noble Truth, the path leading to the end of suffering, needs to be cultivated. Gradually I began to realize how naive and idealistic I was in wanting to get enlightened quickly. I'm a slow learner, but one filled with gratitude for my great good fortune in meeting a wise teacher, and learning about this wonderful way of awakening.

It is hard to find a being of great wisdom;
Rare are the places in which they are born.
Those who surround them when they appear
Know good fortune indeed.

–The Buddha

CHAPTER TWO

A Stab to the Heart

Thanissara

Dharma is in your heart, not in the forest. Don't believe others. Just listen to your heart. You don't have to go and look anywhere else. Wisdom is in you, just like the sweet ripe mango is already in a young green one. With even a little intuitive wisdom you will be able to see clearly the ways of the world. You will come to understand that everything in the world is your teacher.

–Ajahn Chah

Dharma teachings, and the forms used for their transmission, serve us best when we remember they are signposts. The teachings, various schools and their methods, are not an end in themselves, but reminders that point directly to the heart. They are there to support awakening, not to bind us up. At the end of the day, while various practices and teachers can really help, we must be our own guide. Before his death, the Buddha said, "Be a lamp unto yourself, be a refuge to yourself. Those . . . who take themselves no external refuge, but hold fast to the Truth as their lamp and refuge . . . it is they who shall reach the highest goal."[1] Teachings are not ultimate truths, they just point the way. It's just like food: There are many different kinds of foods, some we prefer and some we can't digest. The point of eating is to be nourished, so we need to find what nourishes us the best. What encourages and what brings about insight and realization. Methods should be supportive and empowering, flexible rather than too rigid. Saying "This is the only way it can be done" is too rigid. Sometimes teachings contradict each other. That doesn't mean to say that one is wrong and the other is right. They are appropriate to time and place. Their deeper purpose is to bring us into balance.

Ajahn Chah gave this analogy: It's like watching someone walk down a path. If they veer too much to the right side and are in danger of falling in a ditch, the teacher will say, "Go left." So the diligent disciple writes down, "The teacher says go left." Another disciple may go too much to the left, so the teacher says, "Go right." Meanwhile the diligent disciple says, "No, the teacher definitely said, go left." They get into an argument, write academic papers: "Awakening is instant," "No, it's gradual," "No, instant," "No, gradual." And so it goes on. Ajahn Chah also said the Dharma is like honey: you can dispute what it tastes like, but once you taste it, all arguments cease.

Practice happens within the context of what our particular tendencies and capabilities are. Our practice needs to encourage our strengths, and highlight our weaknesses, so we can attend to them. Ultimately this is an individual thing. If we bear this in mind, we can directly investigate for ourselves. Sometimes teachers can sound like there is only one way to approach spiritual life, which has to suit everyone. Yet, even practices that are attributed to the Buddha are not necessarily found in the Pali Canon.[2] That doesn't mean they aren't true practices, it just means that Buddhism is a very flexible, open-ended approach to finding peace and ending suffering. We don't have to be rigid, cultish, or fundamentalist about our particular way.

For example, with mindfulness of breath we are taught to pay attention to the breath at a particular focal point in the body, say the nostrils or the belly. We can even argue about which is best: holding attention to the sensation of the breath as it enters and leaves the nostrils, or staying with the sensation of the rise and fall of the belly. However, whenever the Buddha talked about working with the breath there was very little direction in terms of where to place attention. There was no particular mention of staying with the breath at the tip of the nostrils, or at the belly, in the Pali Suttas, which are considered the earliest recording of the Buddha's teaching. When I began practicing that's how I was taught, to hold the attention in a certain way, in a certain place in the body.

I attended the same retreat near Oxford that Kittisaro attended in 1976. We were both beginning our fast track to enlightenment! This was also the retreat that sent Kittisaro off to Thailand in haste. We were all impressed that this American was so keen. It was a stretch for me to travel fifty miles to the retreat center, never mind zooming off to a mysterious place like Thailand. However, Kittisaro and I were similar in that we both found our first ten-day retreat challenging. After five days of extreme discomfort and gray loneliness, I devised an escape route. I was there with some friends, but wasn't able to speak with them as we were under a strict code of silence. Even eye contact was frowned upon. I could only hope they would understand when they saw my piled-up cushions at the back of the hall without me perched on top of them.

The retreat was being held in a collection of huts at the back of a large, stately home, which has since been sold by the Burmese family who owned it. More recently it was used to film the sitcom *Waiting for God*. The mansion has a wide driveway that sweeps up from the road to a grand entrance. To each side of the main door were large bay windows where retreatants would sit at meal times.

I really didn't want anyone to see my exit. However, I had timed it badly: everyone was drinking their herbal teas as I began my break-out. One glance behind, at seventy intent eyes focused on the driveway, was enough to convince me to speedily jump over the fence, and continue my escape through the next-door field. The only problem was that the field was full of stinging nettles and large, sharp thistles. Still, I couldn't turn back now. I bravely fought my way through the overgrown paddock and finally made it to the road. There I met my second obstacle. As a poor student, I couldn't afford a train fare back to my lodgings. So instead I took my chances at hitchhiking. No one stopped, of course.

A few miserable hours later, I fought my way back up through the undergrowth to my small cell in the estate, and unpacked my suitcase. Defeated, I sat back on my perch to continue with the breath. I didn't know whether to feel happy or sad that no one had actually noticed my little drama. At the end of the retreat all my friends said it had been an amazing experience. I had found it grim, but had to concede there were a few moments, being with my breath, when I actually did experience peace. It seems it was enough for me to continue. I knew meditation was important, in spite of my woeful attempts at it.

While Kittisaro and I shared the same retreat, our backgrounds were very different. I grew up in an extended working-class Anglo-Irish family in London. Those were more innocent days, when children could play for hours on the streets without fear of harm. Most weekends my grandparents, aunts, or uncles would be around. There was no real pressure at school. We had no ambitions beyond getting a good enough job according to our class situation. I had three brothers, all of whom left school at sixteen to enter apprenticeships, the work market, or the military.

None of us had particularly shining academic careers. School was something to get through, to learn the basics, rather than a means to higher education. At eleven I took an exam called the Eleven-Plus, which was standard for all English youngsters at the time. Basically it filtered those headed to higher education from those destined for the slush-bucket of unskilled labor. I landed in the slush-bucket. My hopelessness at exams continued, leaving a residue of academic inferiority.

From a young age I was attracted to some aspects of Christianity. I particularly liked the soulful picture of the Sacred Heart on our wall at home. My father's family was Catholic and my mother's Protestant; my parents baptized us in both churches. We went to Church of England school by day and Catholic catechism class by night. Preparing for First Holy Communion in the Catholic Church, I was trained to go to confession. One day, sitting behind the grill, with a shadowy priest on the other side, I faltered when reading the little card, "Forgive me, Father, for I have sinned. . . ." My voice dried up. I felt anxious and unsure. Then a feeling from within me spoke. It wasn't the usual me. The usual me would hardly say a peep. Instead an unexpected clarity said, "I'm not doing this, I don't believe in it." Somewhere from the depths, there was an urge to speak an inner truth. It wasn't out of disrespect for the priest or the Church, but something stopped me from trusting a process that didn't feel right. In the spiritual marketplace of teachers, gurus, and practices, I've always been glad for this inner prompting.

In spite of my poor school record, I was an avid reader and spent many hours in our small local library. I was particularly interested in books about India. When I was fourteen, I stumbled across a book on yoga. I started to teach myself and, much to the incomprehension of my family, became a vegetarian. At that time both yoga and vegetarianism were unheard of in our working-class culture. At seventeen I left school, and began working a number of jobs, including as a domestic worker in Paris. I needed to earn money for my application to art school. I had hoped that in Paris I would meet a Toulouse Lautrec or Van Gogh at the Moulin Rouge, but instead it turned out to be quite a lonely and despairing experience. I was glad to get back to England, where I put together a portfolio and, amazingly, was offered a place at Southampton College of Art.

During this time, my boyfriend introduced me to awareness-raising workshops that were just breaking on the far-flung shores of mainstream society. New and exciting doors began to open. I moved from my family home to live in a small commune in the heart of Southampton's red-light district, which was also the area where Indian and Jamaican immigrants lived.

Immersed in an alternative culture, we were like a tiny dinghy bobbing alongside the ocean liner of British society. In our parallel reality everything was up for questioning. One winter evening, while I was lying in front of our small wood fire, raptly reading *The Lord of the Rings,* a friend dropped by and introduced me to the book *Be Here Now.* It was the book I had been waiting for. Besides clarifying many aspects of an ancient path, it introduced me Ram Dass, a teacher who became a significant guide.

Be Here Now exuded a radical and liberating energy that had a lot to do with Neem Karoli Baba (affectionately called Maharaji), one of the greatest saints of our contemporary era.[3] Ram Dass had "stumbled" upon Maharaji during his journey to India in the early 1970s. In his lucid talks and writings since then, he has shared the impact of meeting Maharaji. Forty years later, in his book *Be Love Now,*[4] Ram Dass commented:

> This old man wrapped in a plaid blanket was sitting on a plank bed, and for a brief uncommon interval everyone had fallen silent. It was a meditative quiet, like an open field on a windless day or a deep clear lake without a ripple. I felt waves of love radiating toward me, washing over me. I opened my eyes and looked over at my guru. He was just sitting there, looking around, not doing anything. It was just his being, shining like the sun equally on everyone. It wasn't directed at anyone in particular. For him it was nothing special, just his own nature.

In 2012, Kittisaro and I spent time with Ram Dass, in his eightieth year, at his retreat in Hawaii. He talked of coming across the most extraordinary and precious jewel. This was Maharaji. Even though Maharaji discouraged publicity about himself, his whereabouts, or his miracles, Ram Dass said it was impossible to hide such a gem. Neem Karoli Baba became an inspiration for my journey.

Back in 1975, I had a miniscule taste of the consciousness embodied by Maharaji, through our alternative experiments. I tasted a pure consciousness beyond the usual parameters of everything I had known. That tiny taste set my path. All else faded into the background. I was not interested in a career, marriage, or anything else. Instead I was on a quest. With my friends I attended festivals at Stonehenge, where people were Druids or Earth Goddesses for the weekend. We listened to Krishnamurti's[5] "pathless path" at his school, Brockwood Park, in Hampshire. On one occasion we attended a workshop with Douglas Harding,[6] the guru of "having no head." My "dropout" friends and I walked around for a few weeks with no heads. Instead of the world being *out there,* as boundaries dissolved, we experienced the world *in here*. It was all within our minds, just as the

Buddha said. In the thirst for new understandings, we read books about Eastern mysticism, shamanism, or anything that threw light on altered states of consciousness. I avidly read everything Don Juan[7] had to say about "losing self-importance" and "death as an adviser."

My explorations started to translate into guidelines for my life. They didn't come from a religious tradition; instead they just evolved from the openings I experienced. At that time, I didn't really have a sense for Buddhist practice, but I knew I wanted to live in harmony with the Dharma, though I wasn't exactly sure what that would entail. While I was unclear how to proceed, the seed of awakening had been planted, and my life set on a new course. Overall the impact of our freewheeling explorations opened up important insights and gave me a glimpse of a deeper awareness. However, I had no way of bringing my insights into language or daily life. I didn't know which way to go. I sat listening to Krishnamurti, whose truth and "teaching" was lucid and beautiful, yet his denial of any methods left me stranded. Even though it was difficult, I knew meditation was important. It wasn't about finding something; I'd found more than I had bargained for. Rather, it was about accessing the semblance of freedom I had stumbled upon.

Unsure what to do, I headed out to join a tepee village in Wales for one glorious summer. However, there was also a shadowy side. One morning, after our fringe community ushered in the summer solstice, I sat quietly by a beautiful Welsh stream. A man came over to speak with me who looked like a complete wreck. He was disheveled, incoherent, and had dropped so far out of society I doubted he'd ever find his way back. Could that be me in a few years? It was time to move on. That afternoon I packed my bags and hitchhiked out of the Welsh Valley to the Oxford retreat center. Alas, the doors of perception only stayed open for a mere glimpse. By the time I was pinned to my meditation cushion, the door had slammed shut and I was crashing down to earth.

What Kittisaro and I both first started with was a form of Vipassana (insight) meditation from the Burmese school of U Ba Khin. It became global through the work of Indian teacher Satya Narayan Goenka. As one of the most influential meditation teachers in the world, Goenka and his sonorous voice—*three days are over, seven days left to work*, and so on—has been heard by thousands, if not millions, of meditators. In my efforts to stabilize my own awakening experiences, I attended dozens of these meditation retreats. Finally, after leaving my early experiments in the Southampton commune, my boyfriend and I joined a meditation community in West Sussex that was involved in hosting the first of Goenka's Vipassana retreats in England.

Over the next few years, I found the increasingly narrow interpretation of Dharma practice unsettling. However, I stuck with it. I was now part of a community, and its daily practice of an hour sitting in the morning and evening gave me stability. Eventually, I left the movement. While it was too rigid for me, I was grateful for the focus on ethics, *dana* (generosity), and the discipline this school offered.

Different practices suit different temperaments at different times. For example, the monastic life Kittisaro and I later lived was highly disciplined and focused. It was shaped by numerous observances and a demanding daily schedule. The disciplined lifestyle itself was the method, so the meditation practice tended to be informal. It mostly focused on the cultivation of awareness and inner inquiry as to the nature of suffering, grasping, letting go, and realization. In other words, the Four Noble Truths. The monastic style of Ajahn Chah's monasteries emphasized wise reflection more than technique.

However, I've noticed that in lay life, which is more dispersed, structured methods of meditation can be helpful. Sometimes people use meditation to overly control themselves, and life around them, particularly if they feel insecure. In that case it's important to soften control, and explore working with the experience of uncertainty. For other people it is the opposite: they really need an internal structure to make progress. Otherwise, without any focus they just daydream. A teacher or system with just one approach, insisting "All of you must do this," doesn't allow for people's various temperaments. It's interesting to see that the Buddha discerned what a person could hear, and when they could hear it. It wasn't a single "one teaching suits all" approach.

An example is the story of Suppabuddha the leper, who was attracted to the crowd gathered around the Buddha. It is said in the Sutta[8] that the Suppabuddha was "a poor, miserable wretch of a person." Further, it makes clear that he was only interested in drawing near to the crowd because he thought he would get something to eat. Most people would assume that such a character would be the last person whom the Buddha would respond to. However, the Buddha assessed the capabilities of the entire group and came to the conclusion that this very person, Suppabuddha, was the most able, and so pitched his teaching to him. The Sutta goes on to say that after teaching a graduated approach on virtue, the accumulation of blessings, the drawbacks of sensory experience, and the fruits of renunciation, the Buddha saw that Suppabuddha's mind was "malleable, open, bright and free from hindrances." At that moment he gave the teaching "peculiar to the Buddhas," which is the teaching of the Four Noble Truths, at which point Suppabuddha realized *nibbana* and freed himself from suffering. The Buddha claimed his teaching was a raft only, made from readily available materials, to get from one shore to the other, from the dream to waking up. When we are in tune with the Dharma, teachings arise spontaneously in response to what is needed. Everything teaches us. Ultimately, teachers, traditions, and methods are all limited. Eventually we will probably become disillusioned with them. This is an important part of maturing. It doesn't mean we have to dismiss them, or get bitter because they may disappoint us. There can also be enormous gratitude and appreciation for what we received. Nevertheless, eventually we need to outgrow external spiritual authority and replace it with our direct inner authority.

It was with this attitude of open-minded discernment that I approached my early experience with the Dharma. As I continued attending meditation retreats, my interest in my art career fell away. It just seemed unimportant when there was enlightenment to pursue! Instead I devoured whatever Dharma books I could find. My favorites were the stories of Milarepa, Marpa, Naropa, and Gompopa. I was also particularly attached to a small Zen book called *The Teachings of Huang Po.* Although it wasn't permitted to take books into Goenka's Vipassana retreats, I would always sneak Huang Po in as my ally. I really didn't understand what he was saying, but I liked his perspective that there was nothing to attain.

My passion for Krishnamurti continued, in spite of my being confounded by the application of his teachings. I would go and see him whenever he was at the summer gatherings at Brockwood Park. I devoured all of his books. Then one day while I was attending his teachings, he was so irritable that I began to question the sway he had over my mind. Sitting in the hot marquee with thousands of adoring listeners hanging on to every word, I couldn't quite equate the message of "no teacher and no way" with his authoritarian style. While I admired his "pathless path," the truth was that I needed a path. As Krishnamurti's talk went on, I started to get a migraine. I couldn't put together the inconsistencies rumbling around my increasingly confused and chaotic mind. To meditate or not? To be on a path or not? To have a teacher or not? At the end of the talk, I saw Krishnamurti walk back across the neatly trimmed English lawns to his lodging. A large number of people stood at a distance watching him. No one approached him or went near. I had the feeling he was utterly alone.

While I was struggling with the great question of enlightenment, I was also struggling to figure out my livelihood, which wasn't going so well. I had abandoned art school, and instead worked as a housekeeper at a home for the elderly. Most of my workday, I would lean on my mop and discuss the Dharma with my friend Loeci from our meditation community, who also worked at the home. One day, while cleaning the room of an elderly woman, I sat next to her bed for a while. She was in a state of advanced dementia, rambling about her life as if she were still young, completely unaware of her present circumstance. This encounter deeply affected me. I saw my own future as an old person. It scared me, but it also spurred me on. I was being confronted by aging and death, what Buddhists call a heavenly messenger. It was sobering.

Being sobered was not much fun. I became depressed. I could feel a sense of encroaching limitation. Life was good, but my world was closing down. I had lovely friends, but I was unable to enjoy things in the same way as before. My cleaning job was getting me down, and I couldn't see a clear way forward. One thing that brought me joy was cooking for other people. My mother was a great cook, and my English grandmother Nan, from the East End of London, had also been a consummate cook, particularly of pastry dishes. When my mother and grandmother got into the kitchen, we were in for a treat—and they passed their love and knowledge of cooking on to me. Although I am now a bit rusty, there was a time when I was a good cook. I put this skill to use by volunteering my services at many a meditation retreat. Two great things happened for me while cooking on retreats. The first was that I was offered a ticket to India by a group of Americans who liked my cooking. The second was that I met Ajahn Chah.

Ajahn Chah was on his first visit to England. He came to the retreat center near Oxford with Ajahn Sumedho, who was his attendant. When they walked into the meditation hall, there were about seventy of us young people sitting quietly. I was bowled over by the power of their combined presence. They conveyed a sense of purity and freedom. I was intoxicated just looking at them. That evening, I left the retreat to hear Ajahn Chah speak to Oxford students. During his talk, which was translated, I kept thinking, "Wow, this is good, this is wonderful, this is great." At the end of the talk Ajahn Chah said, "If you think this is good or bad then you haven't been listening properly." Wow, that was really good! I was hooked!

After this meeting I became increasingly overwhelmed by inner turmoil, confusion, and depression. I was trying to sense my way forward. I needed to do something with my life beyond being an all-around domestic. I had been through the highs of alternative culture, and the challenge of sitting through some pretty grueling retreats. I was not inspired by the options available to me in regular society, yet I didn't know what lifestyle to live. One afternoon, in despair, I wrote a list of possible choices. One was getting married: my boyfriend seemed up for it and our friends were doing it. One was teaching English in Japan. Friends were doing that, using the income to keep returning to India to do retreats. Another was working in the gardens of the Krishnamurti School, an attractive option but perhaps too much hard work. I can't remember all the options, but I listed ten. At the bottom of the list, I rather shakily wrote down the possibility of monastic life.

I had been back to see Ajahn Chah, this time in London. He was staying at the small Buddhist *vihara* (monastery) in Hampstead, which was the home for several years of the first four Western monks who were the initial founders of the Forest School in the West. They were Ajahn Sumedho, Ajahn Khemadhammo, Ajahn Anando, and Ajahn Viradhammo. I had bought a train ticket to Hampstead, but on the way I thought about my boyfriend back at the Vipassana community in West Sussex, so I got off the train, crossed to the opposite platform, and headed back. I settled into my seat and then started thinking about Ajahn Chah. I got off the train again, crossed back to the other platform, and caught the next train to London. The next stop, I got off the train and crossed back to get the train to West Sussex. I was in a state of total confusion bordering on panic. Each direction of the train represented a life choice. In the end, a ticket inspector got on the train, looked at my ticket, and said, "You are going the wrong way." He sent me back to the other platform and so I got the train to London. That was it—the ticket inspector decided.

However, as there were no lodgings for women, it wasn't easy to stay in the house in Hampstead, so I had to go back to the Vipassana community. As my confusion deepened, on the very day I made my list of options, Ajahn Chah unexpectedly visited our small meditation community. He was with Ajahn Anando, who had brought his parents from the USA to show them a quaint English village. As they sat down, I sat next to Ajahn Chah. In Thailand it was a gross breach of etiquette to sit right next to such an eminent monk, or any monk for that matter. I didn't know that then, though Ajahn Chah wasn't bothered. A small group of us were gathered around the dining room table. I was riveted. Ajahn Chah looked at each of us. He seemed bemused by this young community intent on enlightenment. After a while, he simply said, "Have you had enough yet?" I felt as if I'd been swimming around in choppy waters forever and he had just thrown a life raft. He had cut to the quick. Yes, I had had enough. I wanted out of *samsara*.[9] Ajahn Chah always said the Dharma was the escape hatch. He had opened the door and was calling from the other side.

After Ajahn Chah's visit to our community, I accepted the offer from the Americans to go to India. This was in 1978 and by now I was twenty-two years old. I spent five months on intensive retreat at the Vipassana Center in Igatpuri, after which I traveled to Sri Lanka, Burma, and Thailand. While in Thailand, I visited Ajahn Chah at a small monastery on the Mekong River on the border of Laos. I had been on my way to Burma (Myanmar) to stay at the U Ba Khin center in Rangoon (Yangon). However, I felt compelled to travel up to the northeast of Thailand to visit Ajahn Chah's monastery. On the way through Bangkok, I left the small group of friends I was traveling with, to catch an overnight train to Ubon, with the specific intention of seeing Ajahn Chah again.

Even though I was very nervous about the forthcoming trip, I had been so affected by his presence in England, there was no question that I would find a way to do it. A friend of mine decided she would come too. However, when we arrived at the train station she got anxious about mosquitoes and communists in the north of the country. I really wasn't that bothered by such things, but it became clear that she had decided to go back to the hotel, so I made the journey on my own.

I was disappointed when I got to Wat Pah Pong and Wat Nana Chat that Ajahn Chah was at neither monastery. However, I stumbled upon a Westerner who could speak Thai and could take us to the small monastery on the Mekong where Ajahn Chah was in residence. When we arrived and went to pay our respects, I didn't really know what to expect. I don't think I wanted anything other than to be in his presence. Although I wasn't sure why I was there, I was certain I was in the right place.

Ajahn Chah was with one other elderly monk. He graciously received me and allowed me to make some offerings of incense and candles. He asked me some questions about what I was doing and where I was going. Similar to his reaction to Kittisaro, Ajahn Chah didn't seem that impressed by my enlightenment search, which was taking me all over the place. Instead he encouraged me to go right within my own heart, pointing directly to the middle of his chest for emphasis. He then sent me to "be a nun" with an American nun at Wat Nana Chat. She was delightful and we spent a few happy days together. I felt very drawn to stay, but I knew it was important to go back to the West. I wasn't quite ready to ordain. I still had my family to check in with, and my boyfriend! A few months later I was back in England, and so was Ajahn Chah. In fact we were staying at the very same Oxford retreat center again, he, of course, enlightening those who came into contact with him, and me cooking. I was delighted to have the opportunity to be in his presence again. However, this time I got a bumpy reception.

First of all, Ajahn Chah asked why I had come back to the United Kingdom, why I hadn't stayed in Thailand as a nun. He was very persuasive when keen for someone to be, or stay, in robes. Once, one of his Western monks in Thailand was pining for his girlfriend and Ajahn Chah suggested he ask her to send some of her excrement in a vial so he could take a whiff every time he felt lust and longing! Ajahn Chah wasn't one to waste an opportunity! As I knelt before him, I was feeling a little mortified that I hadn't stayed in Thailand. I tried to explain about having a Western karma and needing to sort out some of my relationships before ordaining, but I could tell he wasn't that impressed. I do remember that one of the monks sitting next to Ajahn Chah was sympathetic; it was Kittisaro. I didn't realize then that he was the "keen American" we'd all been so impressed by when he left Oxford, a few years earlier, to go to Thailand. Regardless, I was glad he was there at that moment, saying he understood what I was trying to say.

Even though I felt a bit berated by Ajahn Chah, I was still glowing from the contact with him. I was never someone to keep a good thing to myself, so I immediately called up a dear friend and encouraged her to come to the meditation center, saying, "You *have* to meet this master." I dragged her to Ajahn Chah's meditation hut. I just went up and knocked on his door; I didn't know you were supposed to make an appointment with his attendant. The door was opened, and I suddenly had this feeling, *Oh, no, I'm just about to step into the lion's den,* because I could see that Ajahn Chah didn't look overjoyed to see me. In fact, he looked stern. There were a couple of monks with him; they'd been having tea. He invited us in.

My friend and I sat down and Ajahn Chah just looked at me. I felt uncomfortable. He asked me a few things about meditation. Like Kittisaro when he first met Ajahn Chah, I bumbled on enthusiastically and confidently about my understanding of meditation. Ajahn Chah didn't look convinced. He sat there and sort of snorted, "Hmmph." Then he asked, "Do you understand non-self?" and being an idiot I said, "Yes." He looked at me and I started blabbering on about "non-self" while my sense of self grew and grew, invading the whole room. All I could feel was "me," like I was in Technicolor with strobe lights going off all around me. I was aware I was looking more and more foolish. Meanwhile Ajahn Chah got very empty. The whole room got increasingly empty, as I got fuller of "me."' I was mortified. This wasn't what I had in mind when I invited my friend "to meet the master"! I felt as if I was walking the plank, dangling over a precipice. I was in serious trouble. I was blown up like a balloon full of hot air, thinking I knew what I was talking about, while increasingly realizing I had no idea what I was talking about. The more I tried to cover my tracks, the worse it got.

Eventually my speech petered out and I stared intently at a spot on the floor, into which I hoped to disappear. Ajahn Chah said something in Thai to the monk who was translating. He refused to translate it. Ajahn Chah was insistent; he leaned over to his translator and said it again. The monk turned to me and said, "Ajahn Chah says you're very ignorant!" It was as if someone had taken a pin and popped my balloon. The whole inflated sense of "me" went *Pheeeeew* onto the floor in a puddle.

Although it was excruciating, it was okay to have one's balloon pricked by someone like Ajahn Chah. Actually, it was a great honor, and even though I'm sure my face was as red as a beet, I knew I was receiving a precious transmission—and it stays with me to this day. Ajahn Chah, in a very kind way, proceeded to talk about the simplicity and peace of non-self; clearly he was someone who knew the territory! When he had finished, he sent my friend and I out the door. As we left his hut, we collapsed in a fit of giggles. I don't remember all Ajahn Chah had said, but the energetic communication was of freedom. His "stabbing the heart," a phrase he used to describe his Zen approach, which went straight to the core issue: he got my "self" by the scruff of the neck.

For me Ajahn Chah personified the fruit of the practice. He was very free. He wasn't out to please or impress, which was why he could be so effective. Neither did he need approval or adoration. He used his interactions with people to wake them up. His stabbing the heart usually had its desired effect. However, he didn't seem particularly bothered to promote his way as "the only way." Once, when he was in England with his attendant monk Ajahn Anando,[10] Anando kept encouraging people to shave their heads and ordain. Ajahn Chah told him, "Put your razor blade away!" It seems that Ajahn Chah saw the need to be flexible in transmitting the Dharma, at one point even saying, "If you need to call it Christianity, then do!"

Another time Ajahn Sumedho, who was the first Westerner to ordain with Ajahn Chah, took a group of English disciples to visit the international monastery of Wat Nana Chat in northeast Thailand. The group was very excited about visiting an ideal monastery, practice, and teacher. One of the attractions was to meet Ajahn Chah's first Western nun, the American I had stayed with on my visit to his monastery in Thailand. She had been ordained for five years. However, when they arrived, she had converted to a fairly fundamentalist style of Christianity. She hadn't disrobed yet, and so was still in the monastery. She took the opportunity to try and convert the freshly arrived British Buddhists. She told everyone that Buddhism was completely wrong and that Ajahn Chah was the devil. Ajahn Sumedho became very upset and went to Ajahn Chah to complain about her. He wanted Ajahn Chah to get rid of her, protesting she was offensive and was upsetting everyone. Ajahn Chah listened for a while and then said, "Well, you know, Sumedho, maybe she's right!"

Buddhist teachings are guidelines only. They are not there to make us right, or to make us perfect, nice, spiritual people. They are meant to wake us up! When religious people present themselves as ultimate authorities on the nature of God, the human soul, and morality, and see themselves as representing "the way" rather than "a way," they do a real disservice. They undermine personal and collective maturity. As soon as religious traditions replace inner authority with outer control, they have lost their true purpose. They put us to sleep rather than act as guides to the beyond.

Buddhism also falls into this trap. Sometimes practitioners undermine their inner discernment with undue idealization of teachers, traditions, and practices. If teachers become inflated and narcissistic, aided by the projections of their students, they lose touch with the best interests of those following them. There are safeguards, however. One of them is the willingness to both give and hear feedback. Teachers need to be humble, and not so entitled that they become invincible or invisible. In the end being a teacher or a student is a role; neither are ultimate identities, they are just skillful means we use. Eventually we all need to take responsibility for our own awakening, as the Buddha encouraged, and apply the wisdom of discernment. These practices and teachings are just a means to an end, an end that is accessible, right here, right now, when we listen into our own heart.

After having Ajahn Chah "stab my heart," I returned to my meditation community in West Sussex. I was in considerable turmoil. It was now 1979 and I was twenty-three years old. My difficulty in knowing what direction to take was about to clarify. I had moved into a small caravan at the bottom of the garden, parted from my boyfriend, and was learning some Buddhist chanting. I started to consider how to get back to Thailand.

Around this time I heard that Ajahn Chah's Western monks had moved into a rundown Victorian mansion in the hamlet of Chithurst, which happened to be just thirty miles from our community. One afternoon I persuaded a friend to drive me over there. When I arrived I was told that three other women had asked to ordain. The inevitable was happening. I sat in front of a mirror in the attic of this old house, and cut off all my long hair until it was unsightly stubble. Within a month the four of us were ordained as eight-precept maechees or "white-robed mothers." We were the first women to take Theravada robes in the West, incarnating from Pat, Françoise, Katy, and Binny (my nickname), into Sisters Rocana, Sundara, Chandasiri, and Thanissara. Giving up all worldly possessions, friendships, and aspirations is symbolized by shaving off one's hair. I felt like a plucked chicken, vulnerable and ugly. But I also felt a wave of relief. My life was firmly set in the direction of nirvana, or at least that's what I thought!

I had never quite been able to tell my family of my shorn head and white flowing robes. I would call my mother and update her about the meditation community, but did some filtering of the truth. One day my dear Irish aunt was at the hairdresser's reading the popular *Women's Own* magazine when she did a double-take. Next to a photo of a rather forlorn group of stubble-haired women was my name. She called my mum: "Is that our Linda Mary?" Within a finger snap my parents arrived at the ramshackle monastery.

"Oh, hi Mum," I said. She thought a young boy was greeting her. When she finally realized it was her daughter, she burst into tears. Eventually my three brothers also came to visit, finding the whole enlightenment thing rather amusing. By the time it came to my ten-precept ordination, four years later, I wanted to include my family in a much more skillful way. This time everyone came—grandparents, aunts, and parents.

My father struggled with my life choice. He really didn't approve. He was a hardworking man who had dedicated his life to family and duty. He came over from Ireland as a young man, and landed in North Africa in the war effort of the 1940s. Like all my Irish family, he worked for Guinness. He first met my mother at the Guinness St Patrick's dance at Hammersmith Palais.

It was a stretch for him to have a daughter with a shaved head and Buddhist robe, to say the least. It was not his idea of a success story. However, in spite of my father's difficulty in accepting my life choice, and in spite of the fact that Buddhist nuns were a rare occurrence in England at the time, my grandmothers gave me their full blessing. My Irish Gran thought it was great that I was getting out of this "wicked, wicked world," and my English Nan not only gave me her blessing, but also blessed many of the monks, going around grabbing a corner of their robes and saying, "Bless you, darling!"

The first years of my monastic life were inspiring, but also extremely tough. While the lifestyle was profound and simple, it was also challenging. Instead of being lifted beyond the trials and tribulations of the world into some kind of nirvana, I had unwittingly taken on an immense struggle. I struggled to keep up with the discipline, the work, and the relentless schedule. I struggled to get along with my fellow nuns. We were quite competitive as we negotiated our place at the bottom of the pile. But at the heart of my difficulty was the reactivity of my own mind. I was experiencing a lot of suffering and wasn't quite sure how to deal with it.

Usually, when challenged, our brain chemistry conditions us to fight, flee, or freeze. These are our survival strategies. It became increasingly untenable for me to be in a situation where none of those strategies helped. In monastic training you are bound by the limitations you've put yourself in. Eventually you have to find another way, beyond fight, flee, or freeze, to respond to the suffering—which is heightened through the lack of distraction built into the lifestyle.

We were up at four a.m. and worked most of the day, between morning and evening chanting, meditation, and lengthy Dharma talks. Once a week we would sit up all night to meditate. We ate one meal a day, before noon, though later a thin porridge in the morning was introduced into the diet. The regime generated an altered state where bodily and emotional needs were subdued. This basically set me up for a nuclear meltdown; all that was needed was the trigger.

One day I was finally confronted with the full force of the monastic cage I had put myself into. It was winter and freezing cold. At the time, the small cottage we nuns lived in had no electricity and very little heating. On this day, after working on improving the monastery road, I was looking forward to returning to a warm cottage and hot shower. However, the fire I had lit in the morning was dead. The whole place was freezing. I was overwhelmed with despair at the thought of having to go chop wood to remake the fire. I was upset that the nun whose job it was to tend the fire had let it go out. It was her job and she didn't do it! I was ready to walk out, explode, or curl up in a ball.

Ajahn Chah said, "When you can't go up, down, or sideways, then practice really begins." I guess this was the moment. As it turned out, some of the teachings had seeped in. I applied some mindfulness to my breath, body sensations, and mind states. I started to locate a ball of fire in my heart center. It was anger—enough anger to heat the whole monastery!

There was also desolation. I felt like such a failure at the enlightenment path. All this effort and I was like a three-year-old in a tantrum. *I DON'T WANT TO DO IT!!* As I stayed with the emotional pain, I realized the only strategy left was to open to suffering. As the Buddha pointed out, "*Dukkha* needs to be understood," not blamed, projected, or even personalized. In that way I began to see "the pain" instead of "my pain," and in the process saw how we were all struggling in the community. As my understanding deepened, compassion arose for myself and my fellow nuns. I was able to go out, chop some wood, and make a fire.

We all run from suffering, which may bring temporary relief, but its shadow will follow. When we finally turn to face it, we become less idealistic and more realistic. We work with where we actually are, and what we're faced with.

It sounds simple, but in fact it's very hard to simply be with "how things are." We move to the next thing, hoping it will be easier. Ajahn Chah had a knack for pointing beyond our fascination with the next new experience. He was a spell-breaker. We are often seduced into thinking that a new "something" —teacher, experience, location—will make the difference for us. Instead, Ajahn Chah pointed to the feeling of disenchantment as really important to acknowledge. It is a prerequisite for deeper insight into the Dharma. In the consumer culture of our times, to feel an utter weariness at the endlessness of it all is seen as a problem, something that Prozac will cure. But it is a healthy and natural response to the loss of soul that is prevalent in our day and age. Human beings are not just consumers, here to devour the resources of our planet.

When we take a consumer attitude to meditation, trying to squeeze what we can from our mind, body, teachers, and traditions, we lose sensitivity. We may get all sorts of skills, knowledge, and acclaim, but we haven't really entered the Dharma. The Dharma is not the teachings; they just point the way. The true Dharma is *sanditthiko,* here and now, *akaliko,* timeless, *ehipassiko,* inviting investigation, *opanayiko,* leading inward to the source, and *paccattam veditabbo vinnuhi'ti,* to be experienced individually. This Dharma is always revealing its nature, but we don't see it. Ajahn Chah said we don't see because of our views and opinions. While mastery is the fruition of the path, being an expert on all things isn't. In true Dharma practice, we become more inwardly naked, with nothing left to hide.

Once, when I had been a nun for about eleven years, I was on pilgrimage in India with my attendant and friend Pamela Bruckshaw. Besides visiting the Buddhist holy sites, we had the opportunity to stay at the ashram of Neem Karoli Baba, in the foothills of the Himalayas. I was thrilled to stay at Maharaji's ashram. After all, he had been the initial inspiration for my spiritual life. His ashram had a very pure vibration; however, as often is the case in India, things didn't go as I expected.

Just a short while before, we spent some wonderful days at the home of two of Maharaji's devotees in Allahabad, an elderly couple affectionately known as Didiji and Dadaji.[11] They received us with enormous hospitality, sharing stories of Maharaji and his miracles while we sat on the veranda sipping endless cups of chai. When we moved on from Dadaji's home to the foothills of Kanchi, it felt as if we were flowing in a current of grace. Our days at the Kanchi ashram were also blessed, although nothing particularly out of the ordinary happened. On some imperceptible level I wanted some kind of "transmission" or affirmation. While it was wonderful connecting with the power of Maharaji's blessings, which were still tangible, there was this subtle, gnawing need for something more.

When it came time to leave, we made our way to the bus station in Nainital and waited on an overly crowded bus that was to take us to our next destination. I was anxious, as the bus was late in leaving and I needed to get to our next destination before midday so I could eat my daily meal in accord with monastic discipline. But the bus just sat there while more people piled on. I watched the chaos of the bus station through the window—people pushing and shoving, vendors selling all manner of things, cows and rickshaws—while all the time I could feel my agitation grow. As I gazed into the crowd, out of the corner of my eye I saw a crazy and disheveled guy with red betel nut juice all down his grubby white shirt. He was barefoot and lurching from side to side, moving through a throng of people toward our bus.

For a British person, the worst experience one can endure is to be in the middle of some kind of public spectacle. As the crazy man got on the bus I tried to be as invisible as possible, hoping he would sit down quietly (as people do in England) and disappear. However, he immediately honed in on me and made a beeline to our seat. "Madam," he shouted, in perfect English, "this isn't like England, where buses are on time. This is India!" I was completely taken aback by the incongruity of his appearance: his drunken-like behavior and his perfect English accent. Immediately all eyes on the bus were turned in our direction, as he continued to poke fun at my impatience. Although I was completely put out, I was trying hard to appear cool and in control, detached and a little spiritual. Underneath, however, I was unraveling under the gaze of the crowded bus and the giggles that were beginning to fill it.

Suddenly the man turned his gaze directly on me, penetrating into my soul, and demanded, "Madam, where are you going?" I mumbled something about going to various holy sites. "Madam," he said, "if you think you know where you're going, you don't know anything at all!" With that, he turned and got off the bus. I was completely floored. I looked out the bus window, but he was nowhere to be seen; he had totally disappeared! It wasn't the spiritual experience I was looking for, but it did confirm what I already knew, that the path of Dharma is the way of "unknowing."

We begin with unknowing when we enter this world, then come to all sorts of things, but in the end we must return to unknowing. We all have to surrender, one of these days, into the mystery of our existence. Once I was leading a retreat when a rather arrogant man called out, "I want the Buddha's teaching in a nutshell. I don't want to waste my time. I paid for it, so give it to me." Actually, he had paid for his room and board. In the spirit of the Buddha, the teaching is freely given. At the end of the evening, his demand rippled around my mind. I wondered if he conducted all his relationships like that, if he was ever subtle enough to sense the beauty and poetry of life.

You can't expect the Dharma to yield its fruits if you treat it like a prostitute. In entering the domain of the Dharma, there has to be some humility, a willingness to be patient and discerning as we listen beyond our reactions, views, ideas, and desires. We need to allow ourselves to feel uncertain, to know that we don't know. It's not easy to feel unsure or to allow for this sense of disenchantment, but it's important. As Ajahn Chah often pointed out, world-weariness and despair have their place. They are the doorway through which we become unassuming. We don't know what to expect, but we trust something intangible, a deeper flow. In doing so, the mind becomes ready for the Dharma. Something new will open in our lives, something unexpected.

Looking for peace is like looking for a turtle with a moustache: You won't be able to find it. But when your heart is ready, peace will come looking for you.

–Ajahn Chah

CHAPTER THREE

A Steady Mind

Kittisaro

A mind that has samadhi, a mind that is gathered, will naturally see things the way they actually are and be freed from confusion.

–The Buddha

Meditation is the cultivation of a steady mind.[1] In its natural state the mind is like a mirror. Just as a mirror is completely unaltered by what is reflected in it, be it demons or angels, so too the natural mind is untainted by what appears within it. A mirror is essentially empty, and so is the mind. Although empty, the mind is also luminous and aware. It is conscious. This consciousness is endowed with a natural intelligence; it "knows." The constant parade of the mind's activity, however, obscures its innate clarity and clouds this clear knowing. The Thai forest master Ajahn Tate[2] described the essential purpose of meditation as discerning the difference between mind and the activity of mind. In order to see the difference, there needs to be steadiness of attention. This steadiness is called *samadhi*. *Samadhi* is usually translated as "concentration" or "one-pointedness," though this term can give the impression that the mind has to be narrow, like an ice pick. For many meditators, just the word "concentration" starts to make them feel uneasy and tense. I prefer to translate *samadhi* as "gathered" or "centered." In *samadhi*, the energies of body, speech, and mind are suffused with awareness and become unified.

Samadhi is the second component of the threefold training, the first being ethics, and the third, wisdom. This relates to the Eight Fold Path leading to the end of suffering, which is the Fourth Noble Truth. Each aspect of the path illuminates the mind's tendencies, such as thoughts, feelings, habits, and intentions, in particular those that are associated with suffering. The ending of suffering comes about through the application and development of the Eight Fold Path. Impeccable and blameless living (ethics) increases self-respect, frees us from remorse, and strengthens presence of mind or *samadhi*. This in turn creates the conditions for clarity and insight. When the mind is gathered, collected, and unified, it naturally leads to wisdom, as it sees things realistically, the way they actually are.

According to some meditation teachers, *samadhi* is particularly difficult to master. To illustrate the three aspects of the path, another Thai forest master, Ajahn Lee,[3] uses the analogy of a bridge that crosses from a dangerous shore over a turbulent river to a place of safety. The bridge is a metaphor for moving from suffering to the end of suffering. He said that the two support columns on the near and far side, ethics and wisdom, are easier to build because the current in the shallows is not so strong and fast. But in the middle of the stream, where the current is deep and swift, the work is very challenging. While all three trainings are difficult, ethics is relatively straightforward and tangible, and wisdom arises effortlessly when the mind is composed. The central column of *samadhi*, however, is easily swept away by the turbulent currents of the heart when it is not firmly established. The practice of *samadhi* requires a lot of persistence and patience in order for it to bear fruit. Just as it is difficult to plunge the supporting column of a bridge into the middle of a fast-flowing river, it is very challenging to develop steadiness in the midst of the fast-flowing currents of the mind.

We are so easily swept away and flooded by our thoughts and feelings. We become intoxicated when we feel inspired, and devastated when we feel hopeless, sometimes to the extent that we think we'll solve the problem by taking our own life. This is killing the wrong thing! If we are going to kill something, it should be our delusions. With presence of mind we begin to see these delusions. If we float along on a river, dozing away, we won't necessarily notice where the currents are taking us. However, if we try to stop and stay still, making contact with the ground, we'll clearly discern the powerful pull of the stream. In the same way, when we're swept along by the moods of the mind, we don't tend to see them. When we are still, in meditation, the activity of the mind becomes clear.

The Buddha likened the mind to a monkey jumping all over the place. He talked of the mind as restless, slippery, and hard to control. He also compared the training of the mind to taking a fish from water: "Just as a Fletcher shapes an arrow, so the wise develop the mind which is so excitable, so uncertain and difficult to control. Like a fish which on being dragged from its home in the water and tossed on dry land will thrash about, so will the heart tremble when withdrawing from the current of Mara."[4]

How true! *Mara* is the force that deludes and confuses us. We are carried along by the flow of habitual and unconscious states of mind. When we challenge this by committing ourselves to silence and stillness for periods of time, the tendency to follow agitation and restlessness is inhibited. The mind is like that fish pulled out of water, thrashing about. The sense of self flails around, thinking, I'm so restless. I need to get up and do something. It will feel like a death. If you listen to the voices that arise when you challenge the restless mind, they scream and shout and whimper, *I can't take this; I'm dying.* What is actually dying is a state of mind, a limitation of the sense of "me." If we stay steady and learn to allow that mental formation to flop about and subside, we can get a sense for what remains. There is an underlying silence, a presence, a knowing. What is left is a mind that is actually deeper than the thrashing and limited sense of self. Let it flop, flail, and die. You will notice that the listening remains. There is still presence, *the one who knows,* the Buddha.

My teacher Ajahn Chah encouraged us to view all the activities of the mind in the same way we would regard a cobra.

> A cobra is an extremely poisonous snake, poisonous enough to cause death if it should bite us. And so it is with our moods also; the moods that we like are poisonous, the moods that we dislike are also poisonous. They prevent our minds from being free. . . .
>
> If we don't interfere with a cobra, it simply goes its own way. Even though it may be extremely poisonous, we are not affected by it; we don't go near it or take hold of it, and it doesn't bite us.
>
> When we no longer identify with and cling to happiness and suffering, we are simply left with the natural way of things.[5]
>
> —Ajahn Chah

If we go into a dark room where there is a cobra, we are in a dangerous situation. But if we light a candle and see what's inside, we can wisely respond to whatever appears before us. When difficult states of mind are illuminated by awareness, they go their own way and we are not troubled by them. Sometimes they dissolve as we observe them, and even if they don't, we don't have to be entangled in their stories.

Sometimes awareness is likened to a candle flame, which is a universal symbol of wisdom. Developing *samadhi* can be compared to making a candle. The arising of wisdom is like lighting the candle. The flame that lights the room depends on the candle wax as a reliable source of fuel. Without the candle, the light of a match would be short-lived, and the room would return to darkness. Just as a candle is the underlying basis for an enduring flame, a steady and focused mind is the foundation for liberating wisdom. Naturally, as the mind clears, the light of understanding shines forth and illuminates the space. We can see what's going on. With a cobra, it's good to be wary and help it find its way out. Mind states, what we like and what we don't like, are like a poisonous snake, and they can really cause a lot of harm if we are not mindful. We need to know how to work with them.

At Dharmagiri hermitage in South Africa, which Thanissara and I founded in 2000, the cobras, called *rinkhals,* tend to be really shy, but they move very quickly. We don't see them that often, and thankfully they rarely cause trouble. However, we also have puff adders, and they're a different story. They don't usually move away if someone is coming. They move slowly, but strike lightning-fast. If someone accidentally steps on one, that person is in trouble, for the puff adder is extremely poisonous. When I find one in a place where someone may get hurt, I catch it in a bucket, prodding it gently with a stick to get it inside the container so that I can move it safely somewhere else. Basically I'd rather just leave them be, but sometimes I have no choice. I can hear Ajahn Chah laughing, "Be careful!" In the summer season, when the snakes are out, we have to watch where we step. If I need to relocate one, I approach it carefully and speak gently, "Little friend, I'm sorry to disturb you. May you not be harmed, and may I not be harmed." I wish it well and move it to a safer place. When we see clearly, we can work with the reality of the situation more skillfully.

The Buddha said the root of all suffering is ignorance, or not seeing clearly. Without a measure of *samadhi*, steadiness of mind, it is very difficult to have clarity. In the dark we bump into things and get frightened about what might be there. We don't skillfully negotiate the situation, and end up crashing into what we don't see. If we see, then we know what we're dealing with. We understand the danger of poisonous mind states, our own or others, and so respond appropriately.

The Buddha had plenty of cobras in his life. He was severely criticized, blamed, betrayed, and maligned. His close cousin even plotted to kill him and take over the monastic order. The Buddha faced starvation, social ostracism, bodily sickness, and family conflict. He didn't live in a bubble. He lived in a very real world with very real challenges. He met each challenge with a different response. He responded with truth, skillful words, letting karma take its course, compassion, debate, and sometimes he even walked away and let difficult people just get on with it. However, before he did that he tried everything he could. He didn't just say, "Oh, that's how the world is," and huff off, abdicating responsibility. He tried to avert further conflict or disaster.

Once he tried to stop a war that was imminent between those in his home country of Kapilavastu, and the neighboring king of Kosala.[6] He tried three times but was unable to avert the bloodshed. He had to accept that this was a karmic result he couldn't stop, but it didn't mean that he didn't try. On leaving the area, it is recorded that his beloved attendant Ananda asked him why he was so sad, to which the Buddha replied that his people would be massacred within the week. Sometimes, when situations have a lot of poison in them, there's nothing that can be done; one has to remove oneself. However, if we don't see clearly what is going on, we can get overwhelmed and destroyed.

The nature of life includes praise and blame, pleasure and pain, success and failure, honor and dishonor. These experiences are unavoidable, but if we attach to the positive dimensions of these worldly conditions, it's like picking up that poisonous snake heedlessly by the tail. We get bitten and suffer. During my monastic life I received a lot of affirmation and support. Although I struggled with sickness and couldn't always join in work projects or the daily routine, the monks would come to my room to take a breather, enjoying the space without any pressure. I had time to listen and hang out, and as a consequence often found myself helping to negotiate conflicts or tensions that arose between various individuals.

In general I was well liked, and when it came my turn to run a small monastery in Devon, the West of England, I received a very positive response to the public talks and teachings I would offer. My three years as abbot of that monastery were very happy, and a good sense of community developed around me. Of course, being popular is not the aim of monastic life. But nevertheless, the positive camaraderie was supportive of my well-being in the midst of my struggle with ongoing sickness.

However, I have also received blame and harsh criticism, particularly since leaving the robes after having been a Buddhist monk for fifteen years. I like to be liked, so being criticized has been a fierce and powerful teacher. It takes a lot of steadiness of mind and internal reflection to not perpetuate resentment, particularly if the blame seems unfair or untrue. The great Chinese meditation master Master Hsuan Hua,[7] whose transmission of the Dharma has profoundly influenced my practice, encouraged me to receive criticism as "sweet dew." I first came across Master Hua early in my monastic life, through a series of books written by his American disciples Heng Sure and Heng Ch'au, which recorded their awesome pilgrimage along the West Coast of the U.S. They followed an ancient Chinese Buddhist practice of taking three steps and one full-length bow. In 1977 they spent two and a half years completing their bowing pilgrimage from downtown L.A. through San Francisco to the City of 10,000 Buddhas in Mendocino County. They covered 800 miles, dedicating their efforts to world peace. They inspired me, and their books opened the door to my exploration of Chinese Mahayana, Chan (Zen), and Pure Land teachings.

I was particularly helped by the devotional and meditative practices around Kuan Yin,[8] and years later when Master Hua was visiting our monastery, I went to see him to ask his further advice. Not long before that meeting I had finished my yearlong silent monastic retreat, and during that time I frequently encountered an intriguing and yet baffling experience. On many occasions, usually in meditation, I would sense the approach of a subtle, sacred presence that seemed blessedly kind, beautiful, and wise. Sometimes it would tap me on the head and communicate, not in words, but in whole thoughts and meanings. Usually I experienced the interaction as encouragement for my spiritual practice, but occasionally it would be criticism or disapproval. I knew I was very inexperienced in the psychic world of visionary phenomena. I trusted that Master Hua understood these realms and their dangers. I was wondering, *Was this presence Kuan Yin, an evolved spiritual being, or maybe a demon? Were these experiences trustworthy or just imaginary delusions?*

In my question to the Master, I was hoping for confirmation about what was happening to me, or some kind of esoteric transmission on the Kuan Yin Dharma Door. A cryptic teaching on taking criticism as "sweet dew" was the last thing I expected, or particularly wanted. He said: "As for getting flak and disapproval—that's not a problem. We should accept any criticism that comes our way. We should simply change our faults as they arise. If the criticism is inaccurate and useless, then you can happily ignore it: 'It doesn't matter.'" Then he quoted from an ancient sage:

Let them slander, they can curse as they please;
They are simply holding a torch aloft,

Trying to burn the sky:
Certainly they will tire themselves out before long.

When I hear this harsh talk
It tastes to me as fine as sweet dew;
When smelted through,
Suddenly we enter an inconceivable state.[9]

Master Hua went on to explain: "If you can take the slander as your Good and Wise Adviser, then it acts just like fertilizer for your wisdom field. Drink the sweet dew of harsh words. Once you are smelted through, your work is done, your state is inconceivable. In fact, this opposition is what brings you to success. Not simply because there is slander, but because you have been able to contemplate the cursing as level and equal. You have turned a very difficult situation into fertilizer for the crops of your merit and virtue garden."[10]

Perplexed, I thought, "Why is he saying this? Maybe he didn't understand my question." Little did I know that within the year I would be in the midst of a fire storm of criticism, due to my decision to leave the robes to be with Thanissara. Or that our subsequent years of work in South Africa would involve many crises, challenges, further harsh criticism, blame, and devastating betrayals of trust. The Master's response wasn't what I was looking for, but in retrospect it was perfect for what lay before me. He was giving me a teaching about the true nature of *samadhi;* it is not just about refined states of concentration. Whether demons or angels appear, the mind is unshaken. It can receive praise and criticism without losing equanimity. When I fell in love with Thanissara, and finally decided to leave the monastic life to be with her, it was like a bomb had been dropped in our community. Being attached to harmony, I was mortified to be the cause of so much controversy. It's an abbot's nightmare for a senior monk to fall in love with a senior nun, so it's not really surprising that our situation created a lot of turmoil. A beloved teacher I had treasured for years told me heatedly that my action of disrobing to be with Thanissara was extremely selfish, and would destroy the Sangha.[11] I was also told that I hadn't learned anything, that I didn't know how to practice, that this was just delusion, that to disrobe in this way was like jumping out of one wedding bed into another. My abbot was "tired of hearing about marriages made in heaven!"

One senior monk told Thanissara that by leaving the monastic life she was committing spiritual suicide. It was a painful and emotionally charged time for many of us in the community. I genuinely cherished the monastic life, and the last thing I wanted to do was cause harm and distress to those in our community who had given me so much for many years. I was trying sincerely to listen to my heart and discern the wise course of action. "Trust your own wisdom" had been the mantra in the monastery for years. It was a powerful and poignant dilemma.

Master Hua's teaching helped me reflect on the harsh words, and not blindly react to them. I can't say that the criticism became "sweet dew," but at least I knew I had to remain open to it and reflect upon it all. Maybe the criticism was true? Master Hua's responses were never predictable; he cut straight to what was needed, often in a way that would contradict all expectations. He gave me a glimpse of how much Dharma practice goes against the usual stream of worldly values; that it has to deepen beyond only seeking peace and calm. For so many years of my life I had been the recipient of praise and honors—wrestling championships, athletic accolades, academic achievements, the Rhodes Scholarship, praise from my monastic teachers and fellow monks and nuns, loving approval from the Buddhist lay supporters, and success as the senior monk of a small monastery.

Having received so much affirmation in the past, this torrent of controversy and criticism was difficult to bear, but it felt important. As time went on, and I continued to contemplate the unreliability of praise and blame, I gradually let go of the resentment and the sense of unfairness I sometimes felt. To leave the monastic life is a big thing, and I'm grateful that my dear teachers and colleagues in the monk's life challenged me not to take the decision lightly. After all, my ordained name was Kittisaro, "One Who Is Worthy of Honor." Not "One Who Always Gets Honors."

It's a false assumption to think that if we are doing well in meditation, we'll just experience positive things and people will only like us. That's part of the delusion that keeps us in *samsara,*bound to the wheel of rebirth. *Samsara* is represented as a wheel because it just keeps turning endlessly. What keeps it turning is ignorance. If we are not mindful when we meditate, we do the same thing. We look for pleasure and ease, and very quickly feel a failure when confronted with difficulty. It's natural to want peace from meditation; however, it doesn't arise unless there's some skill and some ability to negotiate the reality of our habitual tendencies. Little by little, the cultivation of *samadhi* does lead to a steadiness of mind, but it takes practice. As proficiency grows, we can work with whatever we are confronted with, not only in our still and quiet times, but also in the midst of daily life.

Meditation matures us. It enables us to be more realistic and to work with the actualities of life, without being poisoned by the negativity that arises in the face of difficulty. To do this we need to illuminate the *suchness* of our human experience, which means being very patient, to not move with every impulse. If there is no equanimity with regard to sensory experience, then it is hard to develop *samadhi.* If we only want pleasurable feelings, we can't really develop much skill. However, as we learn to steady the body-mind within presence and awareness, we can access well-being, vitality, and a sense of brightness. But this doesn't happen if we are just swept along by the currents of a mind that seeks distraction. It develops by practicing being with the whole range of feelings, sensations, and mind states, whether pleasant or not. With trained attention, we cultivate the skill of letting experience be transformed through our capacity to be rooted in present-moment awareness.

In meditation we will experience a variety of feelings, which initially intensify through the power of attention. Sometimes the mind can feel light and happy, and sometimes it is caught in conflict. Mostly it's a mixture of both. Ordinarily, when there's a feeling of restlessness, desire, or discomfort, we move. Most of us have a daily routine where we're on automatic pilot following various habits of body and mind. But in periods of formal meditation, we're encouraged to stay with a posture, and to stay with what we are feeling. This limitation goes against the habitual movement of the mind. It can be a real struggle. Feelings of heaviness, agitation, rebellion, discouragement, and disorientation arise. When we stop, we find ourselves meeting our karma, which is challenging. In essence, karma is the sense of being pushed onward, it is the momentum of the mind's activity as it seeks to create, think, and strategize.

Each of us has unique accumulated tendencies of body and mind. In meditation these tendencies are amplified and made conscious. Rather than getting discouraged, see this as an opportunity to be realistic. We need to make contact—skillful, sustained, present, nonjudgmental contact—with the body-mind as it is. Within the cauldron of awareness, there is an opportunity to allow a mysterious transformation to happen. What we find difficult becomes an occasion for developing patience. Patience deepens our capacity to stay with challenging states of mind. When there is an uncomfortable or restless impulse, we usually skip to something else. We're restless *here*, so we go over *there*. We don't like what we see, so we change the channel. This is just being pushed along by the momentum of karma, being "moved by conditions." This means we are constantly reacting to whatever life brings. There's nothing wrong with that, but if there's no choice, it's a kind of slavery. When we're turned by the conditions, we become shaped by them and enslaved. We become restless, struggling like mad. No one has done anything to us, but it's as if we are in a prison cell. There's no light, and no way out.

In staying present, we make contact with our experience, however it is, without getting shaped by it. Perhaps there is restlessness, anxiety, or discomfort. We can stay with it, breathe into it, and bring attention to it. In the process of maintaining attention, we see that these states are impermanent, in and of themselves. Master Hua called this "turning the state around rather than being turned by the state." We can learn to stay steady with a challenging mood, and let it *turn*, recognizing that states of mind shift and change. If difficult states of mind come up, nothing is going wrong. Instead there is the opportunity to cultivate skill and steadiness of mind. This is the practice of *samadhi*, which enables the body, speech, and mind to gather within awareness. We train the mind to be steady, so instead of being swept along by various feelings and mind states, we maintain balance. We're teaching the heart to stay with what we're doing, to abide at ease with how things actually are.

Meditation trains awareness no matter what posture: walking, standing, sitting, and lying down. Awareness receives the energetic experience of the body-mind and breath. If we are patient with these experiences, breathing with them, then little by little they change into something more refined. Patience mixed with awareness will transform whatever is present into a wholesome state. For example, if there's an upset feeling, then breathe with it and stay with it. Little by little it will transmute. We can actually notice the difference. When we guide attention to be with the body, there is a brightening. This process of guiding awareness to body also includes feeling the rhythm of the in- and out-breath. Steady the attention on the whole of the in-breath, and then steady the attention to the whole of the out-breath. We can stabilize attention on listening and receiving our present experience. As we do so the mind becomes less scattered and we'll feel freed up.

Applying awareness to the experience of breath within the body enables the middle pillar of *samadhi* to ground itself solidly through the currents of the mind. We aren't just being swept away by the fastest part of the stream. Instead, we connect down to the earth. We connect to attentive awareness, which stabilizes the mental and physical energies. It brightens and refines them. In this way *samadhi* has a healing dimension. It lets all the stress and residue of unacknowledged feelings be digested and integrated. When *samadhi* is well developed it literally dissolves suffering. The heart-mind—when gathered, focused, present, and aware—metabolizes suffering and transforms it into luminous ease.

So, yes, the heart will tremble on withdrawing from the current of Mara. However, this is not about crushing or killing the mind, but about enabling a deeper realization. We are not trying to destroy, but to illuminate, so that we get to know the tendencies of mind which lead us all over the place, telling us If I get it all just right, I'll finally find peace. Or, If I just go over there, to the next guru, teacher, or retreat, then everything will fall into place. However, when we get *over there,* there is still something that's not quite right. This tendency, to always be leaning into the next thing or getting rid of something we think is obstructing us, is *samsara*. We know *samsara* by its flavor, which is the taste of never being satisfied.

It is stressful to hold on when things keep changing. Stress comes from wanting the changeable not to change: wanting praise never to turn to criticism, energy never to turn to fatigue, certainty never to change to doubt. It's the same as wanting summer to never become winter, or wanting the in-breath to never become an out-breath. We want just one eternal in-breath. But just try it, breathe in and in and in—keep going. At some point you will be bursting to breathe out. You'll feel utter relief to breathe out. At some point you'll be exhausted with being spun around by the kaleidoscope of the mind. You will want to let go. You'll tire of endlessly being turned around, feeling It's *not quite right yet, but it will be in the future.* You'll grow weary of incessantly leaning into the next thing, searching for security.

The problem is, we're leaning on something that won't support us. This is like leaning on the wind. It's obvious that if we do that, we'll fall down. If we depend on the daylight, we'll collapse when dusk comes. If we rely on praise, we falter when it turns to criticism. In the practice of *samadhi,* we're shifting our balance inwardly, onto something else. We learn to relax into the body and its slower rhythms, which ground more deeply into the earth. We are aware of breathing, how it swells and subsides, changes and fluctuates. We train to stay connected with a rootedness to the earth through our body, and to the ground of the mind, which is awareness.

When I first began to meditate, I discovered my attention had always been focused outward, always looking for the right situation. My sense of worth was connected to external affirmation. There had always been this sense of acquisition. Getting more athletic awards or more academic recognition was highly praised in the community in which I grew up. These are the things that are impressive in America, where, for example, a lot of importance is placed on being able to win an argument by having a convincing point of view. For many people the driving force of life is the desire to succeed and rise to the top of the pile. Sometimes we mistake these worldly accomplishments with spiritual insight, or transfer those same standards onto spiritual life. We think spiritual maturity is like being some kind of super spiritual athlete that knows everything and never has a doubt. Ajahn Chah wasn't so impressed with all the gains and unrealistic ideals of his Western disciples. He did recognize that we had done a lot and that we knew a lot, but he likened it to having a larger house than those of the village people around him. This large house had more cluttered rooms that needed a lot of effort to clean out.

Once, when Ajahn Chah first visited London in 1977, a sophisticated and knowledgeable woman asked a convoluted philosophical question about the Abhidhamma.[12] The Abhidhamma is a complex Buddhist treatise on all possible mind states, whether mundane or transcendent. It was an impressive question. Ajahn Chah smiled kindly at the earnest woman and said, "Madam, you are like one who keeps chickens, but goes out in the morning and collects the droppings rather than the eggs." He pointed out what we were doing, in vivid and memorable ways.

Even though Ajahn Chah poked fun at our convoluted sense of self, he also always encouraged his disciples. He was impressed by the dedication of his Western disciples, saying that when our houses were cleared out, we'd have a lot of space. He said that while Buddhism in Thailand was like an old, dying tree, in the West it was like a young, strong sapling, full of potential and new life. He was impressed when he visited the Retreat Center in Oxford, and the Insight Meditation Society in America, where people would sit for hours and were passionate about enlightenment. That he wasn't caught up at all in the criteria of success, however, according to our American standards, was a great relief. Instead of looking outward, as I had been conditioned to do, Ajahn Chah encouraged me to look inward: to be with the simplicity of breath, of one step at a time, one day at a time, while contemplating suffering and its end. Rather than the mind attaining something, he encouraged me to notice the mind itself.

As I noticed how impermanent my feelings and thoughts actually were, I started to get a taste for an inner sense of presence and awareness. We can also call this *inner listening*. Ajahn Chah called it the *knowing*. When a breath begins and ends, what remains? When a sound emerges and then subsides, there's still something; it isn't a "thing" but a presence, a silent listening. As we practice, little by little, with less identification with "my moods," we learn to savor the peace of dispassion. We find our refuge in the depth of knowing, in the intimacy of the natural, aware state of mind. From that perspective, aversion, doubt, desire, or discouragement are seen with more equanimity. Sometimes, when the activity of the mind subsides, we notice silence, stillness, and space. We get a feeling for letting be, letting go.

Ajahn Chah taught, "Do everything with a mind that lets go." He taught a letting go that doesn't push things away. Pushing things away is something else entirely. Thinking we are letting go, we can just be averse, not wanting to be bothered by anything. But he described letting go as *touching and letting go.* Allow things to be as they are. Allow sights, feelings, thoughts, praise, blame, and all conditions to change. It is the nature of conditions to change. We can also practice allowing people and events to be as they are. It's not that we should never respond to or improve life, but it's important to know we can just let everything be as it is. This is equanimity. There is great relief in letting things be. Let things change according to their own nature. Let them come and go. This allows us to rest in a spacious knowing that is aware of sounds and silence, the dawn and the dusk, the beginning and the end. Ajahn Chah also called this *knowing the refuge. Samadhi* enables us to discover and maintain this refuge.

> *Do everything with a mind that lets go. Do not expect any praise or reward. If you let go a little, you experience a little peace. If you let go a lot, you experience a lot of peace. If you let go completely, you will know complete peace and freedom. Your struggle with the world will have come to an end.*
>
> –Ajahn Chah

CHAPTER FOUR

The Practice of Presence

Kittisaro

Your task in practice is to realize the difference between mind and the activity of the mind. It's that simple.

—Ajahn Tate

The Buddha taught skills that support the cultivation of *samadhi*, the art of presence. These qualities are called *jhana* factors. *Jhana* means the mind is stilled and steady. In *jhana*, the luminosity of the mind infuses the body and the slower rhythms of the body steady the mind. Mind and body are thus integrated and unified. *Jhana*, a deep state of *samadhi*, is developed through the skill of gradually steadying the attention on an object of concentration, for example the breath, which is a good starting point. As this skill develops, the body-mind eventually becomes immersed in its own radiance and immovability. The taste of this absorption is very peaceful. When that peaceful and powerful mind reflects on its experience, it sees clearly the impermanence of all conditions, which in turn gives rise to equanimity. *Jhana*, known as *dhyana* in Sanskrit, means "meditative absorption." The hallmark of this state of mind is lucid awareness. The term *dhyana* became *chan* in Chinese Buddhism and *Zen* in Japanese Buddhism. *Jhanas* have become a very popular topic in meditation circles in recent years, generating a whirlpool of views as to what they are and how they are attained.

In public situations Ajahn Chah didn't teach much about the *jhanas*. He wasn't primarily a meditation technician and didn't approach this subject in the way of some schools and teachers, which lay out a lot of technical detail. He was, however, unshakably present, very mindful, and there's no doubt he had great facility with deep states of *samadhi*. Instead of talking about first, second, third, or fourth *jhana*, and so on, he emphasized knowing when the mind is peaceful, a little more peaceful, or deeply peaceful. A difficulty in discussing *jhana* is that it tends to activate a lot of ambition, which ironically can become a stumbling block in our practice. Or it can generate a sense of impossibility, particularly if one reads all the detailed definitions and then compulsively keeps comparing one's own meditation with what the books say. Nevertheless, it's helpful to have guidelines, but we need to approach this territory in a way that empowers rather than intimidates. Having some capacity for *jhana* and *samadhi* is clearly important, according to the Buddha's teaching. These skills will enable the mind to metabolize stress and suffering, and help the body maintain well-being and health.

Also most important in the path of meditation, *samadhi* is the foundation for insight. A refined state of concentration is not an end in itself; it's a means to the primary concern of liberation of heart. Ultimately there has to be some wisdom to discern, as Ajahn Tate taught, the difference between the mind *(citta)* and the activity of the mind. It is this insight that frees us from suffering. At the same time, there has to be *samadhi* for wisdom to arise. *Samatha* and *vipassana*, the calming and investigative aspects of meditation, are mutually supportive. The Buddha emphasized that in the service of awakening, these two qualities should work in harmony together, calling to mind an image of two oxen that pull the plow in tandem. Attaining highly refined states of consciousness was the preoccupation of the yogis that the Buddha trained with before his awakening. In the end, even though he was extremely accomplished in accessing subtle states of formless, meditative absorption, he abandoned that path as he saw that his mind was still susceptible to the hindrances.[1]

Ajahn Chah would say that developing deep states of calm, or *jhana*, without wisdom is like putting a stone on grass, the grass being an analogy for the mental hindrances. It's only a temporary solution, for once the stone is removed the grass grows back. We might think the afflictions are gone but they are only in abeyance, what the Buddha called "dormant or underlying tendencies." Given the right conditions they will arise again. Ajahn Chah was the master of disturbance. If his disciples were too attached to their peaceful states of mind, he would find a way to test how really calm they were, like sending them to a noisy village festival or having them work with people they didn't like. Ajahn Chah was Zen-like, making his point in very direct ways.

There is a funny story from the Zen tradition that reminds me of Ajahn Chah and his unorthodox methods. A diligent young student lived across the river from his Master. One day the student sent an inspired enlightenment poem to his teacher, proudly announcing, "Sitting still upon the purple golden lotus, the eight winds[2] cannot move me." In response the Master wrote the word "fart" across the poem and sent it back. Full of indignation, the student rushed out of his house and ordered the ferry to take him quickly to the other shore. Outraged, he felt he deserved an apology. When he got to his Master's door, he found a note saying, "The eight winds cannot move me, and yet one fart blows me across the river." Deflated and humbled, the young student realized how blinded he was by his so-called spiritual "attainment."

Ajahn Chah saw that his disciples could get obsessed with *jhana*, always wanting more calm, anxious that they didn't have enough *samadhi*, and forgetting to use the capacity they already had to look into the suffering at hand, here and now. He said that relying too much on subtle states of calm that are dependent on the controlled conditions usually necessary for *jhana* meditation, is like relying on a good lawyer to get us out of jail. We can use powerful conditions, like a silent meditation retreat or will power, to spring us out of trouble, but we don't yet understand what got us into trouble in the first place. It takes discernment and investigation to penetrate the causes of suffering and uproot the hindrances.

But even if we don't have a lot of *samadhi*, we can still embark on that journey. This is why at the end of the day Ajahn Chah would say, somewhat controversially, that if we have enough concentration to read a book, we have enough *samadhi* to be liberated. The conditions are right there to cultivate the mindfulness and wise reflection that can free us from suffering. We can see the mind caught in hindrances. Sometimes, however, without sufficient steadiness of heart, we may not have enough strength and clarity to overcome them. Let me be clear, Ajahn Chah didn't discourage us from strengthening our *samadhi*, but he wanted us to see our attachment and views, and remember that calm and insight work together. Training in *jhana* and *samadhi* is important. It's not the end of the journey, but it's an essential part of it. The Buddha exhorted his disciples to develop this ability, because a concentrated mind lessens suffering, increases well-being, and supports the arising of wisdom.

The Buddha recognized five skills that support the deepening of *jhana* and the flowering of *samadhi*. Each of these mental qualities is doable and practical. In the same way we learn any skill in life—playing a musical instrument, gardening, or navigating a new piece of software—we can cultivate the five *jhana* factors. This can be done either in formal meditation practice or in our everyday lives. As we begin, we shouldn't set the bar too high and thereby undermine our confidence. In approaching this territory it's helpful to have a "beginner's mind" and faith in our ability to practice these skills. Everyone can cultivate these *jhana* factors. Even if we are not concerned with the goal of liberation that the Buddha pointed to, developing the five *jhana* factors will help us negotiate our daily life with more ease and clarity. Mastery of *samadhi* is not just a process of genius or luck; it is generally understood that it comes about through patient, persistent, and repetitive practice.

THE FIVE JHANA FACTORS

The First Factor: Vitakka, *Thought That Directs Attention*

The key for the development of *samadhi* is the training of attention. Attention is directed by thought. Thought is not an enemy; however, when thought is unconscious, it is problematic. It propels the attention back to the past, and lunges forward to the future. We start thinking how we should be somewhere else, or we get lost in worries and anxieties: "I don't know if I'm ever going to get anywhere." Then we remember, "Oh, yes, I'm supposed to be present." We get swept away again and again, and end up feeling helpless. We've become a victim of thought. Thankfully, thought can be trained, and as the saying goes, it makes a good servant, but a bad master.

There's a certain kind of thought that is called *vitakka*. This is a "conscious, directed thought," which is an aid. It is the first of the five skills or trainings that support a deepening of presence. Many meditators hopelessly battle away, making thought an adversary that has to be squashed. However, this is unrealistic. Thoughts move like flocks of birds; they can't be eliminated or controlled through aversion. Actually, thought that is guided by wisdom and awareness is a great ally. We can guide attention with a quiet thought, like "Be aware of the body" or "Mindfully I breathe in" and "Mindfully I breathe out." Using thought to direct attention is the first aspect of cultivating the skill of *samadhi*. To use the analogy of Ajahn Lee, it begins the process of plunging that middle pillar of a bridge *(samadhi)* solidly into the ground through the fast-flowing river (the currents of the mind). Attention follows thought. When thought is habitual the attention gets swept haphazardly all over the place by anxiety, desire, worry, anticipation, and so on. We become the prey of thought. *Vitakka* directs attention to awareness, to the present moment. This is the first skillful factor that establishes *samadhi*.

The Second Factor: Vicara, *the Receptive Aspect of Attention*

Once we've directed attention to something, what is it that allows us to receive into awareness the rich, ever-changing texture of that experience? For example, a thought like "What's happening now?" brings attention to the body. We may notice the shoulders; we feel them and observe, "Oh, they're hunched up." As we connect with the experience of tension and receive it fully, the nature of receptive awareness becomes clear; it informs. In this regard, *vicara* reveals what we need to adjust:

for example, to soften and let the shoulders drop. We can also adjust our effort. Sometimes trying too hard makes us tense, so we need to relax our effort, maybe focus on the out-breath and let go a bit more. Sometimes we're all over the place, resisting being present with the body; the mind just wanders around and suffers. In that case we need to apply more effort, more energy.

So the first *jhana* factor directs thought and brings attention to an object within the field of our present-moment experience. The second *jhana* factor, *vicara,* is a more receptive aspect of attention. After we have connected with how it is, *vicara* explores and feels into the nature of the object, receives the experience, and then adjusts. It adjusts for the sake of balance, and tunes into what is needed for well-being and steadiness. Without *vicara,* there is no bonding, and the attention keeps sliding off our object of contemplation. As we become more present, our energetic experience is refined and the body naturally balances; it's a gentle process, not a bullying one. So, we bring the mind to the present, and then receive carefully how it is, tuning our effort, relaxing the body, or perhaps bringing more energy into our posture.

If we bring attention to the body and it's agitated and tense, we can focus on the out-breath, on softening, relaxing, smoothing. If we are sluggish or dull, we may adjust the in-breath and breathe in more fully to energize the body and mind. As the directed and receptive aspects of attention work together, they root that middle column through the turbulent river of the mind, right down into the earth, which is stable. The pillar doesn't stop the flow of the river. The stream still flows by. We still might have all sorts of thoughts, worries, and doubts. They come and go, but we are rooted here and now. The mind is centered in its own presence, in its own ground of awareness. As awareness develops and infuses the body and mind, naturally the currents of the mind will begin to settle.

The second *jhana* factor of *vicara* is the capacity to stay connected with the moment. It is often neglected by those cultivating meditation. There is too much emphasis on willfully directing attention. Like flogging some poor old horse, we keep chastising the mind, "Back to the breath!" which makes the mind and body tense. There has to be a balance between the directed and receptive aspects of attention, which support each other. "Be with the breath" or "How is it now?" are thoughts that direct attention. Once we've come into contact with our experience here and now, we need to sustain that connection. This second factor also means something like exploring and evaluation; it enables us to stay with how it is.

To enjoy the first deep level of *samadhi,* we need to employ our own thought to help us stay with the breath. Ajahn Chah encouraged his disciples to use the popular mantra of the forest masters—BUD-DHO. A mantra guides and protects the mind. It is a skillful use of thought that helps steer attention to the present moment. Once you have encouraged attention with the question, "How is it now?" then receive and steady awareness on the breath using the mantra BUD-DHO. Breathing in BUD—breathing out DHO. BUD-DHO is the nominative case of Buddha and means the awakened one, wisdom, or primordial intelligence. Not just the historical Enlightened One *out there,* 2,500 years ago, but the one *in here,* this awakened heart. *Buddha* or *buddhi* means the faculty of *knowing,* which is the essence of mind. This *knowing* isn't the same as having accumulated lots of knowledge about things; instead it's an inner, immediate, aware intelligence.

The mantra BUD-DHO is also related to the Sanskrit word *bodheti,* which means to awaken or cause to blossom. As we practice the second *jhana* factor of *vicara,* the receptive quality of attention, there is an opening of mind, just as the petals of a flower open to receive the warmth of the rising sun. We hold attention in a way that allows for this receptivity. Using the mantra BUD-DHO, particularly if we align with its inner meaning, supports this opening presence. In this way *vicara* is a skillful means to sustain attention within awareness of body and breath. You might also find your own word, phrase, or mantra—even better if the words you choose encourage a sense of heart, gentleness, receptivity, and trust.

I would like to highlight this receptive quality of attention, as it is so undervalued in our contemporary culture. We are inclined to be focused on a willful approach to life. We don't receive life. We tend to just keep pushing on to the next thing. We override our body and feelings to achieve, conquer, and overcome. But do we ever take time to listen more deeply into how it really is? In cultivating these two *jhana* factors we are learning about the basic building blocks of skillful relationship. The place to start is with our selves. Directed attention is *yang*, while receptivity is *yin*. Both aspects are needed to sustain attention within the present. If we only direct attention, but don't receive what we've brought our attention to, it's like being in a conversation where somebody is talking at you but not listening to you. They ask, "How are you?" but then don't bother to listen to your response. They talk on about this and that but you feel as if you're invisible; there's no space to be heard or received. If we only have directed thought in our meditation, it's a little like that. We might tell ourselves, "Be with the breath. Come on!" but we become so goal-orientated that there's no ease. Instead, a question like "How is it?" invites attention. It encourages us to receive our experience in a way that commanding the mind can't. What if we patiently and humbly notice the body, with its sensations and feeling tones? What is it like to be with what you are experiencing now?

It's really important with this training to not browbeat ourselves. Instead, we encourage ourselves to be more fully present by guiding attention with gentle application. As we patiently feel into what is present within the body, heart, and thinking mind, we sense how to adjust. For example, we explore a feeling of heaviness and realize, "I'm not breathing deeply enough." So breathe more deeply and drink in the vitality of the breath energy. Or notice if the body is agitated and tense. We can adjust by focusing on the out-breath, softening, relaxing, and smoothing the energy body. If attention wanders, we can also use these quiet thoughts to continue to guide it, like "Mindfully I breathe in, mindfully I breathe out." In this way we encourage the mind to gently rest and abide with the rhythm of breathing.

Being with the breath is like a mother standing behind a child on a swing. She gently receives the child as he arrives and *lets go* as he swings away. Awareness is the mother; it is just there, receiving and letting go. It touches the breath as it comes into the body; it touches it as it goes out. So our relationship to the practice of being with breathing is light, gentle, and easeful. When *vitakka* and *vicara* are in balance they support sustained attention on the body, breath, mind, and heart. The body begins to fill with the presence of awareness. This refines the bodily energy and brings ease. We find that even if uncomfortable, the body enjoys attention and begins to relax. This in turn grounds the mind. In other words, the two work together. The mind steadies on the sensation of the body, while the body is filled with the natural awareness of the mind.

The Third Factor: Piti, *Fullness of Being*

The first two *jhana* factors, inviting attention and sustaining attention, develop into the third *jhana* factor, which is called *piti*. This is usually translated as "rapture." The experience of piti is fullness of being. The body and mind become suffused with awareness. We can access *piti*, even in a moment, when we remember to savor our experience. Bring attention to your body, and then take a slow, long breath. As you breathe out, relax and consciously enjoy the sensations. Do this a few times and you will experience the seed of *piti*, the pleasure that is possible in meditation. *Piti* also means to enjoy and to be filled with bliss. These words can make piti seem out of reach. *Am I supposed to go into ecstasy?* However, the essence of bliss is learning to be filled with presence. The pleasure of *samadhi*, in fact the great discovery of *samadhi*, is that within this present moment, right here and now, we uncover and recognize something that's beautiful. Rather than thinking enjoyment is always around the corner, always somewhere else, we notice the root of joy is right here within the heart. This is one of the fruits of *samadhi*.

Vitakka directs the attention to the present moment, *vicara* receives the moment, and *piti* learns how to savor, enjoy, and be filled with the moment. We start by encouraging ourselves to be with the moment. We can cultivate the seeds of *piti*, even with uncomfortable sensations. Simply be with the sensations that are present within the body, whatever those sensations are, and be interested in them, care for them, and fully receive them. This way the energy of the mind/heart wells up to permeate and gladden the body and mind. One helpful image of the gradual development of *samadhi* described by my dear friend Ajahn Sucitto[3] is of a boat beached on the sand. When the tide starts rising, the boat lifts. It is still beached on the sand, but gradually it will begin to rise. At a certain point it is lifted free; it is not stuck anymore. The ocean supports the boat. In the same way, there's an uplifting feeling of buoyancy with the birth of *samadhi*. Being spacious and open, the body fills with awareness and breath energy. The body becomes the container for this energy of *piti*. The body feels both spacious and grounded. It is important to note that spaciousness doesn't exclude being grounded; the two go together. When you are centered and at ease in the ground of the body, not clutching outwardly for stability, you will recognize and generate a sense of spaciousness. This relaxation enables the life force to show up and suffuse the body-mind.

The Fourth Factor: Sukha, *Ease and Relaxation*

Being relaxed is a very important dimension of *samadhi*. As we savor our present-moment experience, we're inducted into *sukha,* the fourth *jhana* factor. We begin to feel satisfied. There is ease and relaxation. Why is relaxation so important? Unless we relax we keep generating energetic blocks: in our jaw, shoulders, and through our body and mind. The third *jhana* factor of *piti* gives rise to this fourth factor, *sukha,* which means ease and happiness. They also balance each other. If we make too willful an effort or get too excited, we create more tension; instead, as we relax, the energetic blocks in the body start to release. This fourth factor does require effort, but it's a very subtle effort. It's an effort that's not trying to go somewhere else, but to be simply present and at ease, accessing the happiness right here. It's the effort to stay with how it is, to relax the tension in the body, and to let things be. We allow the body to be more open and the mind to relinquish its preoccupations. With this subtle focus on ease and relaxation, energy flows through the body.

People often experience these *jhana* factors when they do a sport, work out at the gym, or do a discipline like yoga. They feel an increased sense of presence, buoyancy, and ease. The cultivation of *samadhi* is just a different kind of sport, one that works more subtly with the energies of mind and body. We allow the energy of the body and mind to be as it is.

Rather than trying to change anything, we bring attention to the reality of what is present. We receive and breathe with our experience and just stay there. We stay connected, relaxed, and soften the tensions on the out-breath. From there, a quality of presence and stillness naturally arises.

Even if there are uncomfortable sensations, savoring what is present creates ease. The aim is not to change the sensations, though they may change, but to bring about the fullness of awareness that allows for a depth of relaxation. Another way of understanding relaxation is that we stop battling and struggling. There is ease, well-being, and healing. The body and mind, held within *samadhi*, come into balance.

The Fifth Factor: Ekaggata, *Unification*

The final *jhana* factor encompasses the previous four. Together they give rise to a steady, gathered, radiant, easeful, and mindful presence. The fifth factor is called *ekaggata*, which means unification or single-mindedness. As we relax more deeply and have ease within the moment, our boundaries begin to dissolve, along with the sense of *me* "doing it." The perception of my feet and my hands, my body, my mind, the sense of "here" and "over there" all become unified and rooted in awareness. The body/mind is alive and whole, not different bits and pieces and the feeling of "me" locked inside it. There is simply a sense of embodied presence that is balanced and unified. *Ekaggata* is rooted in the word *eka*, which means "one." We are not fractured, not split, and cannot be divided. This "oneness" even extends beyond the boundary of the body, as all becomes unified within the awareness of the mind. At first when we try to meditate, we usually start with a willful effort, pushing the mind around. But then the effort becomes more subtle, as we repeatedly bring attention to the present. At a certain point effort is relaxed and begins to flow; we touch a more effortless ease. This natural sense of stability and gathering power of unification allows the body, heart, and mind to be flooded with the light of awareness.

The Buddha understood that when a practitioner consciously withdraws from seeking outwardly, he can remain in this peaceful abiding.

The word *viveka* means to withdraw from the tendency to seek all over the world after the objects of the five sense pleasures—sights, sounds, smells, tastes, and tactile sensations. The five *jhana* factors are supported by *viveka,* which is a fundamental attitude we can cultivate. We can train the mind to withdraw from its chronic preoccupations, its aims and ambitions. In the teaching of the Four Foundations of Mindfulness, which lead to the development of calm and insight, the Buddha encourages the practitioner to remove the mind from its preoccupations, its *distress* and *longing* with regard to the world. The training of the Four Foundations begins with this skill of *viveka,* which can also mean seclusion or detachment. *Kaya viveka* takes the body *(kaya)* to a quiet, secluded place for the sake of meditation, while *citta viveka* withdraws the mind *(citta)* from its entanglement with the world.

While *viveka* supports the *jhana* factors, likewise the *jhana* factors support *viveka,* particularly the first factor of *vitakka* or directed thought. When the mind is caught in distraction, we can use the thought "Not now" or "Let go" to guide attention back to body and breath. In the Viveka Sutta, we come across a *deva* (angelic being) who appears to guide a monk who's faltering in his meditation. The monk is "thinking unskillful thoughts connected with the household life." It is recorded that the deva admonishes him: "Desiring seclusion you've entered the forest, and yet your mind goes running outside. . . . Subdue your desire for people. Then you'll be happy and free from passion. Dispel discontent, be mindful. Let me remind you of that which is good. . . . Don't let the dust of the sensual pull you down. As a bird spattered with dirt sheds adhering dust with a shake, so a monk—energetic and mindful—sheds the adhering dust."[4]

It is necessary to have some capacity for removing the mind from its obsessions in order to cultivate *samadhi.* We don't always have to be out there on the front lines trying to fix everything, thinking about this, analyzing that. Learning to "let things be" is important in order to regenerate our own inner sense of well-being. The maintenance of well-being and healing of heart, body, and mind is one of the fruits of *samadhi.*

The Buddha talked of four fruits of *samadhi.* The first is the cultivation of a pleasing, abiding here and now. We are able to be with simplicity.

We enjoy just breathing, walking, drinking a cup of tea, the everyday moments of our life. Our well-being isn't so dependent on external events. We learn to maintain inner balance, clarity, and strength, and in the depths of meditation we are refreshed. The second fruit is that we are mindful and alert. We are present for our life, and can live skillfully. Discernment arises regarding the mind, its intentions, and the actions of ourselves and others. By being really present it's possible to touch into the unfolding truth of the Dharma. We see everything is teaching us; everything is moving in its own way according to karma. We connect with authenticity and experience contentment and potentiality. The third fruit is that we have knowledge and vision. When the mind is steady and deeply focused, the subtle dimension of things becomes apparent. As Ajahn Tate said, we see the activity of mind as different from mind itself. We see clearly the impermanent and the permanent. When this understanding is perfected, there is the realization of the last and ultimate fruit of *samadhi:* the unshakable liberation of heart.

THE BUDDHA'S ANALOGY FOR THE EXPERIENCE OF *JHANA*

The Buddha illustrated the cultivation of the first *jhana* in the following way: "Just as if a skilled bathman . . . would pour bath powder into a brass basin and knead it together, sprinkling it again and again with water so that his ball of bath powder—saturated, moisture-laden, permeated within and without—would nevertheless not drip; even so the [practitioner] permeates and pervades, suffuses and fills this very body with the rapture and pleasure born from seclusion. . . . There is nothing of the entire body un-pervaded by this [feeling]. . . . This is the first development of this Right Concentration."[5]

At the time of the Buddha there were people whose job it was to prepare a bath for others. So the analogy used here would have been something that everyone was familiar with. When someone took a bath, the bathman would heat water in a big container and then place a special kind of fragrant dry powder or crystals into a brass bowl and sprinkle it with water. As the powder became permeated with water, it would be kneaded by the bathman so that little by little what was granular and dry transformed into something different, something fragrant and cleansing. It changed into a malleable ball of suds.

The images illustrate the cultivation of first *jhana*. The brass bowl is a metaphor for the container of awareness. Everything is held within awareness. The bath powder is a metaphor for the body when it's fractured and dislocated, not conscious and balanced. When the life force isn't spread evenly through the body, it feels heavy and disjointed, like lumps of dry soap powder. The moisture is a metaphor for sprinkling the body with mindfulness, bringing moments of attention to the various parts of the body. Kneading and massaging the powder with water is an image for the rhythmic power of the in-and-out-breath, suffusing awareness into every part of the body. The ball of moisture-laden powder does not drip, illustrating how all the energy of the outwardly dispersed mind returns and transforms the body.

We are aware of the entire body held within a spacious, golden, luminous sphere of awareness, drenched with well-being. The tensions, pressures, and discomfort are recognized within awareness. As we notice a knot or pain, we sprinkle a little more water (attentiveness) there, breathe into it (the hands massaging), and soften the tensions on the out-breath. As we relax into the sensations of the body, we get the feeling of the body opening up and the knots dissolving. Little by little, applying the skill of the *jhana* factors, the body-mind unifies. Untangling energetic knots, awareness fills the body and suffuses it with light and calm. As body and mind merge, there is bliss and contentment.

If attention is directed to where we feel heavy and dull, or feel pain, then little by little there is mysterious transformation. The mind is steadied by the body and the body is embraced by the mind—mind and body unified. The body-mind resonates with well-being, constrictions open up, and boundaries dissolve. There is oneness within and without as even the perception of "inside" and "outside" disappears. This is the happiness of meditation.

WORKING WITH ILLNESS AND PAIN

It's important to be patient with this practice. All of us can do it. Even if many times we may find ourselves feeling hopeless, we can always start again. We always begin here and now, little by little, cultivating an abiding of well-being whatever the circumstances. One of the great trials of my monastic life was almost dying of typhoid fever in Thailand, which led to years of sickness. I was completely changed by this. My body had been very athletic and I had a lot of energy and positive willpower. But, due to my illness, I lost a lot of weight and all my energy. I spent three years in bed, and then for years afterward I struggled with low energy and debilitating exhaustion. I kept thinking, *I'm a meditator, I should be able to heal myself.* But I couldn't.

Illness wasn't a teacher I would have chosen, but there was nothing I could do about it. Until that point I had basically been able to accomplish whatever I wanted through willpower, study, and persistence. I'd been able to bend circumstances to my desires. My sense of self was intimately connected with my success. Then I spent years struggling with chronic pain, overpowering weakness, and digestive disorders. The Buddha said that sickness, old age, and death are heavenly messengers. They wake us up; certainly they became very real to me. There was no way I could live in denial of these truths. Though I saw doctors and healers and underwent myriad treatments, I couldn't overcome the illness. Unable to participate in the normal monastic routine, I felt like a failure. However, one day my abbot Ajahn Sumedho came to my bed and said, "Kittisaro, I want to apologize to you. I've wanted you to get well all this time, remembering how strong you used to be, but I realize that's putting a strain on you." Then he said, "Kittisaro, I give you my permission to die."

I felt so much relief at his statement that I cried with joy. I felt like I was given permission to deeply accept my situation. Before that there had always been this resistance to sickness, that it was wrong and a personal failure. Also, though it was with good intentions, the pressure from friends, family, healers, and myself to "get well" had become a burden. After Ajahn Sumedho said that and released me, although I still took my medicine and saw doctors, I became more accepting of the reality of my condition. I stopped believing that I *had* to get well. I began to deeply receive my situation. As I lay on my bed, I would spend hours being with the sensations in my body. I would hold the body in awareness. And just as I've explained, I would take attention, with the breath, right to the places where there was pain. And just stay there, with great patience and gentleness. This is how I got a real feeling for the power of *samadhi,* not only as that which focuses the mind, but also as that which heals.

With this practice I have been able to regain a lot of strength. I never thought my life force would return, and even though I still experience the effects of that sickness, I have been able to do things that would have once seemed impossible. Even so, it's important that I have time every day to reenergize myself through this practice of *samadhi*. The training of awareness in this art of presence is a magic wand unlocking the secret of a mysterious alchemy.

Most important, my illness taught me how to die—in other words, how to surrender to what I couldn't change. I had to make peace with the painful and confused states of body and mind that I encountered. My capacity for patience deepened, and in moments when I wasn't feeling sorry for myself or wishing my life were otherwise, I discovered a depth that is never sick, that never dies. My unyielding illness, which refused to follow my orders, took me to a place where I lost everything I had thought I was. Then I found *what remains*. I found that which no one can take away.

The training of *samadhi* is not easy. The Buddha said it is easier to conquer 10,000 warriors on a battlefield than it is to truly train the mind. So why do it? Well, when we don't, we make all kinds of assumptions that lead to conflict and endless suffering. Like that of a snake, this poison will slowly undermine our well-being. On a more global scale, the unchecked poisons of greed, hatred, and delusion have driven us to a collective precipice. Our future looks increasingly precarious, so there's a real urgency to see our lives, both individually and collectively, through a clear lens.

When the mind is composed, it sees clearly. When I had science classes as a child, we would put a drop of water on a microscope and see the microorganisms in the water with great precision. But if the eye isn't focused and keeps looking around, then we just get a distorted picture. That which sees clearly, which can focus, discern, and know the reality of the situation, is called the "Eye of Dharma." With *samadhi* we enter a realistic relationship with the elements of our world: the body and mind, and its moods, feelings, thoughts, and intentions. We can let conditions be as they are and in doing so notice the larger context of awareness itself.

Even though this contemplative process is a gradual training, it's good to remember that freedom is always here and now. Right in the midst of any given moment, whatever the condition, the essential nature of everything, including the mind, is freedom. Just as a mirror is unaffected by the myriad appearances that come before it, the inherent state of the mind is untainted. Its innate nature shines through. Right in the midst of the most constricted states or the most difficult circumstance, there is the pure essence of awareness. The Buddha called this innate freedom the "original brightness" or the "luminosity of heart." This freedom is our natural state.

> *You say that you are too busy to meditate. Do you have time to breathe? Meditation is your breath. Why do you have time to breathe but not to meditate? Breathing is vital to our lives. If you see that Dhamma practice is vital to your life, then you will feel that breathing and practicing the Dhamma are equally important.*
>
> –Ajahn Chah

CHAPTER FIVE

Two Kinds of Peace

Thanissara

Concerning samatha (calm) and vipassana (insight), the important thing is to develop these in our own hearts. When I practiced, if a thought of hate arose, I asked myself why. If a thought of love arose, I asked myself why. Just investigate this one point until you're able to resolve feelings of love and hate. When I was able to stop loving and hating under any circumstance I was able to transcend suffering. Then it doesn't matter what happens, the heart and mind are released and at ease.

–Ajahn Chah

After my first ten-day meditation retreat, which I barely survived, I came back to the student house I shared with my friends and boyfriend and set up a meditation space. The first time I sat down on my cushion, fully prepared to enter a sea of deep and peaceful calm, an ice cream truck pulled up right outside my window. It played the same squeaky, inane tune over and over again, trying to attract customers. Before long I abandoned my "peaceful" preoccupation and went to ask the poor ice cream vendor if he could *please* move on because he was disturbing my peace. When I sat back down, it occurred to me that maybe I had missed something about meditation!

For years I just wanted meditation to make me peaceful and enlightened. I had my ideas of what enlightenment was, and it certainly had nothing to do with being confused or depressed, which is how I tended to feel in everyday life. I did everything possible to avoid mundane things that everyone else seemed to be preoccupied by; in my estimation, everything was humdrum and boring. I lost my appetite for pretty much everything. I looked at the world and it was an iron cage. Sometimes it had golden bars, beautiful people, and delightful experiences, but I was still in prison. I traveled far and wide to intensive retreats, to avoid the world of commonplace things. I was a serious seeker. I would sit for hours, endure all sorts of pains, and I gave up all sorts of things. In the process I developed some facility for deep states of calm. I experienced altered states of consciousness, extra-sensory perception, and sublime states of peace and lucidity.

However, as soon as the retreat finished I'd fall back into confusion and would feel lost. Eventually, after I completed six months of silent intensive meditation at Dhammagiri, the Vipassana Center in India, I realized that while refined states of consciousness were peaceful, they would not liberate me from my suffering.

Yet I wasn't quite sure how to proceed. The variety of teachings available today didn't exist at that time. Instead I kept reading my small book of Huang Po, who said there was nothing to attain, which I intuitively felt was true, even though I still wanted to attain something. Over time, I became so sensitive that the sensory impingement of the world became intolerable. Every time I left the controlled space of the meditation center, I'd become overwhelmed. As my retreat experience of peace increased, so did my inner turmoil in everyday life. I also started to experience mind states that I had previously disassociated from or repressed. While on the one hand I was in a highly refined and sensitive state, on the other hand I was plunged into a swirling sea of discordant emotions and confusing mind states. When I finally entered monastic life, it slowly dawned on me that disturbance wasn't a problem; it was the path.

I began to understand that I didn't need to escape to anywhere else, even into very subtle and peaceful states of mind, but to embrace the reality of what was right in front of me. I knew I had to come to terms with suffering and limitation, and for that I needed all the tools in the Buddhist arsenal, which basically meant I needed a better understanding of meditation. Just trying to get peaceful was definitely not cutting it. One day the abbot of the monastery said to someone who was complaining about the world, "The problem isn't the world, the problem is the mind." I understood at that moment that I needed not only to calm the mind, but to have insight into the nature of mind itself.

Ajahn Chah taught that there are two types of peace: that of tranquility, which is still shaky, and the peace of wisdom, which is unshakable. These two types of peace are developed through two complementary aspects of meditation. These two central forms of Buddhist meditation are *samatha* and *vipassana*. *Samatha* means "the stilling of thought" and is associated with *jhana* and *samadhi*. *Vipassana* means "insight" and is associated with wisdom. These two aspects of meditation support each other. Ajahn Chah likened them to a candle and its flame. The practice of *samatha* and *samadhi* is like building a strong candle; while lighting the candle to see what's going on is the activity of *vipassana*.

The meditation practice of *samatha*, calming and steadying the mind, happens when attention is brought to the present moment in a particular way, as discussed in the previous chapters. *Samatha* uses an object of attention that is calming. It can be the breath, bodily sensation, sound, or a mantra or prayer. The breath, generally speaking, is neutral experience, as it is not associated with a sense of self, with its worries and obsessions. Although the breath energy is an intimate and necessary aspect of our life, we don't usually associate a sense of "me" with how the breath is; it's just a function that is happening. If we bring our attention to the realm of thought or feeling, that's more personal. We associate with thoughts and feelings and are defined by them, whereas the breath is neutral and impersonal. When we are with the breath, it doesn't usually activate our inner story lines and psychodynamic material. This is why meditation on the breath is most often used to bring about the calming of the body, mind, and heart.

When *samatha* is highly developed as a meditation method, it can lead to refined states of consciousness, where we experience the mind's energy in a more subtle way. We experience the mind in its formless and spacious aspects. We can also experience the body filled with the awareness of mind, which gives it a sense of light and ease. The breath, which at first is the coarse experience of the inhalation and exhalation, becomes more refined. There is still the rhythm of the breath; however, we also notice the subtle breath, which is just the energetic experience of the body. This includes awareness of subtle currents of energy and sensation, which, when focused on, can give rise to pleasant feeling. As *samadhi* develops, sensory experience can also appear in refined ways. The sense spheres include sight, sound, smell, taste, touch, hearing, and thought. For example, sound can manifest inwardly as a sort of vibratory sound, like the sound you hear when you put a large seashell to your ear. This is sometimes called "the sound of silence," which is just a high-pitched or low-pitched hum. It is also called the *nada* sound, which means the sound of emptiness, or the sound of the cosmos. Sometimes there is also inner sight, which can appear as light, colors, or images. There are also subtle manifestations of the other senses, such as subtle smell or subtle taste, though those are rare.

In Buddhist understanding, thought is also considered a sense. When there is subtle thought, it becomes less coarse and distracted, and more lucid. When thought is functioning in a healthy way, it enables cohesion for the self. From the information that flows through the senses, we construct meaning and thereby give placement and continuity for the self by means of our thought-based narratives. Thought clarifies our perceptivity of the world, assessing appropriate responses. In this regard, thought is an important function. It enables us to negotiate the world. We formulate our understanding with thought. However, our thinking processes are often chaotic and susceptible to all sorts of influences, such as inner obsessive stories that are symptomatic of unresolved emotional wounds. We are also influenced by the thoughts of others and mainstream narratives that shape societies and our global consciousness.

Thought is very powerful. It frames the realities we find ourselves compelled to live within. However, we can also use thought in very positive ways, such as to reframe a situation in order to reduce stress. For example, if I start thinking in negative ways about someone that upset me, the suffering just becomes more and more compounded. If instead I consider their struggle, it begins to soften my heart. I feel more compassionate. Thought can guide the mind, like the consideration that it is better to cultivate a kind heart than a resentful one.

However, working skillfully with our thoughts is not enough. We also need to get perspective on them. We first calm the thinking process, and then investigate it. When we bring awareness, which is usually tied up in thought, to the neutral experience of the breath, thought is refined through increased *samadhi*. It is not only lucid, but we can also experience thought and perception as intuitive knowingness, revelation, creative impulse, and quantum leaps of understanding. We may even have an awareness of future events or the minds of others, or a sense for the deeper causes that bring about certain results. These are all natural attributes of the mind. Generally speaking, these positive results are considered side effects in terms of the main intention of meditation.

The primary intention of *samatha* meditation is to calm the mind in order to investigate it, thereby enabling insight. When insight is distilled into wisdom it becomes a tool for liberation of heart. Initially, some skill at calming meditation is beneficial, as it leads to inner tranquility and lucidity. Then, as the mind calms, we can take our attention away from the coarse manifestation of sensory and bodily experience to the more refined emergence of subtle signs, such as inner sound, light, or subtle sensation and thought. These subtle experiences are called *nimittas*, which means "signs." As calm deepens, the experience emerges of *ekagatta* or "unification," which Kittisaro described in the *jhana* factors in the previous chapter. This style of meditation is healing and nourishing. It leads to some significant benefits such as calm, clarity, focus, and extrasensory knowledge.

However, the calm we experience as a result of this kind of meditation is prone to disturbance. It requires a certain amount of control to sustain it. Unless one is very accomplished, or perhaps has a natural propensity, this style of meditation needs a fairly strong and focused will to maintain it, alongside an environment that is free from intrusion. Often people love meditation retreats, where the environment is controlled through silence and minimal contact with others, because they are conducive to calm. Yet all too often they feel the loss of that calm when returning to everyday life. This means that they have yet to understand the importance of a whole other dimension of meditation, which is the ability to wisely reflect on disturbance itself.

Because I did a lot of retreats at the start of my practice and developed some facility for calm, I found the world very coarse and sought to avoid its impingement so I could maintain the interiority I had developed. People were loud and irritating, sensory experience too grating, and the everyday affairs of politics and social discourse was unsavory. I was a spiritual snob. I was judgmental of regular people and felt my escape from the world's demands was a superior vocation. I experienced a great swell of dispassion and had no real desire to make money, get married, seek a career, or acquire possessions. This profound feeling of disenchantment eventually led to leaving my boyfriend, giving everything away, cutting off my hair, and entering the monastery. I'm not sure what ideas I had about monastic living, but whatever they were, they were naive. Perhaps I thought that I would sit in a forest hut floating above the world for the rest of my mortal life and then at death dissolve into a vast, blissful cosmic soup.

Instead I was very rudely awoken in the reality of the spiritual warrior camp that is monastic life. I was living with people I hadn't chosen to live with. I was under pressure to conform to a daily routine, which started at four a.m. and went until late at night, and a discipline that required the relinquishment of my personal freedom to wander round as I wanted. As the workdays were long and hard, and as we didn't eat after midday, I often felt hungry. I was also often tired and on the edge of trying to keep up with the demands of the life. Just as I caught up with some sleep on our "days off" we would launch into our weekly all-night meditation. And while I was trying not to be competitive, in reality I was, which was hard considering the favored position of male monastics over female within an immovable hierarchy. As the youngest and therefore most junior nun, I seemed to be destined to keep going down the pile rather than up it. Consequently I became obsessed with getting to the meditation room first so I could claim my little sitting patch before the laypeople piled in. Those few square feet of space symbolized the last vestige of my domain.

As if my daily obsessive scramble for paltry patches of sovereignty weren't undignified enough, I'd find myself feeling less than kind toward the monk in charge of the afternoon drinks, who had a penchant for reaching his arm into the dark interior of the locked kitchen cupboard, maneuvering past the tins of delicious cocoa only to pull out a jar of Marmite, or if we were lucky, some green tea for our evening beverage. My monastic life really wasn't going that well. It wasn't what I had imagined at all. There didn't seem to be much bliss around. I stuck with it as best I could, and to be fair there were times when the sheer focus and discipline were rewarding, the camaraderie heartwarming, and the transmission of Dharma peerless. Basically, in spite of the ego "wipe out" strategy, I felt grateful.

The intensity of the lifestyle brought about "breakthroughs" usually as a result of being confronted by despair and anger. As I became more open to the suffering within my own mind, I began to see that working with the hindrances of desire, aversion, dullness, restlessness, and doubt was the leading edge of practice. Through the daily process of monastic life, I gradually reached a turning point where I was less interested in trying to escape into some pseudo nirvana, and more engaged in working through my suffering. Actually, I really didn't have a lot of choice, as my inability to control the situation demanded I practice with difficulty rather than avoid it. One of the training principles of monastic life was the more difficult things were, the more opportunity there was to develop some skill. And certainly difficulty was the name of the game at that time.

In the early years of building Chithurst Monastery,[1] being cold, overworked, exhausted, and irritable was a bit of an ongoing theme. For quite a long time I shared a room with a nun who snored. A night owl, she would retire to sleep at midnight, clicking open the latch on our door, only to wake me up. There I would lie, trying to think spiritual rather than murderous thoughts, counting down my few hours of precious sleep until the four a.m. bell. Before I began to work with disturbance, my meditation arsenal was mostly a jujitsu of mind-calming techniques. I really didn't have a deeper understanding of *vipassana* or much of a perspective on my thoughts and feelings. Instead I used a lot of energy to repress the deepening erosion of my spiritual positivity and increasingly fragile "calm" states of mind.

Those early days in the monastery were very raw. There was zero psychological sophistication or understanding of how the shadow plays out, particularly in spiritual communities. However, in spite of the challenges we faced, including the potent reactivity of our minds, there was a great spirit of enthusiasm and youthful idealism. We were the elite team on the fast track to enlightenment. We had the best teachings, a superior vehicle, and a tradition that enjoyed the luxury of feeling a pure and unbroken connection with the Buddha's radical lifestyle of total renunciation. I absorbed the daily Dharma talks and teachings with a great sense of appreciation. I found them nourishing, uplifting, and helpful. The teaching of Ajahn Chah came through the lifestyle. We lived the premise that authentic awakening doesn't begin until "you can't go back, you can't go forward, and you can't go up or down." This was the brilliance of the monastery. It offered a very limited structure within which the suffering of the mind became painstakingly clear.

Being "on the ropes" with no way out, while faced with the failure of my peaceful meditation practice, inducted me into a deeper relationship with the inner workings of my mind and heart. The teachings from our abbot, Ajahn Sumedho, unrelentingly focused on the grasping mind as a cause of suffering. I enjoyed his style of teaching and tried to "let go" as daily encouraged. However letting go just wasn't that easy to apply. Even so, the pressure was on to surrender into the discipline, to the teachings and to the whole way of life. In the midst of this dynamic, while my mind squirmed, trying to find some kind of inner ease, I became increasingly aware of how the mind generated its own prison, or at least that's how I experienced it. Gradually I realized I didn't need to fear suffering; instead I was being offered an opportunity to go beyond its reach.

The heart of *vipassana* meditation focuses on our deep attachment to the sense of self. At times I was able to see the pain of the separate self and its isolation from others and the world around. Applying awareness to the constructs of the self opened up some compassion for the struggle we were in. I knew that I had discovered a whole new dimension, a way beyond our conditioned strategies of fight, flight, or freeze. In those days, I didn't have the language to frame it like that, but I was beginning to understand how to practice. I had discovered the "middle way" of mindfulness and the power of accepting suffering. Before then I had only been trying to escape the world. Now I knew a way of being wise to the world.

The Buddha's own discovery of the "Middle Way" was unique at his time. Before his enlightenment and teaching, *samatha* and *jhana* methods of meditation were the ones most commonly taught and practiced. These methods are supported by the principle of *viveka,* which is classically defined as the ability to "abandon hankering, disappointment, and grief for the world." It is training the mind to renounce its preoccupations. *Viveka* also means "physical withdrawal," which is how the Siddhartha—the Buddha to be—trained with the yogis of his time. This has always been part of the great tradition of the yogis: going to places removed from society—to a cave, forest, or desert—for the sake of refining meditation in order to bring about great calm and transcendent states of consciousness. However, these states can't hold the hindrances at bay. Ultimately this approach offers temporary peace, but not the ability to know peace in the face of disturbance. Besides focusing on developing refined states of consciousness, the yogic traditions of the Buddha's time included great physical austerities, where practitioners tried to crush the needs of the physical body in order to transcend its limitations.

The "Buddha to be" tried this for six years with a small group of dedicated yogis, who one assumes were his close friends. These were the Olympic meditators of the time. Their specialty was the cultivation of extreme methods, rejection of society, and uncompromising focus on catapulting themselves beyond all concerns of the body and mind. They were a tough bunch, and it was recorded that the Buddha was the most extreme of all of them.

In the end, the Buddha rejected this way. By then he was reduced to skin and bone and was on the edge of death. He talked of touching his stomach and feeling his backbone, of touching his head and his hair falling out, of passing urine and falling over in a heap. It was at this moment he thought, *Might there be another way?* At this point two significant events happened. First, he had a memory of withdrawing from a village festival as a child, and sitting quietly in meditation under a rose apple tree. Meditating on his breath was very pleasurable. He realized that the pleasure he experienced was not harmful. He didn't need to crush pleasure. From this innocent memory a new way forward emerged. He understood that "this was the way." Up until then he had been intent on crushing all feeling while denying the needs of his body. But now he realized he had gotten too weak to practice anymore. He was on the edge of death, he knew he needed to eat and regain his strength.

The second event was a compassionate woman who, seeing his weakened state, came to offer him some milk rice to eat. Her name was Sujata. She had been watching his heroic efforts and, moved by his endeavor, she offered him food. The acceptance of his first nourishing meal signified the end of his pursuit of extreme asceticism. He no longer feared pleasure or was lost in it, and he no longer walked the path of pain. Instead he entered the royal road to his own full Awakening. In spite of this, he paid dearly for rejecting the extreme and disembodied practices of the time. On his receiving the milk rice from Sujata, his five fellow yogis severely criticized and abandoned him. He was alone. Alone, but free to pursue his unique and radical way of Awakening, which he later articulated in his teaching of the Four Noble Truths. But even after his Awakening, the Buddha didn't reject *jhana* meditation; in fact, he taught it as an important support for deeper insight.

For ourselves, we may not be able to find a cave in the Himalayas, but we can still develop *samatha,* or calming meditation. At first we do so during formal times of sitting practice, by learning to withdraw the mind from distracted and negative thoughts. Just say to the mind "not now" and bring attention to the object of meditation. This simple method helps steady the mind, supports the increase of well-being, and creates the conditions for insight.

Practitioners who develop *jhana* can sometimes access psychic realms of knowledge, including knowledge of past lives, future lives, and other realms. These abilities are often very attractive to spiritual materialists. In the early recordings of the Buddha's life, it seems he had many psychic abilities; nevertheless, his primary focus took a different direction. He didn't hold up special powers as the goal of the path. While psychic ability can happen, it doesn't necessarily lead to the freedom the Buddha advocated. For example, Devadatta, the Buddha's cousin, was popular, charismatic, a great ascetic, and had impressive psychic powers. He was an accomplished orator and impressed a lot of people who became his followers. But he nurtured serious delusions that weren't uprooted, which clouded his mind. He was very jealous. He connived to murder the Buddha. He didn't succeed, obviously, so instead he tried to split the order. This is an interesting example of how charismatic spiritual teachers may appear impressive due to their abilities and powers. However, it doesn't necessarily mean they've overcome ignorance, ego inflation, or the desire for personal power.

For most of us, how to manage psychic powers is not really our main challenge in life! Mainly, we don't have the lifestyle or the capacity to develop these very subtle and refined states of mind. Even if we experience some of these results in our practice, we shouldn't put all our energy into aiming for that. The intention of meditation, as clearly stated by the Buddha, is to realize the "unshakeable deliverance of heart." This is what the Buddha aimed for, and we are encouraged to do the same. The peace of calm is subject to being shaken, whereas the peace of Awakening is unmoving. To realize unshakable peace is the ultimate purpose of insight meditation.

Sri Nisagadatta Maharaj,[2] whose teaching greatly influenced both Kittisaro and myself, had a concise way of defining the essence of insight meditation or Vipassana. He said, "Use your mind to know your mind. It is the best preparation for going beyond the mind." *Vipassana* is just this, *using your mind to know your mind*. This is the activity of wisdom. Wisdom is the fruit of *vipassana*, a word that literally means to "see into" or to "see directly." We see peace but also what obstructs peace. Actually, peace is always available. The more present we are, the more potential there is to taste peace. This peace, the Buddha said, "leads inward to the source, invites investigation, is timeless, and always here and now." However, the mind gets distracted, and so in *vipassana* we explore what blocks peace. It is a reflective and contemplative style of meditation that doesn't depend on controlling the environment or sensory impingement to gain a peaceful state. That kind of peace collapses as soon as something happens that we can't control. Emotions come up that are difficult to be with, events challenge us, and people upset us.

Even if we are good at accessing refined states of mind, it tends to take a lot of willpower to sustain them. If we get sick or weak and can't sustain our focus, then the unconscious material that we've repressed will surface. There are just so many ways to be disturbed every day. If we don't really understand the importance of cultivating insight and wisdom, we will always feel disappointed with our meditation. This happens for many meditators; they generate an internal war zone, battling to control the mind. Actually the mind, and life itself, is never particularly peaceful; there's always some trouble.

In *vipassana* meditation, we contemplate not only the pleasant and peaceful but also the unpleasant, the things we don't want to deal with. *Vipassana* is not a meditation technique so much as the art of contemplation. Sometimes people find it a lot easier to have very clear directions, such as: repeat a mantra, watch the breath, do ten thousand prostrations, read this text, or believe in a guru. Of course, following directions is helpful and various practices can be supportive; they build capacity, and wholesome tendencies. However, *vipassana* isn't a formula, i.e., "Just do this and you'll have this result." While there are techniques that support *vipassana*, such as naming states of mind, or sweeping attention through the body to note sensations, in essence *vipassana* is formless. Sometimes it is called "choice-less awareness." It is the art of seeing deeply into the nature of mind through contemplative inquiry.

To do this, we reflect on whatever emerges within the field of our awareness. For example, we may start a meditation session being with breath, breathing in and breathing out. Maybe everything's fine, we're quite peaceful; but a few minutes into the meditation a disturbance emerges. Suddenly we feel irritated by someone or we feel a longing to be somewhere else. Sometimes we don't even have a name for what we feel; it's just a vague "something" that is uncomfortable. We can either give attention to the breath for the sake of gathering more steadiness of mind, or open to our present experience in a more reflective way. We can inquire, "What's here? What's present? What's the experience now?" It may be resistance, or dullness, or turbulent feelings in the solar plexus, or constriction around the heart. Or perhaps the mind is agitated or anxious. This reflective type of meditation is an inquiry into the nature of our immediate experience. We can ask questions like, "What's difficult about being here now?" That will reveal a lot, because the mind says, "I don't want to be here now." Then you can ask, "Where do you want to be?" and the reply might be, "I don't really know." Then you start to come into contact with this feeling that clothes every moment of our existence. You might have a name for this feeling—anxiety, worry, longing, or resistance—but you can put all of these under the umbrella of *dukkha* or suffering.

> *It's not just by sitting with your eyes closed that you develop wisdom. Eyes, ears, nose, tongue, body, and mind are always with us, so be constantly alert. Reflect on your experience continually. Seeing trees or animals can all be occasions for study. Bring it all inwards. See clearly within your own heart. If some sensation makes impact on the heart, witness it clearly for yourself, don't simply disregard it.*
>
> –Ajahn Chah

CHAPTER SIX

The Grit That Becomes a Pearl

Thanissara

Having loved enough and lost enough, I am no longer searching, just opening, no longer trying to make sense of pain, but being a soft and sturdy home in which real things can land. These are the irritations that rub to a pearl.

—Mark Nepo

One of the essential messages of the Buddha is that it's really important to get to know the experience of *dukkha,* or dissatisfaction. Not to know it intellectually, not to write a thesis about it, but to get to know it by meeting this experience directly. Until we know *dukkha,* we don't really have a way to end it. The discourse of the Four Truths that the Buddha gave after his Awakening begins not with enlightenment, but with the encouragement to know *dukkha,* to know it in order to overcome it.

To know the experience of suffering can sound fairly straightforward. But the mind is pretty slippery around the experience of *dukkha.* We tend to say, "The problem is it's too hot or too cold, or it's the situation I'm in, or because I got so screwed up when I was a kid, or it's my partner, or my job." Of course external factors contribute to our happiness or suffering, we don't need to dismiss the factors that shape our lives—but in *vipassana* we're not trying to figure out where the *dukkha* came from. Instead we work with pain and suffering as we experience it, without blaming others, repressing it, or projecting it inward onto our self. Meeting *dukkha* in this direct way doesn't preclude challenging or changing our individual or collective circumstance, but it does empower us to stop unnecessary suffering right at the place we experience it, which is the mind.

When we experience *dukkha,* our first instinct is to move our attention away and distract ourselves. We have billion-dollar industries based on entertainment and consumption keeping us distracted from this core truth of life. But are we more content? Conversely, we can become addicted to pain, finding ourselves repeatedly gravitating toward worry, old wounds, and resentments. We can even wallow in suffering, our own and others'. Some people become sufferers, great martyrs thinking "no one suffers as much as me—let me just tell you about it." We all have complex reactions to this everyday experience of unsatisfactoriness. Often those reactions are personalized as "my problem." It is very common for the mind to project suffering onto the "self," interpreting *dukkha* as a personal failure: we are failing because we suffer. Or the mind will project our suffering onto those around us; it's somehow "their fault." In this activity of projection and blame we miss how the mind itself generates an endless stream of *dukkha* through its inability to accept self, others, and life as it is. In short, it's our reactivity that generates *dukkha,* keeping us agitated and therefore unable to contemplate the actual, direct, here and now experience of it.

The Buddha's way of explaining *dukkha* is a great relief. He didn't say, "Well, it's your suffering, it's your fault." Nor was his teaching, as it is sometimes articulated, "This world's just a pile of suffering." That's pretty negative. Actually he put it in a very dispassionate way. He just said, "There is *dukkha.*" Just as one might comment on a fact of nature, saying "It's raining hard today" or "The trees are shedding their leaves." *Dukkha* is inherent within the conditioned realm. Conditions mean anything that emerges from formlessness and comes into form, whether it's the body, feelings, perception, thought, or sensations. Whatever form emerges, *dukkha* is inherent. Things are *dukkha* because they are impermanent and therefore unreliable. Actually, *dukkha* is natural and not suffering. It becomes suffering when the mind identifies with phenomena and grasps. The meaning of *dukkha* that conveys this process is derived from the breakdown of the word into *du*, which means "apart from" and *kha*—or *akash*—which means "space." This gives the sense of being apart from the spacious, the perfect, and the complete. In this way *dukkha* conveys the deepest anguish and dilemma of the self, which is its state of separation from the whole.

In meditation, when we bring attention to "now," it allows whatever is present to be real to us. For example, we notice the breath, the body, our feelings, and whatever impinges upon our senses. Attention illuminates whatever is here, which is often the experience of *dukkha*. Usually, even at a very subtle level, there will be some sense of discontent, anxiety, or restlessness. It's important to know *dukkha*, not to obsess about it, but just to meet it. It's important because if we don't know it, we continue to generate *dukkha* from false assumptions. We actually make *dukkha;* the mind habitually and unconsciously generates *it*.

Dukkha is different from pain. Buddhist thought makes a distinction between pain and suffering. Pain is part of our human experience. For example, getting sick is painful, as is grief at the loss of a loved one; this is natural and appropriate. However, we then tend to generate a whole extra layer of suffering, through our difficulty in accepting how things are. When we resist the natural flow of life we create suffering, stress, and struggle. When we assume ownership and permanence in a world that is constantly changing, we become burdened. In essence, it is the ignorance of the mind, when it doesn't see the true nature of reality, that produces suffering. And so, our relationship to "how it is" becomes the conditioning factor for either generating or reducing suffering.

We are doing the suffering; no one is doing it to us. It is because of this that we can free ourselves from unnecessary *dukkha*. This is not always easy to do. "How it is" can really challenge us. Yet even though it is difficult, this is a doable practice, otherwise the Buddha would not have taught it for regular people like us.

For example, I suffered when the unethical behavior of someone I trusted came to light. It had a devastating impact. I felt betrayed. The theme of betrayal became a powerful contemplation, particularly as there was no resolution. In the end this situation taught me a lot. I kept reflecting on where the suffering really was. Was it in the behavior of the other, in the divisiveness that followed, in the blame that was projected? I wanted more truth to come out, but it didn't, it stayed hidden in a web of lies. When lies are covered up, it leaves those abused without recourse to justice. This is a powerful theme that runs through human history: people manipulating others for their own ends, while at the same time distracting from their behavior by shifting blame elsewhere. We'd be naive not to understand that the conversion of lies to "truths" is pervasive in contemporary political and corporate culture. When apprehended correctly, such experiences become the sharpening stones for our wise realism.

To have a conscious relationship to suffering is different than having an unconscious one. We will all experience pain, simply due to our incarnation into form. It is part of being human. We experience bodily pains, ill health, fatigue, hunger, thirst, and as we get older we will feel the pains of aging. That's just the way it is. Freedom from *dukkha* doesn't mean eternal youth, or that we are never going to have a headache, never going to feel irritation, or loss, or get betrayed and hurt by others. Freedom from *dukkha* is not abdication from the human race, but a deeper acceptance of how we are, an acceptance that brings both equanimity, and also a clearer response.

Dukkha is also categorized as the pain of things ending. Even within pleasant experiences there is *dukkha*, because the nature of conditioned things is to pass. All things already have their endings within them. If we become attuned to this, then we can appreciate the moment. We can appreciate the extraordinary fact of our unique and precious lives. We can even appreciate *dukkha*, rather than resisting it. We understand that the experience of suffering is a portal to our awakening. We don't wish for suffering, but once we understand how to be in relationship with it, it becomes the means through which we mature as loving and wise people.

The Buddha placed the contemplation of *dukkha* at the heart of his teaching. The foundation of Buddhist teaching is formulated around his Four Noble Truths: "There is *dukkha*," "*Dukkha* has a cause," "*Dukkha* has an end," and "The Eightfold Path which brings about the ending of *dukkha*." Each of these truths has a corresponding practice. In response to the first truth, the practice is to "meet, understand, and contemplate" *dukkha*. The practice for the second truth is to "let go or abandon" the causes of *dukkha*. The third is to "realize or recognize" the end of *dukkha*, and the fourth is to "develop or cultivate" the path leading out of *dukkha*. Sometimes this teaching is misrepresented as a negative view on life, such as "Buddhists are just into suffering." Actually, it's a very positive message, as it says we can do something about the *dukkha* we unconsciously generate and then experience. This simple teaching is actually extremely profound and direct. It offers a clear diagnosis of the fact of suffering, an insight into the causes of suffering, and a remedy and cure for suffering.

The Four Noble Truths may not be a very fashionable teaching, but it's an extremely profound one. Wherever we are, when *dukkha* arises, we have a pathway to peace. In calming meditation, we develop strength of mind through the practice of steadying attention on the breath, body, or our chosen object of contemplation. In insight meditation, we take that same strength of attentiveness and bring it directly to the experience of *dukkha*, as it is felt within the body and heart. We do this in a very particular way, by neither justifying nor trying to fix the pain, neither being overwhelmed nor shaped by it, nor repressing or distancing ourselves. The art of meditation is to meet *dukkha* directly, to breathe with it, and inquire into it. This is ultimately less painful than avoiding it.

I remember as a young nun I suffered a lot. I trained in a male monastic hierarchy deeply ambivalent to the presence of nuns. Initially, I didn't see the impact, but as time went on, I noticed it generated a painful and divisive power dynamic. I was grateful to live as a monastic, but the fine line between "training" and the blunt use of power was unhealthy—particularly when as nuns, we had no agency in the decisions that shaped our lives.

However, there wasn't much I could do about the situation. Basically, it was just a lot of suffering. One day, I was contemplating the pain in my heart due to some new rules that had been handed down without consultation, which I found churlish. I was just right there, holding attention to the sensation. It felt like a knife in my chest and a hand around my throat. It was very visceral, and although the trigger was a controlling hierarchy, the feeling felt ancient. It was the familiar pain of powerlessness. In the middle of my walking meditation, I stopped and stretched out my arms, like Christ on the cross, and screamed out, "I accept this suffering!" It sounds dramatic (and somewhat inflated), and fortunately I was well hidden in the monastery forest! But something profound happened. I realized I could be with a painful dynamic and not suffer. My suffering was there because I didn't want things the way they were. In my acceptance, the suffering turned to compassion. I felt compassion for the monks and nuns, for myself, for everything and everyone. Meeting experience *as it is* empowers. We may not always be able to change a challenging situation, but we can be better resourced to engage with it.

Ajahn Chah came from a farming community in Northeast Thailand and left school at thirteen. He tended to put things in unacademic, immediate, and straightforward ways. He often pointed to the fact that *dukkha* arises because the mind is caught up in "wanting and not wanting." We want what is not here and don't want what is here. This is very simply put and yet challenging to really see. However, framing it like this, Ajahn Chah points to a direct practice. With some steadiness of mind, we can reflect on desire, and its internal narrative of always wanting things to be different from what they are. We frame our experience: "I don't want it to be like this; I want it to be different." Each moment we want, long, wait, and look for something that is not there, we generate *dukkha*. Conversely, when there is resistance or aversion to how it is, we generate *dukkha*. We resist what is "now." The push and pull of the mind undermines our capacity for contentment. When we look into the Second Truth of desire and aversion, we get perspective. What we struggle with can be okay. It is workable. We can work with all of it, people blaming us, pains in the body, emotional turmoil—instead of continually adding *dukkha* through our judgment, "It shouldn't be like this."

A lot of the time we feel, "It shouldn't be like this!" It should be somehow different. We should be in a heaven-like world. But we weren't born into heaven; we were born in this world, with its wars, environmental degradation, suffering, exploitation, difficulty, and pain. Accepting the reality of *dukkha* isn't an abdication from response, it is a way to understand that the most effective way we can change the world is through the quality of our own awareness. As we work to resolve our personal *dukkha*, we lessen the possibility that our actions will increase the suffering that already exists.

When Kittisaro was a novice monk, just before his full ordination, his parents took a trip to Thailand, all the way from Chattanooga, Tennessee, to find out what he was doing. In the process they met Ajahn Chah. Kittisaro's father is a very astute political observer and at that time he was concerned, as were most Americans, with the war in Vietnam and the threat of communism. He was concerned that the monastery, which was on the border of Laos, would be invaded by communist guerrillas. Ajahn Chah said that the thing he should really worry about was the "communist guerrillas in the mind." I guess nowadays he would have pointed us back to the "terrorists of the mind."

This is where we begin and end. We take everything back to the mind. As we experience life, all sorts of feelings, thoughts, and reactions arise. Our problem isn't so much "what is" but our relationship to what is. When I consider my own suffering, so much of it comes from the fact that I simply cannot accept life, and people as they are. I get upset by what people do. Ajahn Chah said it's like hollering at a person who upsets you. Then someone comes up and says, "You know, that person is crazy." You relax, because suddenly there's perspective. Until we are mature human beings, we're all a little crazy; we all produce suffering. So it means we are going to learn patience! The ongoing inquiry into the nature of suffering is a patient process. These Four Truths are a deepening hologram: wherever we touch them we enter the process of contemplation. When we locate clinging, desire, and aversion, then, as encouraged by the Buddha, we let go.

Letting go is the Third Noble Truth. Vipassana insight meditation reveals where we hold on. Where we hold on, right there is *dukkha*. Right where there's *dukkha* is the place of letting go. In insight meditation we contemplate the nature of suffering and its release. Actually, the mind in its natural state is open, aware, and present. It is reflective. But the mind, when tinged by ignorance, has a tendency to constrict around thought-forms and desire, generating a sense of self that feels "It's not enough" or "I'm not enough." Our lack of inner freedom is often born from this feeling of "not enough." The constriction around "I need to be something more" or "I don't want what is here" is a constant irritation. Ajahn Chah likened it to a dog with mange. He goes into the shade, to the heat, from place to place, running around everywhere trying to find relief, scratching here, scratching there. The dog keeps feeling each place is the problem, not realizing his discomfort is due to his own skin.

In a moment of just stopping and relinquishing our addiction to "wanting and not wanting," a whole other dimension opens up. When the cause of *dukkha* is released, we recognize a timeless abiding, always here now, which is the heart/mind's natural state. Recognizing the mind in its natural state is not something to attain; it's a realization. When grasping and resistance cease, the endless chasing of one thing after another, then the mind recognizes the taste of its own nature, which is the taste of peace. This peace is *nibbana*.

Just as the grit in an oyster becomes a pearl, so *dukkha* has its function. Awakening quickens through wise contemplation of suffering. Instead of blindly reacting to the experience of *dukkha*, shifting around it or blaming someone else for it, we apprehend it directly, and more quickly. A conditioning factor for this process is what the Buddha called *nibbida*, which means "disenchantment." We finally come to a place in ourselves when we know another experience isn't going to alleviate our basic sense of discontent—the next holiday, the next acquisition, or the next exciting distraction. In our contemporary society, when we feel *disenchanted* it is seen as a problem. We are encouraged to go shopping, take medication, or find some other escape. We think, "If I sit on the beach today I'll be much happier than staying here." So we go to the beach. We're happy for a few minutes and then think, "If I just had a nice coffee, I'd feel better." Or we think, "It's too hot here. If I go up into the mountains where it's cooler,

I'd be happy." This seeking drives us on and on. It's a good sign when we begin to be suspicious of endless pursuit; it means we're not buying into it so much. Periods of retreat bring us into direct confrontation with what we've been trying desperately to avoid—this basic feeling of dissatisfaction. This isn't to say that things like anti-depressants and holidays don't have their place. But even when we get life as perfect as we can, the underlying message of *dukkha* still crashes in. It prods us until we respond to the invitation to contemplate our experience more carefully. Sometimes when we acknowledge the presence of suffering, we immediately want a solution. Fix it quick! Get a Band-Aid! Take it away!

This is kind and careful work. When circumstances generate pain or anguish, we can lessen *dukkha* by patiently containing our reactivity. Then, at the place of suffering, the journey of transformation opens up. As beautifully articulated in Mark Nepo's poem, we become "a soft and sturdy home in which real things can land." This describes perfectly the quality of awareness and receptivity needed to undertake the journey through suffering. We "no longer try to make sense of the pain." We create space and allow awareness to provide a gentle holding for the "irritations that rub to a pearl." This is the work of *vipassana*. As we inquire into the moment, *dukkha* becomes dharma, or nature, rather than a "me" that is wrong or bad. As we listen more deeply to suffering, we begin to notice non-suffering. The heart realizes its innate courage, strength, and invincibility. This journey through pain and suffering burns away the impurities, and what is revealed is something pristine, clear, and beautiful, like a moonlit pearl: the tender, merciful heart, and its infinite ability to receive the cries of the world.

When we're with suffering, it's as if we are with a child that's very unhappy. If the child is wailing and wriggling, wanting to get away, wanting something but it doesn't know what, we kindly hold the child. Sometimes we can experience our minds as the child and the awareness as the mother. The child of the mind can be really hurting and screaming, "I can't bear this. I'm hopeless!" Or, "No one is there for me," or just an unnameable pain that seems so familiar, so ancient, and so intractable. But the mother, our aware, present heart, just sits it out and waits patiently for the deeper truth to emerge. She is breathing with the pain while gently holding the mind and body with kind awareness. Then something else happens; something beyond the re-activity of the mind. Instead the heart softens. It sees its own nature: spacious, non-suffering, peaceful, and timeless. Here is freedom. Here we find the courage to bear suffering in order to overcome it.

All the world is full of suffering. It is also full of overcoming.

—Helen Keller

CHAPTER SEVEN

Desire: The Core of the Matrix

Thanisara

Know and watch your heart. It's pure but emotions come to color it. So let your mind be like a tightly woven net to catch emotions and feelings that come, and investigate them before you react.

–Ajahn Chah

From the Buddhist perspective, the matrix of unconscious desire feeds our suffering and discontent. Desire always points to the next thing, a better situation when everything will be alright. Desire motivates us, but when it's unconscious it becomes a tyranny. It undermines our capacity for contentment. In the sphere of spiritual life, it prevents deeper realization. When we are under its sway we have the illusion that if we really had the right kind of life or spiritual practice, teacher, or circumstance, then we'd get more peaceful and enlightened. However, until we understand desire and illuminate its limitations, we will never get to know true peace. It will always drive us on.

Desire never points to itself; it forever points to the new valley over the next hill. We literally become what we desire. When we've had enough, we want to stop. We don't want to experience the results of our desires. Have you ever gotten something you really desired, but then it wasn't what you wanted after all? When I was a nun I hardly traveled for over a decade—I spent day in and day out within the walls of the monastery. Sometimes I would look up at planes on their flight paths, longing to travel to interesting places. Since leaving the monastery, our teaching work means we continually travel, so now my big desire is to stay in one place! It's wonderful when our desires are fulfilled, but if you pay close attention you will notice that the idea of what we want is often better than the reality of it. Ajahn Chah used to joke that we want to be alone when we're with others, yet when we're alone we pine for company. That's how desire works. It's a constant agitation. Even if we get what we want, very soon it becomes stale and we find ourselves swept up with new desires.

The endless parade of desires is sometimes called "the flood of becoming." If a log gets caught in a flood it gets bumped along. In the same way, we get shaped and pushed along by our desires. However, in the process we miss being here, right now. The peace the Buddha pointed to, which is another way of talking about *nibbana,* is recognized when we come out from under the sway of desire. With some mindfulness and wise reflection, we can recognize desire as an object, rather than "me," and can contemplate its nature. This is why mindfulness is called the "flood stopper." Mindfulness reverses the endless flow of the seeking mind and brings it back home.

One of my favorite teachings is from the Sutta Nipata, in a chapter called "The Way to the Beyond." It records conversations between the Buddha and sixteen students who ask about the goal of his teaching. It is clear from the tone of their questions they have great love for the Buddha and a deep interest in understanding his message. The Buddha answers each of them succinctly, touching on themes of *nibbana.* It is said that in hearing the Buddha's responses, each became enlightened. Here is one of the dialogues, recorded from over 2,550 years ago.

The Brahmin student Jatukanni asked the Buddha, *"I had heard . . . that there is an ocean-crosser, the hero desiring the desireless, and so I have come to ask a question of this man without desire. Tell me this, eye of instant seeing-knowing: what is the state of peace? Please explain it to me as it really is."*

The Buddha replied to Jatukanni, *"Lose the greed for pleasure. See how letting go of the world is peacefulness. There is nothing that you need to hold on to and there is nothing that you need to push away. Dry up the remains of your past and have nothing for your future. If you do not cling [even] to the present, then you can go from place to place in peace. There is a greed that fixes on a person. When that greed has completely gone, then there will be no more poisonous taints, without which you are immune from death."*[1]

Peace is the relinquishment of desire. This isn't to say desire is bad or wrong. We need desire to get things done. However, when we are driven by unconscious desires that always seek a better situation, we never know peace. The practice of mindfulness illuminates the energy of desire. It's not about placing a value judgment on desire, but seeing it clearly so it can be transformed. When desire is guided by wisdom and compassion, it transforms into aspiration, enthusiasm, and the capacity for wholesome action. It can be used in service of the Dharma. However, even the desire for good is never-ending. It compels us to keep going, endlessly trying to get the world sorted out, but the world will never be fixed. The Buddha continually pointed beyond desire—to *nibbana,* to peace. Another way of talking about *nibbana* is "the end of desire," and with it the end of the tyranny of time. Desire keeps us revolving on the wheel of becoming, always moving, whereas *nibbana* is stillness at the center.

We don't get to the end of desire by repressing it. Instead, we need to understand the energy of desire so that we can free ourselves from its demands. The Buddha explains to Jatukanni that when greed is gone, there will be no more "taints." The original word, translated here as "taint," is *asava,* which means "flood." Sometimes *asava* is also translated as "outflow." The four classical "floods" that shape the self are desire for identity; views and opinions; desire for sensory pleasure; and ignorance of reality. Each of these floods contracts the pure awareness of the mind around a particularity of constructs that we call my "self." The personas and roles we abide by, the views and ideas we hold to, the experiences we seek, and the ways we try to leave our "mark" upon the world.

The "flood of becoming," or the desire for identity, preoccupies a huge amount of energy. For the most part our identity is defined and socially constructed by the gender, nation, religion, race, country, and economic class we are born into. However, increasingly this is not the case: we live in a time when our identities are very fluid and are more inwardly identified than externally designated. Just in my life I have witnessed the changing arc of personal identity. My English grandparents never doubted their identity or place in society as members of the British working class. They were happy with their lot, and lived it out to the best of their ability. My parents pushed the edges by marrying outside their "tribe," and by leaving our extended family in London to seek fairer shores.

However, now there is a great fluidity in terms of identity. Everything has dramatically changed: gender roles and gender identity, geographical and religious affiliation, dietary choices, and educational and economic possibilities, to name a few. We are moving to a multifaceted identity that is no longer tribal but global. Maybe ultimately we will come to understand our transpersonal identity, which Nisagardatta sums up as "I am one, but appear as many."

However, until we evolve into the "one appearing as many," the "floods" continue to feed our dualistic consciousness and its perpetual search for belonging and permanence. The maintenance of self-identity depends on a narrative sustained by our views, which don't always take into account a subtle and complex interconnected web of change. The self also feeds on sensory consciousness: what we feel, think, see, and hear, which are in a constant state of flux. When we try to find stability in the transient, we set ourselves up for stress.

Once, I was teaching a meditation class, when I mentioned the Buddha's encouragement to Jatukanni: "Dry up the remains of your past." One of the students objected, saying, "Without a past I would be nobody!" Being a "nobody" is probably one of the worst putdowns we can receive. However, for one who is developing the art of contemplation, being nobody is freedom. It frees us from the obsession of "my life" and its successes and failures. Instead we know ourselves as part of a seamless reality. The self needs a past to exist. It also needs a future. It is wedded to time, so the stress of its maintenance —with its stories, aims, and concerns—becomes ever more fraught as we race against time. The fundamental paradox of self is that it seeks durability, constancy, and coherence, when in reality it is in a state of flux and full of inconsistencies. It feels it is independent from the rest of existence, and it ignores its inevitable powerlessness.

Take, for example, King Canute, a Viking warrior king of England about 1000 CE. Legend says that he proclaimed, while seated on his throne by the seashore, with waves lapping round his feet, "Let all people know how empty and worthless is the power of kings. There is none worthy of the name but God, whom heaven, earth, and sea obey." Canute had heard his flattering courtiers perpetuate the myth that he was "so great he could command the tides of the sea to go back." So he had his throne carried to the seashore and sat on it as the tide came in, while commanding the waves to advance no further. He made a point that is still relevant today, particularly to the powers that be in this world, and their delusions of grandeur.

From a Buddhist perspective, the sense of self, however successful it may be, is associated with *dukkha*. Fundamentally the self is coupled with each of the *asavas*. These four *asavas* can be summed up as "ignorance." Basically, we ignore the true nature of reality. Even against our rational knowledge, we assume that things are more enduring than they are. We assume more control than we actually have. We also assume ownership of things that actually we simply can't hold onto. These are some of the illusions that we labor under. Even if we understand their obvious falseness, we still set about each day with these assumptions firmly in place, often at an unconscious level. In doing so, we create the cause for anxiety, disappointment and struggle. No one is doing this to us. It is ignorance, within the mind, that causes our ongoing sense that life is somehow not quite right.

Each of these floods is completely entwined with the energy of desire. Without the root cause of desire the flood of becoming dries up. The Pali word for desire, *tanha,* gives a more potent sense of its energy. It means "thirst" or "craving." The thirst of desire is unrelenting. A friend summed this up well. He was a very accomplished businessman, a top executive director of a huge corporation and partly responsible for thousands of jobs and the investment of millions of dollars in the stock market. His job was highly stressful and in part he coped with it by planning for fantastic holidays where he hoped to truly relax. Yet when he got to the holiday he confessed that he usually felt very irritable. His mind was habituated to always moving on to the next challenge. Nothing was good enough. He simply didn't know how to relax. I think we can all relate to the dynamic, if not the circumstance. We plan for a future where everything will be easier. This leaning into a better and brighter future is fueled by desire. However, when we get there we still experience a sense of unsatisfactoriness.

Kittisaro and I were once invited by this same friend to a dinner party at his beautiful home. We sat, rather oddly, alongside bankers, politicians, and CEOs. As the wine started to flow and people relaxed, this friend spoke to me very honestly about the high levels of stress and fear involved with the overwhelming responsibility of his job. How he suppressed his feelings, and how he had nightmares. When I asked whether it was possible to stop, I was amazed by his response. He said he could only stop when he was successful. Although he was considered successful by anyone's standards, he did not feel it. Success was always something just beyond his reach. It begs the question: What exactly is success and how do we measure it? Our corporate-media-consumer world seduces with all sorts of compelling images and ideas of success, but do we ever really get there? Do we ever really feel successful? We may have moments of feeling successful, but grasp them and we will condition their opposite. Inevitably the feeling of failure will be waiting for us. In this way desire, when it is unconscious, is associated with the experience of restlessness and disappointment.

THE THREE SPHERES OF DESIRE

Just know yourself, this is your witness. Don't make decisions on the strength of your desires. Desires can puff us up into thinking we are something, which we're not. We must be very circumspect.

–Ajahn Chah

Desire is designated into three aspects: sensory desire, which is called *kama-taṇha;* desire for existence, *bhava-tanha;* and the desire not to exist, *vibhava-tanha.* We can't really practice with desire until we become conscious of it. In monastic training, one way to bring desire to the surface is to frustrate it. The training within the Forest School of Ajahn Chah made an art form out of frustrating desire, called in Thai *toramahn*, which roughly translates as "torture"! This conveys the more extreme warrior-type approach of that school. The premise is that if you want to go beyond desire, you need to challenge it, endure it, and allow it to burn out. The training focused on frustrating the desire for food, sleep, sex, and personal power. None of this was particularly kind to the body or ego, and I'm not totally convinced it is the best approach, but there is no doubt that it is a powerful way of getting to the essence of the issue.

The First Sphere of Desire: *Sensual and Sexual Desire*

To live as a young, celibate monastic is challenging. Usually the assumption is that monastic life is a nonsexual life. Quite the contrary: sexuality is placed under the microscope of investigative awareness, as is every other aspect of desire. Sexual desire is complex in that while it is a bodily instinct, it also is connected to our need for love, intimacy, and security. However, sometimes love can be confused with sexuality. Consensual sex is a way of deepening a loving relationship, which is a very beautiful part of our human experience. And yet, there are so many other ways human sexuality is used. Sex, it seems, is not straightforward. It can also be used for personal gratification, in ways that exploit. Some people view others as simply a way to assuage their lust, which can also implicate them in lies and betrayals of trust, all of which lead to some extremely painful consequences. Throughout history, sexual brutality has been an insidious way to exert power, control, or revenge. Our collective history of rape, abuse, and incest has generated a complex inheritance of sexual wounding. For millennia, religions have instilled guilt and veered from guidance to control of their adherents, through advocating repressive sexual morals. Even within the secular liberties of our times, sex is co-opted. Every day a barrage of soulless sex is used to sell stuff we have absolutely no need for. We soak in myriad images and narratives where sexual prowess is equated with acquisition, which should render us more lovable, successful, and wealthy. In the aging process there can be a natural waning of sexual desire. Being the object of media consumerism, however, doesn't end when we become less attractive and sexual appetites start to decline. Now there are nips, tucks, facelifts, and Viagra to keep it all going. No wonder sex is such a confusing tangle of complex feelings, needs, and conflicts.

Sexuality is one of the most defining characteristics of human life, and because of that, it sways the mind. We are all alive as the result of sex, and it is essential to the continuation of life. Although we interpret the sexual drive personally, it is really impersonal. At its most basic, it is simply a force of nature. Our sexual energy is deeply connected to our creativity, and our life force, the most elemental being the ability to procreate. Bringing children into the world weaves our identity into family, tribe, and nation in very compelling ways.

The Buddha, through the formation of his homeless, celibate, mendicant community, created a radical life choice. In its aim to cut through familial and national identity, it confronts the very core of our energetic system. Freed from the complexities of romantic and sexual pursuit, the quest for achievement and wealth, the demands and duties connected with livelihood, family, society, and nation, one's energies can be directed to the task of enlightenment. This is the outline of Buddhist monasticism as laid out by the Buddha.

While this is a coherent and compelling template for a dedicated life, without real care, circumscribing and repressing sexual and creative energies can be too blunt an instrument. It doesn't always go well. It can lead to frustrated sexual energy being acted out through distorted and unhealthy power dynamics. A healthy monastic life aims to contemplate sexuality without either acting out or repression. The intention is to use sexual energy in service of awakening: to transform the need for personal intimacy into intimacy with life. However, as with every ideal, there is a distance to travel to bring about the actuality.

As a young nun I had plenty of opportunities to contemplate sexual energy, from its coarse bodily effect to its impact on the mind and emotions. Living within the small community that founded the first Forest Monastery in the West was more like living on a building site. At that time Chithurst House was a decrepit Victorian mansion, an absolute garbage dump. The gardens were overgrown; dozens of abandoned and rusting cars were strewn around the grounds, while indoors dry rot ravaged the wooden timbers holding up the house. The whole place was about to fall down. There weren't the financial resources to employ building contractors, so instead the monastic community became construction workers. We were also the cleaners, gardeners, cooks, and hosts for the most colorful range of visitors. Whatever was needed we did ourselves.

From time to time, I would find myself infatuated with one person or another. Nowadays, this is called a "*vipassana* romance," a common occurrence on meditation retreats. You see someone you are attracted to, and your mind becomes intoxicated with desire. You have all sorts of notions about them, which are usually false, but which you project onto them anyway. You may not have even spoken to them, you may never speak to them, but in your fantasies you court them, have romantic outings, have great sex, have a nice little imagined life and possibly even marry and divorce, all within the space of a few days, hours, or even moments. It's an absurd but seductive occupation for the mind. I found myself reasonably adept at *vipassana* romance. If there wasn't someone who fit the bill, I'd make them up. I guess it was a less than skillful way of managing my intimacy needs.

Eventually I got tired of these cotton candy mind states and wanted to get clearer about the energy of romantic desire, so I started to investigate the dynamic more closely. Taking sexual desire less personally allows for perspective. We can observe its nature. Sexual desires can obsess the mind and in reaction we can repress, indulge, or get embarrassed by them. However, with increased mindfulness there is more skill in containing the heat and power of the energy. Beyond the obvious clichés of romantic love that my mind would embellish, I started to get really interested in inquiring into the layers of its effect.

During this time, I was on a work crew that had the task of burning endless piles of wood and garbage from the extensive grounds. Also at that time I had been struggling with infatuation, so I had a very tangible experience to work with. One day, while tending the fire, something really clarified around the energy of sexual desire. Looking at the burning fire, into which I was throwing logs, my mind shifted into a more focused state. I saw that each log was like the bodies I had incarnated into over and over again. The fire of desire, in particular a deep longing for intimacy, just burnt through one body after another. In the process of moving through the layers of longing I arrived at the depth of the aloneness of the self. The parades of desires were all surrogates for the primary need to belong and to be loved, seen, and understood. I also saw the essential delusion of desire in its search to be satiated. It screams out or gently seduces or hammers away, obsessing and compelling the mind. Thinking just one more log will quench the fire of longing, we keep throwing on logs. Instead the fire just burns brighter and stronger. The more logs thrown on, the more the fire burns.

I was touching into a major cog in the wheel of *samsara*. I saw that sexual desire, with its romantic packaging, fueled endless incarnations, one after the other. It burns through one body after another, but is never satiated. It eats through a million bodies, the whole of creation, and it still rolls on. I'd never get to the end of it. *Samsara* means "just keep going," round and round, looking for perfection, in this case looking for love. *Samsara* is usually posited as the opposite of *nibbana*. It is the endless search for happiness and security driven by desire.

On that cold winter's day, looking into the roaring flames of my bonfire, I felt how endless it all was. As a great weariness welled up I shifted my inquiry to sensual desire and the addictions of the mind. The way we seek to absorb into pleasurable or soothing sensations: into anything that will fill the gaping void. There is nothing wrong with enjoying sensual experience; however, when it's compulsive, it robs us of our inner strength. We keep feeling we can extract fulfillment from food, drink, drugs, TV, the Internet, our smart phones, from a new situation, from whatever we can absorb into. There is a rather graphic Buddhist image for this: a dog gnawing on an old bone that has no meat. Eventually its teeth get worn down to the gums. Trying to milk pleasure out of every situation eventually jades our senses and our soul.

Ironically, a common experience in meditation retreats, which give very little possibility for indulging sensual pleasure, is that people find their senses heightened. They enjoy the most simple of things: a cooling breeze on a hot day, the sounds of birds, or the way the light falls on the bark of a tree. We don't need as much as we think to live a happy existence. There is a saying, "Rather than cover the whole earth with leather, put leather on the soles of your shoes." Instead of trying to fulfill all our collective desires, which have consumed the earth's resources, better to get to the end of desire itself. In doing so we connect with the eros energy of life itself, as it transmutes into fulfillment.

The Second Sphere of Desire: *Aims and Ambitions*

The second sphere of desire is called *bhava-tanha. Bhava* means "to become." It is the endless seeking for placement and identity, the underlying itch we need to be better. We become driven by projects, aims, and ambitions. The desire to become is seductive, it is based upon the feeling that "I am not enough." It fuels the subtext of our lives: "I've got to get or be more." We translate that into our meditation, thinking, "I want to be more peaceful. I have to become wiser. I've got to become more compassionate." This is not to say there isn't any truth to these thoughts. Such thoughts can motivate us in a positive way, but when they pull us along compulsively, we don't know contentment. *Bhava-tanha* is rooted in our deep feeling of lack. We just keep being driven, running on the wheel, never able to rest. There's a lot of *bhava* energy in the world. We don't often hear the message, "You are fine as you are." Rather, it's all about what we need to achieve and produce. The love and acceptance we get is based upon that.

Psychologically, the energy of *bhava* is a complex dynamic in our lives. It's not a question of crushing it, or crushing any desire for that matter, but of illuminating it with awareness and mindfulness. It's important to make it more conscious. We can't pretend we don't want to aspire to anything. The answer isn't to give up and just be some sort of enlightened stone that is unresponsive. It just means we need to be awakened to this energy and negotiate it with skill. It's a great relief to know *This is desire operating, I don't have to be moved by it.* Instead, we can watch the desire move. As Master Hua said, "Seeing the state of mind move, rather than being moved by the state." With mindfulness we can reflect on the various aims and ambitions of the mind as they come and go. We can practice letting them go rather than impulsively following them. In doing so we shift from "becoming" into a whole other dimension; that of "being." When we know "being," we know how to rest, and from there, instead of being pushed by impulse, we can choose what we respond to, if anything. The compulsion of moving to the next thing is lessened when we attune attention to the quality of our being. When we touch into "being," we feel content, open, relaxed, and responsive. We connect with the fullness of our inner authenticity. There's a sense of completeness that *bhava-tanha* can never deliver. Actually we don't have to become anything. Relaxing into being, we feel our deep intimacy with life. We feel ourselves as life. We don't need affirmation through servicing the endless demands to achieve; instead life itself affirms our existence.

In Buddhist understanding, *bhava-tanha* is the force that ensures rebirth. Rebirth is usually understood as incarnating from one life to another, propelled by the momentum of karma. In Buddhism, rebirth is considered within the realm of mundane—or relative—Right View, which is the first factor of the Eight Fold Path laid out in the Fourth Noble Truth. While absolute reality transcends all views—because we can't ultimately define reality—relative Right View aligns our understanding with the Dharma. A sense for rebirth places our lives within the context of skillful action. We understand what contributed to the effects we live through. Our intentions and actions condition the direction of our life, both individually and collectively. In short, what we do leads to our future "birth." This is relatively true, but in ultimate reality there is no independent entity such as a "self" that is reborn. It is more accurate to say that the "self" is a conditioned, interdependently arising process, shaped by what has gone before. However, we live in the realms of time and relativity, where a sense for rebirth can support our investigation into tendencies and patterns that carry from one day to another, one year to another, one life to another. Even if we don't have a feeling for rebirth from life to life, we can still get a sense for the conditioning factor of *bhava-tanha* that shapes the self throughout this current lifetime.

For myself, insights that have come from meditation, depth healing, and psycho-spiritual inquiry have given me a feeling for karmic debts, as well as affinities and lessons, which carry from one life to another. It gives a large perspective in which to contemplate relationships, whether personal, collective, or global. Overall, I find the idea of rebirth supportive. It gives me a useful perspective on how I understand the unfolding of my life. But in the end, unless there is direct knowledge, rebirth tends to be speculative. It can even be a hindrance when we go about creating elaborate identities in previous lives.

In general, it doesn't really matter if one believes in rebirth or not. What is more important is to get a sense of the energy of *bhava*, or "becoming," as it is actually happening. We get an immediate sense for rebirth when we see desire operating. We are "reborn" by the momentum of the past, combined with aspirations we project into the future. In other words, we take shape around what we have desired, and what we wish to become. The more mindful we are of the intentions and desires we set in motion, the clearer we set the course for the future.

Much of contemporary new age spirituality draws from the ancient truth that the intention of mind is a powerful conditioning factor for bending life to our desires. It tells us we can become more powerful, successful, wealthy, popular, and healthy. This approach can also focus on more refined outcomes, such as becoming more spiritual, peaceful, and enlightened. Generally speaking, these outcomes are good to aim for, but they do not constitute the deeper meaning of the Buddha's message. Even if our ambitions are realized, they will not bring about an end to discontent and stress if we haven't fully understood desire. If we think they will, we will be disappointed.

The mind is a delicate instrument. When we understand how to set intention, align our energies, and focus our will, then—outside the wild card of karmic unfolding (and that is a big wild card!)—we set the course of our future "births." When we are less conscious we become driven by repetitive habit, in which case we can expect much the same in the future, as we did in the past. However, as the distraction that drives our habits lessens, there is increased ability to guide the outcome of our lives. At the end of the day, rather than speculating about past or future lives, it is more important to be conscious about the intentions that shape our life now. What we aim for, personally and collectively, conditions much of what we live through, and within the larger events beyond our control, that shape history.

While under the sway of *bhava-tanha* we are always going somewhere else, which means we never really arrive. Even if we become everything we wish to be, if we are still identified with the process of becoming, we will never know freedom. Siddhartha Gautama, the Buddha-to-be, realized *nibbana* on the night of his Awakening. He broke the chain of future births, and emptied the force of becoming. This is why the Buddha said on Awakening:

> Seeking, but not finding the house builder, I traveled through the round of countless births. Oh, painful is birth ever and again. House builder, you have been seen. You shall not build the house again. Your rafters have been broken down, and your ridgepole is demolished. My mind has attained the unformed Nirvana, and reached the end of every kind of craving.[2]

The self, ever seeking a home, roams a myriad of identities, but doing so is haunted by the law of impermanence. At the arising of insight into the utter emptiness of self, all seeking stops. That there is nothing to acquire becomes clear. The spell is broken and the house of the self collapses.

After this utterance it is said the Buddha gazed toward the horizon to see a dawn star rising. At the same time he touched the ground beneath him and called on the spirit of the earth to witness his Awakening. The desire for separate existence was released as the reality of the ever-present Dharma shone through.

The Third Sphere of Desire: *"I Don't Want To Be Here"*

While the first and second spheres of tanha are about getting our desires met, the third sphere of desire is about what happens when we've had enough. It is called *vibhava-tanha,* which literally means "craving to not become." It is the desire for nonexistence or annihilation. In some ways it mimics *nibbana* in that there is an intuitive sense that if we didn't exist, the burden would end. However, like all desire, it still operates under the force of delusion. *Vibhava-tanha* does not have the release of *nibbana;* instead it manifests as psychological desolation, despair, depression, and self aversion. At its extreme it is suicide. It is the shadow of "becoming." Sometimes when people are most successful they are at their most vulnerable. Success can be very hollow, even more so when we heavily invest in its return.

Once a renowned spiritual teacher told how after giving a lecture to thousands of adoring devotees, he went back to his hotel room and felt utterly alone and desolate. This desire for annihilation fuels the secret addictions that go alongside a blaze of glory and public renown. It is the shadow that runs alongside creativity: for example, at the same time that we step out, we also want to disappear from view. That feeling can be a subtle disquiet, or a total collapse of confidence. It can also be felt as an underlying melancholy that makes it hard to just get out of bed in the morning. Although this energy is called "desire" in classical texts, it is actually the underbelly of desire. It points to the play between interest and apathy. At the same time, when we're being productive, there's a feeling of wanting to shut down and not bother. We want to hide away and push out the world. We can experience *vibhava-tanha* as dullness and flatness in the heart. We don't feel alive or responsive. More profoundly, it can be felt as a constant resistance to life, as if we resist the very experience of our incarnation. We don't really want to be here.

Meditation tends to attract people who have strong tendencies toward *vibhava-tanha*. The world is painful and challenging, so we retreat, because we want to avoid life. We want to get out of it, get away; instead of being joyous, we become cynical. This energy played a prominent role in my life, and certainly colored my approach to meditation. That's not necessarily bad, as it initially helped motivate my practice; however, it is ultimately debilitating. For years I experienced a pervasive sense of heaviness and self-doubt. Most often, it would arise in social situations, where I would easily slip into my default mode of invisibility. Of course, the shadow of that is feeling unmet, unseen, and unheard.

As a strategy it really didn't serve me well. Over time, I began to recognize the inner voices associated with this shadowy territory: *I can't do it, it's too difficult, I'm not good enough, and when will it all end?* I just wanted my life as a monastic to get me out. No one was making me suffer; I just found the experience of life burdensome. Buddhism attracted me because it didn't pretend you had to feel happy, it gave me permission to acknowledge the full extent of the anguish that I felt.

Dharma practice definitely helps. It makes conscious the unconscious, and helped me discern this resistance as a mind state, rather than a defining feature of inner being. For a long time it was "me," but eventually I began to get it in perspective through the practice of mindfulness. This enabled me to consciously engage the effects of *vibhava-tanha*. It's like an undertow that pulls one's life force in the opposite direction from where one is trying to go, which takes away a lot of energy.

The practice of mindfulness contains our psychological and emotional experience, so we can contemplate it. The phrase *yoniso manisikara* is often used in tandem with mindfulness. It is usually translated as "wise reflection," meaning mindfulness needs to be accompanied by investigation and discernment. Mindfulness not only focuses on a point of experience in the present moment, it also includes a global awareness of what is present within the "field" of the present moment. Our experience—body, feeling, states of mind—is placed within mindful awareness. It is here, in the dynamic meeting of attention with experience, that insight and transformation happen.

It is not easy to maintain mindfulness when our primary defenses are activated. These defenses are forged in reaction to intense feelings, felt from conception through our preverbal years. Our psychological defenses are not "bad," they are simply strategies we learned that helped us survive as tiny babies. Neither are they necessarily there because of a lack of care. Just our vulnerability or waiting to be fed as babies can evoke powerful feelings of abandonment, fear, and longing. These feelings overwhelm a tiny baby and infant. In response, our defenses were built to protect us from these feelings. However, as we grow up our defenses become imprisoning. They split us away from our innate energy, and we become locked in dysfunctional patterns and end up limping through life rather than having access to the fullness of our energy.

Vibhava-tanha is a common primary defense. As we bring mindfulness to this dynamic, behind the sophisticated ways we deny and disassociate, we *will* encounter unsettling feelings. We will find ourselves faced with our "shadow," a term Carl Jung coined to refer to powerful emotions and beliefs held in the unconscious that influence our life. Behind our "shut down" can be fear, rage, or a fog of confusion. At times when these become triggered, we need to take a lot of care. When touching deep areas of primary feeling, behind our defenses, we need to take space, have kindness, and be patient.

Instead of crashing out, we can be mindful, one breath at a time. Gradually this becomes a strong container to help us withstand our deepest pains without defaulting to self-harming or acting out. This container is strengthened through moments of kind attention and awareness to the feeling tones that are present. When these factors are in place, then as painful feelings emerge, like despair, or the wish to annihilate ourselves in some addictive pattern, we will know an opportunity has offered itself.

As our capacity for awareness strengthens it is possible to tolerate the deeper wounds within the psyche. Often these are disguised beneath the restless momentum of desire and our attempts to fulfill its demands. It's not always easy to get through the swirl and floods of desire and its opposite force of aversion. This is why training mindful attention, *samadhi*, and wise discernment are so important. When there is some stability and inner capacity to be steady in the moment, then whatever is present becomes illuminated. Rather than acting out desire, and the emotions associated with it, we contain the complex energetic dynamic associated with our defense system, so that we begin to release from dysfunctional reactions that are no longer healthy.

Ajahn Chah talked about practice as "preparation for when powerful passions arise." The everyday practice of mindfulness can seem inconsequential, however its true value comes to the fore when we feel ourselves on the edge of overwhelm or in the midst of challenging circumstances. It's in those moments that deeper tendencies become triggered. If mindfulness is strong we will have the capacity to contain what is felt. This then enables the further application of inquiry. Such a skill can avert a tremendous amount of unnecessary suffering.

Desire, in all its forms, is not the problem. It is the unconscious relationship to it that undermines the recognition of our deeper nature. That which knows desire is not desire. It is clear, present knowing. This is our refuge, our harbor and our safe abiding.

THE DEEPER INTENTION OF DESIRE

In the Buddhist map of Awakening there is a term for the positive application of desire, which is *chanda*. *Chanda* is different than the swirl of desire that undermines our inner sense of well being, true worth, and our ability to enter an intimate relationship with others, and with our environment. *Chanda* is the first of the four *iddhipadas*, or pathways to power and success. It is associated with a pure energy. It has a sense of exhilaration, which is illustrated in the Sanskrit etymological root *skandh*, which means "to jump." *Chanda* is sometimes translated as "zeal" and "enthusiasm." It is wise passion aligned with pure intention or resolution. This kind of energy is necessary for the fulfillment of the spiritual path, and for skillful action in the world. A conscious relationship to desire is very different than being caught in a whirlpool of desire. One revolutionizes the world, as the Buddha did; the other only continues to manufacture suffering and degradation.

However, within the distorted energy of desire is a seed of wisdom. With mindfulness and inquiry we can begin to decant what that is. Each form of the three desires masks authentic energy and motivation. For example, sensory and sexual desire *(kama-tanha)* is about our wish to unite and merge with the whole. It is the profound impulse to dissolve the anguish of separation, and to expand into the feeling of love and connection. This is such a beautiful and innocent impulse. It resonates at the deepest level of our being, and makes empathy the currency of daily life. It also supports a web of humane relationship with all creation. When we mature spiritually, psychologically, and emotionally, rather than regressing into an immature merging with the "other," we become conduits for the loving service of life.

The second form of desire *(bhava-tanha)* is rooted in the desire to become something better. It is our sincere wish to fully blossom into our most true potential. We each carry the seed of the *bodhicitta,* which is a wise and loving intention that seeks to serve others. This seed is the same impulse that flowers into a Buddha, a Christ, a Gandhi, and a Mandela. It is the beauty and grace of small, daily acts of kindness and mercy. It is the wonderful aspiration to accomplish what we set our minds to without giving up. And it is the wish to demonstrate our truth within the world.

Lastly, the desire for annihilation *(vibhava-tanha)* emerges from a profound and healthy impulse to remove ourselves from pain. We just tend to go about it the wrong way, often through addictive or distracted behavior. However, as we become more aware, we learn to cultivate skillful ways of alleviating suffering. Ultimately the desire for nonexistence, if understood well, will journey us into the depth of the dark mystery. We will concede our profound lack of ability to truly understand the nature of this extraordinary universe, and of even our own being. In the depth of mystery our small, struggling self surrenders, and in that surrender we discover redemption, awe, and completion.

Ajahn Chah used to say that without desire there is no practice and no path. As desire becomes purified from its coarser objectives, when it is guided by wisdom and compassion, it fuels our awakening journey. However, when desire is unconscious, it thwarts and distorts our natural energy and well-being. We don't need to get rid of these three forms of desire, but to tease out their deeper imperative. Each is a catalyst for awakening. Each can be transformed and used in service of authentic and appropriate response within the world.

As mindfulness strengthens, the ability to contemplate desire becomes more continual. That which knows desire is not desire. As is taught by the masters of the Forest School, it is important to see the difference between mind and the activity of mind. Desire is an activity of mind. Mind itself has a "knowing nature." This knowing, which is the opposite of ignorance, is called *vijja*. Vijja is the innate intelligence of awareness. Ajahn Chah taught *being the knowing* as an immediate way of connecting to our deeper nature. *Being the knowing* is accessed through contemplation and inner listening. We often miss it because we look too far. Instead, relax into the immediate sense of your innate, aware presence, here and now. Pure knowing is completely immune to desire. To be grounded in presence is to move from the ever-turning circumference to the still center. The idea of an aware center is just an analogy, as awareness has no center. It has no location or spatial designation.

While awareness is intimate, it is not a self-identity. The Buddha was careful to not give attributes, which would then make the primordial awareness of the heart a concrete "thing" that we "attain." It is a realization, not a place we get to. It is the recognition of the unmoving *suchness of being*. The Buddha used language like "the deathless" or "the refuge." It is this recognition of our natural state that cools the fever of desire, and quenches the thirst of craving. The Buddha alludes to this when he talks of being "immune from death" and "going from place to place in peace." While mindfulness discerns the objects of awareness, it also discerns awareness itself. This is why ultimately mindfulness is called *ekayana*, which means "the one way" or "the way to one." It is the path of peace that enables us to walk the world, unshaken by the pull of desire.

> *Remember we don't meditate to get anything, but to get rid of things. We do it, not with desire, but with letting go. If you want anything, you won't find it.*
>
> –Ajahn Chah

CHAPTER EIGHT

Dew Drops and a Lightning Flash

Kittisaro

A visiting Zen student asked Ajahn Chah, "How old are you? Do you live here all year round?"

"I live nowhere," he replied. "There is no place you can find me. I have no age. To have age you must exist, and to think you exist is already a problem. Don't make problems, then the world has none either. Don't make a self. There's nothing more to say."

—From *A Still Forest Pool: The Insight Meditation of Achaan Chah*[1]

Toward the end of my monastic life in England, before I even knew I would be disrobing,I spent a year on silent retreat in a small hut in the forest of Chithurst Monastery. Leading up to the retreat, I had been abbot of a small monastery in Devon, which had just been established. For three years, from 1987, I put a lot of energy into helping the monastery take root in the local area, which meant giving numerous public talks, traveling, and teaching, as well as supporting our fledgling community of monks. It was one of the happiest times of my monk's life. I loved the countryside, our small monastic community, and I enjoyed connecting with nearby Totnes, one of England's most green, Buddhist, and alternative towns.[2]

Throughout my time in Devon, I still struggled with poor health. Although I managed the symptoms—mainly with meditation, exercise, careful eating, and regular rest—I still suffered frequent fatigue and digestive problems. In response to my ongoing health issues and debilitation, Ajahn Sumedho suggested I take a year off, on retreat.

By then I had a regular devotional practice centered on Kuan Yin, the bodhisattva of compassion. My interest in this practice came about as a direct result of my longstanding health difficulties. After reading some of Master Hua's commentaries on the Mahayana Sutras, I was introduced to the Great Compassion Mantra of Kuan Yin, which Master Hua said would certainly help those who struggle with sickness. I learned the mantra from the book, and diligently practiced every day. After meeting the two inspiring American disciples of Master Hua, Heng Sure and Heng Ch'au, I received some proper instruction from them on how to recite the mantra. I also delved more deeply into the teachings around Kuan Yin (Avalokitesvara in Sanskrit), who appears prominently in four Mahayana Sutras: the Heart Sutra, the Shurangama Sutra, the Lotus Sutra, and the Dharani Sutra. This led me to explore the Dharma as understood and expressed within the Mahayana School of Buddhism. I asked my teacher Ajahn Sumedho for permission to do the practices I had discovered in the Sutras, and he gave his blessing. These teachings began to complement my practice of the Theravada and deepen my understanding and faith.

Around this time I also had the opportunity to meet Master Hua, who reminded me a lot of Ajahn Chah. Master Hua had an imposing reputation as an accomplished and fearless practitioner. He was one of the great Chan masters, who transmitted a style of Buddhism that predated the Communist takeover of China. One of his teachers was Master Hsu Yun,[3] whose name means Empty Cloud. Master Hsu Yun lived until he was 119; there are striking photographic records of him at this advanced age. When he was well over 100, he was mercilessly beaten by the Red Guard within an inch of his life, and left for dead. It is said that Master Hsu Yun refused to die. Instead he healed himself and continued living, because he didn't want the young people who had beaten him to have the bad karma of taking his life. These Chan masters were of a totally different order! They were fierce practitioners and unswervingly dedicated to the bodhisattva ideal of great compassion. They inspired enormous faith in me. This gave my practice a different orientation and a deeper motivation. I began to consider the bodhisattva intention.[4]

Knowing of my great devotion to Master Hua, Ajahn Sumedho offered to take me for a short visit to the City of 10,000 Buddhas in the early part of my yearlong retreat in the forest. After everything I had read and heard about Master Hua's life, I was in awe. I couldn't believe that I was actually going to meet him in the California monastery he founded. I was so excited that the flight from London to San Francisco was like a dream. As we got off the plane and entered the terminal, I was thrilled to see Master Hua waiting across the entrance hall with a welcome party for our Theravada delegation. Before I knew it I was suddenly standing in front of the Master. I kneeled down before him onto the floor of the airport and bowed, not worrying what people would think. As I stood up I found myself face to face with Master Hua, not quite sure what to say. So I asked him, "Do you like it here?" I couldn't believe that such a dumb question came out of my mouth! The Master looked amused and simply said, "I like it everywhere!"

During my year of silent retreat, Kuan Yin became a tangible presence. Every day I did a slow two-hour devotional practice called "The Great Compassion Repentance Ceremony," which is centered on the vows of Kuan Yin. Master Hua assured me that this practice would help me overcome my illness and other karmic obstacles. As I deepened into this practice, supported by all that I had learned from Ajahn Chah and Ajahn Sumedho, I entered a beautiful state, a depth of silence that revealed a timeless, trusting, intimate listening. This inner listening is considered the essence of Kuan Yin.

Ultimately, Kuan Yin isn't Mahayana, Theravada, or even Buddhist. Kuan Yin is neither male nor female. The true spirit of Kuan Yin can manifest in any form needed to awaken, rescue, and pierce the hearts of living beings with compassion. In essence, Kuan Yin is a metaphor for the deepest heartbeat of the universe: a heart that is empty and yet filled with listening—a listening that is aware, merciful, profoundly wise, and responsive. Through the practices centered on Kuan Yin, I discovered a deep sense of connection with all life. Ironically, even though I was silent, sitting alone in a tiny forest hut, I felt closer to my family, friends, and fellow community members than if I'd been sitting in a room with them. I discovered a prayerful dimension to my practice and plunged ever deeper into this mysterious Kuan Yin dharma door, the crux of which is merciful response emerging from emptiness.

My year of retreat was life-altering. I found a depth of peace and enjoyed undertaking demanding ascetic practices. Throughout the whole time I felt a great sense of connection to the earth. My best friend became a badger who would come round to finish off my daily alms food, which I would lay out lovingly every morning on an offering stump covered with fresh fallen leaves. I loved to wait for him to come by, so I could see what foods he liked; it was a daily blessing. In the end my badger friend evoked a poem, "Ode to a Badger."

As my retreat unfolded, the ties to the community I had lived in for nearly fifteen years began to loosen. I realize now, my contemplative life was moving beyond the framework of one tradition, as I deepened my exploration of the Kuan Yin dharma doors and the lineage of the Chan masters.

My retreat ended prematurely, when my fellow monks became worried for my welfare, and in the end "benched me." I had become extremely sensitive and somewhat vulnerable after a year of silent, intensive practice. Because I was having lots of visions and was extremely thin and weak, they were concerned I might go crazy or even die. I was very grateful for the time in the forest, and even though I found some of the psychic states confusing, new openings had become available to me. Although my understanding of them was embryonic, I began to sense new dimensions of this mysterious world.

Around the time of my reentry into the monastery, Thanissara and I started to speak together. I shared about my retreat experiences, and she talked of her pilgrimage to India. Both of our journeys had opened us in unexpected ways, and revealed an internal spiritual refuge that was increasingly independent from the monastic lifestyle. Our commitment to being in the monastic training was beginning to shift. Around this time, we were invited to a blessing ceremony, which took us through the fabled town of Glastonbury, where we stopped for a few hours. While there, we were invited into a small sanctuary within the Chalice Well Garden, to see their treasured sacred relic, the blue bowl. As we meditated with the chalice, we experienced an invisible yet tangible sense of blessing encircling us. After those timeless moments, it felt like we had just been spiritually married. How strange. Even though we had never physically touched each other, we were falling in love. A deeper current was clearly moving us away from our monastic lives and into an uncertain future.

We told the guiding teachers of the community what was happening for us, that we were thinking of leaving the monastic life to be together. This was controversial, and unleashed a lot of reactivity in the community. Within the month, Thanissara had disrobed.

Before making a final decision myself, I wanted to reflect on my situation in the presence of Ajahn Chah, the extraordinary being who had inspired me to ordain. I went back to Thailand to see him and pay my respects. Ajahn Chah was still alive, although in a coma. After a devastating stroke he had been semi-paralyzed and unable to speak for nearly ten years. This was hard for his disciples to accept, since his former presence had always been so charismatic and dynamic. His illness was in many ways his last powerful teaching. How many countless times had he told us, "All is uncertain. If you look for certainty in that which is uncertain, you are bound to suffer." Health, sickness, being in robes, being out of robes, life and death—all conditions of the world are endlessly shifting and changing. For three days and nights I helped with the nursing care of Ajahn Chah, and told him in my heart of my wish to disrobe and be with Thanissara. I felt his blessing for our new life, and I made my decision. It was important for me to see him, and leave the monkhood in a way that honored the priceless treasures that I had received in that life.

I departed from the monastic life in a simple ceremony conducted by Ajahn Liam, the acting abbot of Ajahn Chah's main monastery during his illness. Ajahn Liam is a quietly impressive Thai monk known for his unwavering mindfulness and humility. When I returned the robes and consciously relinquished the monk's rule of discipline in his presence, he encouraged me to remember all that I had learned in my years as a monk, and to strive to bring those good qualities into the world. His gentleness touched me, after all the heated, emotional turmoil my wish to disrobe had caused back in England. When I told Ajahn Liam I was surprised at his compassionate reaction, he smiled and said, "Ajahn Chah always taught us to be kind."

From the monastery where I'd first met Ajahn Chah fifteen years before, I now left with just the white layman's clothes that had been given to me by the monks. Carrying a large bouquet of purple orchids, I flew to Dublin on Christmas Eve to meet Thanissara. As we got on the bus, we held hands for the first time.

By the following July we were married, at Thanissara's parents' local church in Hedge End, England, in a beautiful ceremony attended by more than a hundred friends and family. It was a tremendous day woven around an interfaith service that reflected our core belief in the ultimate unity of all the great faiths.

Although we found ourselves in a radically different life situation, our practice continued. We both shared a love of the Dharma and very soon found ourselves being invited to teach. After we disrobed we really had no idea what livelihood we would undertake; we hadn't really given it a lot of thought. First we had to set up bank accounts, get drivers licenses, and figure out how to make everyday decisions again: what to eat, what to wear, and where to live. Friends and family helped us out, and for a few years we traveled, teaching retreats in Europe and occasionally further afield.

One day an invitation arrived inviting us to teach in South Africa. Ajahn Anando, who had taught there as a monk, was meant to go. However, by this time he had also disrobed and married, but tragically the gunshot wound he received in Vietnam decades ago—which left a hole in the back of his skull—had developed into a brain tumor. Anando was fighting for his life. After a short but dramatic struggle with cancer, he died short of his fiftieth birthday. It was a great loss. We both loved Anando and considered him a dear friend.

We felt it an honor to teach in South Africa in his place. We had been recommended by two renowned Buddhist teachers, Stephen and Martine Batchelor. That was in 1994, just after the shift of political power that saw the fall of apartheid and the inspiring arrival of Mr. Mandela as South Africa's first freely elected president. It was an exciting and turbulent time to arrive in the country.

We've been working in South Africa since then. Initially, we were guiding teachers of the Buddhist Retreat Center in KwaZulu Natal for about seven years. We then founded a small hermitage on the border of Lesotho, called Dharmagiri, and co-founded two HIV/AIDS response projects. One of the most heart-full experiences during that time was the support we received from our dog Jack. He arrived into our lives as a puppy, with just a tiny string round his neck, having been separated on the mountain from the other dogs in a Zulu hunting party. He was small enough to put in one hand. As no one claimed him, he simply stayed with us for the next fourteen years until he died, also of a brain tumor. In our minds Jack was similar to Anando in that he had an indomitable fighting spirit, a great heart, and he was an utterly devoted Dharma protector.

The years of founding our work in South Africa were as turbulent as the dramatic weather patterns of the mountainous region where Dharmagiri is located: during summer, thunderous lightning and rainstorms; and in winter, extremely powerful winds and sometimes lots of snow. Arriving in South Africa, we found a traumatized country, where both colonialism and apartheid had left deep racial and economic divisions. Swift on the heels of South Africa's political liberation, the AIDS pandemic hit like a silent tsunami. Our practice quickly shifted away from the quest for personal liberation, and instead we were catapulted into a hardcore bodhisattva workout. The merciful response of Kuan Yin was definitely a guiding light, but there's no doubt that without the Buddha's teachings on equanimity and emptiness we would have been lost.

TEACHINGS FROM THE DEPTH

Develop a mind, which rests on nothing whatsoever.

—Huang Po

The Diamond Sutra states, "All conditioned dharmas are like dreams, illusions, bubbles, shadows, like dewdrops and a lightning flash; contemplate them thus." All the dharmas, all our experiences, come and go; they're like shadows. Are shadows isolated entities? A shadow might look like a thing, but it is intimately connected with light that is cast off another object. It's not separate; it's linked to something else. All conditioned dharmas are like dewdrops, they are like jewels on the lawn, but are they independent entities? They're there, but when the sun rises they evaporate. They're there and then they're gone. Are we separate selves? We might think we are, but other things, like the sun, the air, the nourishment we take in, all continually sustain and support us.

The same is true for lightning. In the Drakensberg Mountains where Dharmagiri hermitage is nestled, amazing lightning storms build up in the afternoon during summertime. When they continue into the night, it evokes a sense of awe. Extraordinary bright flashes, tinged with a purple haze, light up the darkness. The lightning flashes are unexpected; you never know where the next one is going to be. It's exhilarating, waiting for the next strike. You can't guess, but when it comes, you try and catch sight of it. It's only there for an instant. In the end, it's stressful to try and catch the uncatchable, to hold for a moment longer what is over in a flash. It took me a while to notice that the lightning and thunder keep dissolving into an immense space and a great silence. The lightning's there, and then it's gone. The thunder's there, and then it's gone. We can't capture the thunder and the lightning, but we can appreciate the ephemeral thrill of their appearance. We can rest and enjoy their flickering dissolution into the unmoving blackness, depth, and silence.

We tend to know only the conditioned world of appearances, the world of impermanence. But trying to find security in conditions is like trying to hold on to a lightning bolt, not wanting it to change. It's like asking the dewdrops not to evaporate. If we *contemplate thus*, however, we are aware of the evanescent nature of phenomena. We realize that language is misleading, implying a solidity and separateness where there isn't any. The Buddhist word for thus is tatha. It means knowing things as they are, in their suchness. When we're *thus*, reflecting rather than reacting, we realize the lightning flash dissolves back into immensity. If we're clinging to the lightning flash, it's stressful, but if there is non-clinging, letting go, we are at ease and free. *Contemplating thus*, we're still and peaceful in the midst of movement, not grasping or rejecting, not afraid. The lightning is there, but we can also appreciate the immensity from which it came, the infinite blackness. We can rest and abide in the *suchness*, and appreciate the flashes, the dewdrops, the myriad transformations of life. Yet our thoughts might lead us to think that present *suchness* is so immaterial that it can't be a real support. It seems so much more solid to grab on to something, so we grasp health and it turns to sickness, we grab onto praise and it turns to criticism, we clutch at youth and it fades into old age. In the midst of change, where is our true resting place? Where is our ground?

The Drakensberg Mountains have one of the highest incidents of lightning in the world. These mountains are powerful. They rise up and level out at 10,000 feet onto the escarpment of the Lesotho Kingdom, which is known as the Tibet of Africa. In Zulu the mountains are called uKhahlamba or "Barrier of Spears," which accurately describe the sharp peaks reaching into the sky. Dharmagiri is situated on Bamboo Mountain. It is also called Mvuleni, which is Zulu for "Place of Rain" or "Place of Openings." It is where local people come to pray for rain. An ancient Khoi-San (Bushmen) painting on Mvuleni depicts a shaman's battle with a rain beast. In the summer season the rumbling booms of thunder and spectacular lightning flashes evoke a powerful dragon-like presence.

Indeed, Drakensberg means "Dragon Mountains" in Afrikaans. This, so the story goes, is because when making their historic trek inland to escape British rule in the Cape, a Boer father and son reported seeing a dragon flying over the cloud-shrouded mountains. Interestingly, in Buddhist cosmology the dragon, or Naga, is a celestial serpent that has power over fire, thunder, and rain. There is a fascinating concord between these names, the Eastern worldview, the drama the Khoi-San art depicts, the actual experience of the primordial power of these ancient mountains, and the elemental weather patterns they attract.

The hermitage is also a great place to contemplate the immovability of the mountain, which is a good metaphor for the ever-present *suchness*, the ground of *nibbana*. When the thunder comes, there is a tremendous rumbling, which can be heard for miles. I love the intensity of these storms; the crack and roll of thunder in the mountains still leaves me in awe. As lightning dissolves back into immense space, so every crash and rumble of thunder returns to underlying silence. When the momentary phenomena disappear, you might say what is left is emptiness. Emptiness means there is no defining characteristic; it's empty of content. When we see a lightning flash or hear a thunder clap, we say "It's purple," "It's close," or "It's loud." These are forms. All forms have characteristics or signs that we designate through language. These distinguishing features of light, shape, and form become more concretized when we give them names.

When we give attention to something, it tends to become a "thing," an "it." It gives the impression of something more static than it actually is. Unconscious attention and perception labels our experience, creates the sense of a solid world filled with discrete, independent entities. The flash in the sky becomes "the lightning," the rumbling sound becomes "the thunder," and the black expanse becomes "the night." In reality each is dependent and woven in with the other. The body also has characteristics that are designated by language. We say it's big or small, tall or short, but each term is only relative to other designations we make. Moods too have characteristics. They are heavy, light, or dull. "I like it" and "I don't like it" are distinctions that can define and shape consciousness, further fragmenting and atomizing our reality. All of these attributes have a certain "thing-ness" and tangibility that have recognizable qualities and characteristics. They stand out from the background, just as the lightning stands out from the night and the thunder stands out from silence.

Normally we use "empty" to mean an absence of form or an absence of observable characteristics. For example, you enter a room and say, "No one is here." You go out and tell your friend, "There is nobody in the room. It's empty." And she says, "Didn't you see Joe?" You go back in again, and say, "Oh, there's Joe in the corner; it's not empty." Where did the emptiness go? Did Joe destroy the emptiness? Another way of looking at it is that Joe occupied the emptiness. You could say that conditions appear *within* emptiness. Form appears within emptiness. But does the form contend with the emptiness? Or does the emptiness inhibit the form? At first glance, emptiness and non-emptiness appear to be two separate phenomena. However, emptiness allows form to manifest. In this way emptiness and form are mutually supportive and not separate. What appears to be two is actually a nondual reality.

From the perspective of Buddhist understanding, the fundamental nature of all phenomena is *sunnata,* or empty. The Buddha taught emptiness in an accessible, down-to-earth way. He would start with what is happening now. He would say, "What are the characteristics that are filling your consciousness now?" For example, if you are reading this book lying in bed at night, you might say, "The reading light is dim; I feel tired." You answer in terms of what you are aware of. Your mind is not empty of that. But you could also answer in terms of what is absent. For instance, where are the experiences associated with work or eating lunch? The Buddha would say, "This present moment is empty of those experiences." To illustrate this point he used the world around him. When in a forest (at that time), there were elephants, trees, and so on. When in a meditation hut, the experience is empty of those things—empty of the perception of forest, animals, trees—but what is here now is here.

Similarly, in the evening, we know that our experience is empty of morning; it is comprised only of what is present now. This was the gradual way that the Buddha introduced the concept of emptiness, recognizing the appearance of forms and their absence. Get a feeling for something that's there and then gone. The lightning appears and then disappears. Consciously bringing into awareness the impermanent nature of conditions is the gateway into emptiness. This is how we can begin to understand this profound principle. It's not taking a stand for or against the presence of things, but rather establishing an aware relationship with this moment and noticing that it is empty of what has gone before.

For the sake of contemplation, the Buddha designated the conditions of body and mind into five categories called *khandhas,* which means "heaps" or "aggregates of existence." This was the way the Buddha described the totality of what constitutes the "world" and the "self." The five *khandhas* (*skandhas* in Sanskrit) are *rupa* (form), *vedana* (feeling), *sanna* (perception), *sankhara* (volition, and the karmic formations that come about due to intentional activity), and *vinanna* (sensory consciousness).

The first *khandha* of form includes the outer as well as the inner sense of the body. It also includes the form and shape of all things, organic and inorganic, near and far, subtle and gross. The second *khandha* of feeling and sensation is less tangible. We can't see feeling, but it certainly grabs our attention. Feeling and sensation are categorized into three aspects: pleasant, unpleasant, and neutral. Every experience, inner or outer, is accompanied by a feeling, a sense of being pleased or displeased or indifferent. Perception, the third *khandha,* frames our world and is connected to memory and familiarity. If I walk in a town I'll be able to recognize streets, shops, and other people, thanks to perception. *Sankhara,* the fourth *khandha* of volitional activity, directs attention. Our world appears dependent on what we give attention to. For example, if my attention is always on the past, I literally start to inhabit a world of memories. This shapes the sense of my "self." If there are painful memories I will feel upset, and conversely happy when I think of pleasant experiences.

Sankhara or volitional formation occurs when will is directed to sights, sounds, smells, tastes, tactile impressions, or mental objects. Generally speaking, the sense of self is influenced by what we hold attention to. As we ingrain tendencies of mind by dwelling again and again on various narratives and thoughts, psychological grooves are created that the mind's energy runs along. These habitual tendencies are *sankharas,* deeply conditioned patterns, which govern the activity of the sense of self. The last *khandha* is sensory consciousness, which includes moments of seeing, hearing, smelling, tasting, touching, and thinking. Sometimes sensory consciousness is likened to electricity moving from one sense to another, generating the illusion of a continuous self that is hearing, thinking, and so on. The Pali term for *vinnana* suggests a dualistic discriminative consciousness, a divided knowing that tends to generate a subject and object.

Naming these five categories is just a way of pulling the threads out from the woven tapestry of our experience, a contemplative aid to encourage the seeker to reflect carefully on the nature of reality. In each waking moment the *khandhas* weave together to support the sense of "me" and "the world." In concert, they create the illusion of cohesion and solidity. However, the Buddha said it is not so:

> Suppose a person beheld the many bubbles on the Ganges as they floated along, and after careful examination saw how each appeared empty, unreal, and insubstantial. In exactly the same way carefully examining the five khandhas we discover them to be empty, void, and without a permanent self.[5]

The words "Ganges River" conjure up a very real entity that we can visit. We can sit on the bank of the Ganges and drink chai and watch the flow of the water. If we try and capture "the Ganges," however, we can't. It will slip right through our hands. In the same way, just like insubstantial bubbles on the surface of a river, these five *khandhas* are empty. There is no solid substance within them. We have a sense of self, but if we try and grasp something called "me," we can't actually do it. We might even imagine that these *khandhas* have an independent existence, but they are like dewdrops. Dewdrops disappear without a trace when the sun rises in the early morning. We perceive something called "dewdrops," and then give them qualities; we say they are beautiful, that they twinkle like diamonds. We may then even want to possess them. They appear to be "things," but when we look more closely the reality is revealed. They are not what we thought they were. Just like the bubbles, the dew is there and then it's gone. Its appearance depends on many other conditions and they cannot exist independently.

This contemplation is profound. It informs what we take to be real and sheds light on the nature of thought. When we see a bubble, perception says, "It is! See, it's real, it's there." When the bubble bursts, someone else says, "It isn't! See, it's unreal, it's gone." *Is, isn't,* the argument rages on. Thought cannot capture the true mysterious nature of things. So, it is said in the Lotus Sutra, "This Dharma cannot be described. Words fall silent before it."[6] As we contemplate the empty nature of phenomena, we begin to recognize the limitation of language, and start to reflect on the unreliable nature of thought itself.

While "things" are "empty" of independent existence, they are also empty of our views about them. Our labels and opinions, including thoughts of *me* and *mine,* are just what the mind projects. A dewdrop doesn't give itself a name. In the same way, all that we take to be *me* is fundamentally empty, in a process of constant change. Its existence is dependent upon a whole range of conditioning factors.

For our meditation practice to be liberating, eventually we have to contemplate the sense of ownership. Ajahn Chah regularly encouraged his disciples to ask the question, "Who is the owner of this body and mind?" For example, he had this to say about anger: "If anger really belonged to us, it would have to obey us. If it doesn't obey us, that means it's only a deception. Don't fall for it. Whenever the mind is happy or sad, don't fall for it. It's all a deception." Anger can be all-consuming, and then it subsides. A moment of praise uplifts us, and then it is gone. Strong emotions are particularly powerful in terms of how they shape the sense of self. In meditation, to get feelings into perspective it's crucial to notice their transiency. If we grasp at something that is continually changing, we immediately create the conditions for stress. How can there be certainty in that which is constantly changing, instant after instant?

Sustaining the direct perception of impermanence, diligently and patiently, is a doorway into the profound truth of emptiness. As we deepen our understanding of the ever-changing nature of conditions, we recognize the futility of grasping, and realize the subtle way in which concepts mislead us. Every so called "thing" is constantly revealing its ephemeral, insubstantial, and essentially empty reality. In this way the contemplation of emptiness brings us to a place of non-possession, a place of relinquishment.

Sometimes when I'm struggling and worrying, I look at the mountain that cradles Dharmagiri, and consider its 220-million-year-old presence. In a few years everything I've worried about won't matter. All the concerns about building a hermitage or promoting outreach programs, the reactions to the opinions of others, the tides of like and dislike, it will all dissolve back into the great void. Even the mountains and this great earth will one day disappear. To attune one's life, day by day, to the fundamental emptiness of reality, is to hone an inner practice of letting go. Acting and letting go. Doing what needs to be done, and then once again putting down the stress that the clinging mind generates. Working in South Africa would not be possible without this inner attitude.

> *In the great void the King of Death will never find you. There is nothing for old age, sickness, and death to follow. When we see and understand in accordance with truth, that is, with right understanding, then there is only this great emptiness. It's here that there is no more we, no* they, *no* self *at all.*
>
> –Ajahn Chah

CHAPTER NINE

Nibbana: *The Beautiful*

Kittisaro

When dukkha is completely stopped, nothing remains. All that remains is an entirely pure awareness. It's not even a Noble Truth. It's the purity of the heart. If you want you can call it Nibbana. All that I ask is that you know this marvelous extraordinary Dharma. Its excellence exists of its own accord without our having to confer titles.

–Ajahn Maha Boowa

The contemplation of emptiness brings us to the most sublime dimension of the Buddha's teaching, the realization of *nibbana* (*nirvana* in Sanskrit). It is here that we taste the peace of liberation. While we still operate from the sense of self, we experience limitation. From the perspective of a self, we feel as if we're moving through life, a "me" engaging events in a sequential way, traveling from the past into the future. But from the perspective of reality, we're not really going anywhere. As a self we might feel we are located inside a skull, or perhaps inside a body, as a thinking, feeling, and responsive individual who makes choices, finds meaning, and goes about daily life. Usually we don't question this assumption at all. The Buddha declared in the Shurangama Sutra that "The primary misconception about the body and mind is the false view that the mind dwells in the physical body. You do not know that the physical body, as well as the mountains, the rivers, empty space, and the great earth are all within the wonderful bright true mind."[1]

The Buddha taught that "This mind is luminous," that we lose touch with the true radiance of heart when we are confused by what moves through the heart. It's not that we need to go somewhere else; rather, we learn to be fully here, where we've always already been. When we investigate the teaching of emptiness, a shift starts to take place, a transformation from "me" thinking about "my life" and "the world" to a receptivity that listens and is aware. We begin to notice what comes and goes. We start to recognize the reality of the unmoving heart that registers the appearance and disappearance of conditions. From this perspective, rather than "me" moving through life, in actuality life is manifesting, dissolving, and then being recreated within the field of awareness. It's mysterious how the myriad appearances of the world constantly come into creation. We can understand and investigate these creations because of awareness. Awareness itself isn't being created, nor is it destroyed. It just is. It's not as if we have to climb up to the top of Mount Everest to find awareness, or that we have to deserve it somehow. We can't help but be aware. It's the very essence of our nature. That we are simply aware is our deepest truth.

Our tendency, however, is to get lost in the myriad creations of the mind. We are mesmerized by the magic show of the mind, as it shapeshifts from one state to another. We are beguiled, amazed, horrified, seduced, and terrified by the mind's creations. While we are under their sway we are a little crazy. We still think there is somewhere *out there* to go, and we grasp at conditions in search of happiness. We are like Nasruddin, a mischievous Sufi sage who ate his way through a bag of chilies, all the while tears pouring from his eyes. "What are you doing!" his friends exclaimed. "I'm looking for the sweet one," Nasruddin replied. Noticing the background of awareness is often preceded by the exhaustion of endlessly fishing around in the bag of life, looking for "the sweet one."

World-weariness is important, not to be dismissed lightly, and yet we override it, looking hopefully for the sweet one, crying all the while. Disenchantment, rather than being a problem, is an important spiritual turning point. Sometimes called "the great reversal," it marks a waking up and the turning of attention back to the heart itself. This was the experience of the Buddha, whose journey can serve as a metaphor for our own. Each aspect of his journey represents an inner process that is relevant for us.

The Buddha-to-be grew up surrounded by an unreal, sheltered world, immersed in pleasures that his father hoped would keep him from looking beyond the bars of his gilded cage. The more unpleasant dimensions of reality were hidden from him in his familiar and comfortable surroundings. Eventually his quest for truth was initiated by the sight of an aged person, a sick person, and a corpse. He described this experience, saying, "The vanity of youth, health, and life, left me when I realized that I too am subject to old age, sickness, and death." Before this understanding arose, he was aghast when he saw someone bent over, aged, with wrinkled and blotched skin and gray hair. He was distressed by sickness and horrified when he encountered death. Like us, he didn't want to acknowledge that death is always before us. However, when the truth of impermanence penetrated his heart, he realized that he was no exception. He was ashamed of his reaction. Everyone forgets that they too will age, even while confronted with the aged. On the full acknowledgement of his common destiny, the question arose in the Buddha-to-be, "What is not subject to sickness, old age, and death? What is secure, truly stable, and truly peaceful? Is there anything that transcends death?"

Being confronted by aging and death is classically known in Buddhist lore as receiving a communication from a "Heavenly Messenger." Old Age, Sickness, and Death are the Buddhist heavenly messengers. Our modern societies hide these "messages" away. They treat old age as something to be ashamed of. We have a multi-billion-dollar industry that offers the illusion of perpetual youth. We have creams to iron out wrinkles and plaster over them. There is plastic surgery to lift sagging parts of the body and popular medicines to keep other parts of the body moving in an upward direction! We hide old people in homes and avoid seeing a corpse or decaying body. But the Buddha's teachings warn us, "No, these signs are very important. They're messengers from the divine. They remind us of what this conditioned realm is really like."

Everything is conditioned, from a whole galaxy to a momentary thought. Everything has the nature to arise, exist for a while, and then cease. The insight into change opens the door to the unchanging. All that arises dissolves back into awareness, the ground of the mind. The Mula Sutta[2] gives a succinct description of how our experience of the world comes and goes. The origin of "the world" is rooted in desire and arises on attention. Desire directs attention. The focus of attention becomes our world. When attention rests on phenomena, there is contact, which in turn gives rise to feeling, the experience of pleasure and pain. The Sutta states, "All things converge on feeling." Feeling is powerful, often generating the "push and pull" of the mind. However, we can also mindfully contemplate feeling. The Sutta continues, "Ruled by *samadhi,* dominated by mindfulness, surmounted by wisdom, and yielding deliverance as essence, are all things." With mindfulness and wise reflection we see that feelings and phenomena are constantly changing. Seeing this releases the mind from grasping at what is ungraspable. Instead we can "let be." Letting be or letting go is a beautiful practice, revealing the spacious freedom that is at the core of every experience. Ultimately it opens the mind to the unchanging. The Sutta continues further, saying that "All things merge in the deathless." This statement points to the unconditioned, to *nibbana.*

The Buddha's quest led him to this insight. After his numerous struggles to attain some sublime, peaceful, otherworldly state, he finally recognized that he had been looking too far away, that freedom had been right here all along. He didn't need to get rid of anything or attain anything. He simply saw that all phenomena constantly revealed reality. He articulated it like this: "There is an un-born, un-originated, un-created and unformed. If there were not this unborn . . . escape from the world of the born, the originated, the created, the formed would not be possible."[3] He realized this unborn true nature of things is always here and now, timeless, inviting us to see, to be experienced individually by each wise person.

The Buddha realized that each so-called "thing" comes to be because of a supporting condition. We are here because of mother and father, because of food, air, water, and so on. "This" comes into being because of "that," and while in reality all things are interdependent, the separative nature of language can disguise this truth, creating a fragmented world. For everyday negotiation of life, the use of concepts to express difference is necessary. We can talk about my favorite tree, what we like and what we don't like; but these are just opinions. Words, concepts, and designations are powerful; they shape our world. However, they are only pointers. Once we develop this insight, we make a distinction between the name and the actuality. The word "tree" is just a label, a symbol for something that can't really be captured by thought. When thought is not reflected upon, we mistake it for reality. To begin to see the limited nature of every thought, is critical in freeing the heart from the illusory walls of the mind.

Consider a beautiful garden. We can distinguish our favorite plants. Perhaps we like the yellowwood, ash, or oak trees, or the different flowers. We can talk about the oak tree as big and strong or the lilies as delicate and fragrant. We can say "tree," but if it is separated from the earth, then it ceases to be a tree. It would be dead, just a lump of wood. So, integral to tree is earth. In the end, whether we like a particular tree or not, all trees merge in the earth. Their "tree-ness" is rooted in Mother Earth. So, although we have separate names for the many trees and flowers in our garden, are they actually separate? When a branch falls off the oak tree, it dissolves back into the earth in the same way as a branch from an ash tree. The roots of each tree go down into the earth, where we can no longer distinguish their differences. In the same way all sensory consciousness merges back into the depth of pure consciousness.

All things merge in the deathless. When we look superficially we see differences, but when we widen our gaze we recognize the ground where all things come together. When we look out into the world, misled by our thinking mind, we see separation: me, you, here, there, beautiful and ugly, good and bad. When awareness is fixated on objects, it loses touch with the ground of being. By persistently and profoundly noticing change, in all the sense spheres, we recognize everything returns to the ground of listening, knowing, pure awareness.

The surface of consciousness is sensory experience. This includes everything we see, hear, smell, taste, touch, and know. Sensory consciousness discriminates and makes things stand out. It constellates the sense of subject and object. The sense of "me" co-arises with the sensory experience "it." In reality, however, there isn't an entity that is a "me" or an "it." Just as with the plants in the garden, that dualistic distinction is misleading. For the most part, when we live on the surface of consciousness it is like we are wandering in that garden admiring all the different trees and flowers, forgetting to remember the ground that makes it all possible.

Surmounted by wisdom are all things. The wise mind is not enchanted by the surface, and so does not lose touch with the ground. The Buddha used the phrase *anidassana vinanna* to describe the mind of an awakened one. It is pure consciousness that is not distorted, a knowing that doesn't create any "thing." It knows that which never dies. This is another way of saying "the unborn" or *nibbana*. Birth and death are ephemeral, but *nibbana* neither comes nor goes. If we try and find it we can't. It has no "signs." We can't actually say it's like this or like that. It is not an object that can be grasped. However, it can be realized directly. What usually blocks this realization is that we look too far away. We try and make it an object that we can know. Or we make it too special. The tree limbs fall back into the ground. Sound dissolves into silence. Where do all things merge, all the distinctions, all the differences?

If we don't get caught in our preferences, we can see that everything has the same nature. All things find a common ground. The last phrase of the Buddha's profound teaching on Rootedness from the Mula Sutta is "Ending in Nibbana are all things." *Nibbana* is completion, the end of imagining "things" that aren't real. It's a homecoming.

On hearing the Buddha's teaching of the Four Noble Truths, Kondanna was awakened and got his first glimpse of true peace, of *nibbana*. Kondanna understood that *everything that has the nature to arise has the nature to cease*. Through this simple realization, he intuitively recognized *nibbana*, the deathless and unchanging element. Just "letting things be" takes us to this same insight. The Buddha taught that non-grasping and non-rejecting in itself is *nibbana*. But when we're so busy getting somewhere, getting rid of things, looking somewhere else, we don't recognize the stability of where we have always been.

We can practice letting things be in very simple ways. Start by using an out-breath. The out-breath is a sign that we can use to take us to the sign-less. It naturally inclines to letting go. When we breathe out there is relaxation. Use the out-breath to let be and get a feeling for resting in presence. Conditions still arise and cease, but presence remains. Every sound still appears, but dissolves back into silence. Sensory experiences appear in consciousness, but then disappear back into the ground of knowing.

This is a patient contemplation. Little by little, we recognize this placeless place. Here there are no distinctions between you and me. It is the place where all forms merge and all sounds dissolve. It is a place of true trustworthiness, what the Buddha called the Other Shore, the Subtle, and the Refuge. He said this refuge is like a harbor. It is secure, a place of safety that can be relied on, which protects from the storms of life. Resting here, there is no need to grasp or reject anything. There is no identification with the self, the world, or even the "knowing." There is only peace.

> A young student came to the Buddha. Sir, said the student, there are people stuck mid-stream in the terror and the fear of the rush of the river of becoming. Death and decay overwhelm them. For their sakes, Sir, tell me where to find an island, where is there solid ground beyond the reach of all this pain?
>
> Kappa, said the Buddha, for the sake of those people stuck in the middle of the river of becoming, overwhelmed by death and decay, I will tell you where to find solid ground. There is an island, which you cannot go beyond. It is a place of no-thing-ness. A place of non-possession: of non-attachment. It is the end, the total end of death and decay and this is why I call it *nibbana*. There are people who in mindfulness have realized this, and are completely peaceful, here and now. They do not become slaves, working for Mara, working for death. They cannot fall into his power.[4]

CHAPTER TEN

Contemplative Ease
Kittisaro and Thanissara

Why don't you listen to your own hearing nature? Hearing does not spontaneously arise. It is because of sound that hearing gets its name. But when hearing returns to its source, it is free of sound. What then does one call that which is set free?

—Manjushri to Ananda, from the Shurangama Sutra[1]

On January 16, 1992, we were still in Ireland, just about to leave Dublin for the west coast of County Mayo. Outside the Dublin house where we stayed, there was a Mother Mary statue in the square. Before leaving, we placed the beautiful orchids from Thailand by her feet. We were thankful for the safe passage from monastic to lay life. As we stood, taking a moment for a silent prayer, we felt a compassionate presence envelop us, moving us to tears. We then picked up our bags and started to walk to the bus stop.

As we passed the neighbor's house, he called out to us and we responded, "Hi, Liam, how are you today?" "Every day is a good day when you're not dead," he said. As we turned the corner, an elderly woman staggered out of her front door, screaming, "My brother, my brother!" We ran into the house as flames engulfed the roof. We were met at the bottom of the stairs by an impenetrable wall of intense heat and thick black smoke. We couldn't pass. By the time the fire brigade arrived it was too late, her brother was already dead. As people gathered outside the house, they talked of the man's drinking problem. "Perhaps he fell asleep with his cigarette still alight," they speculated.

As we traveled onward to County Mayo, our clothes infused with the pungent smell of smoke, we reflected on the paradox of feeling blessed in the presence of Mother Mary, then shocked at the dramatic confrontation with death. A few days later we found out Ajahn Chah had died on that same day. Echoing the Buddha's analogy of the world being like a burning house, Ajahn Chah often talked of the need to get out of the fire of *samsara*. We had received the initiation for our new life together!

A few months later, we returned from Ireland to the UK, to get married in the presence of our families and friends. For our honeymoon, we traveled to Asia on pilgrimage, staying at Buddhist holy sites and various ashrams. We also travelled on to Thailand for Ajahn Chah's funeral. In India, we visited the Jetavana Grove, where the Buddha resided for most of his rainy season retreats.[2] As we walked among the gardens, a Vietnamese monk approached us. "I've been waiting for you," he said. "Kuan Yin told me you would come." That got our attention! We talked for a while, and the monk, whom we called Thay,[3] invited us to visit his monastery in Bodhgaya, the place of the Buddha's enlightenment. A few weeks later, we turned up at his door. Every day at sunrise and sunset we recited the Great Compassion Mantra of Kuan Yin together. As we got to know Thay, he talked of his master. Thay said his master had predicted the war and slaughter that was just on the horizon in Vietnam. He also predicted that a third of the people in Cambodia would be killed, and advised Thay to leave Vietnam and establish a monastery in the holy place of the Buddha.

Thay spoke of the iconic and controversial moment when his dear friend, an elderly Vietnamese monk, immolated himself in protest against religious persecution. This image flashed around the world in 1963. Thay was there. He told us Thich Quang Duc prepared for weeks by continually reciting the name of Kuan Yin. Being elderly, he felt his life was nearly at an end, so out of compassion he wanted to make a statement to bring people to their senses. As Thay recounted the details, we were transported to the emotional moment when the venerable monk gave his handkerchief to Thay, sat in full lotus while gasoline was poured over him, and then lit the match. Thay said they all cried.

During our days with Thay, he spoke so often of his master that his presence became tangible. Thay had only one small passport photo of him, which he wanted us to take to Thailand to be drawn by the skilled portrait artists of Chiang Mai. As we were going there to Ajahn Chah's funeral, we were happy to agree, though we were reluctant to take his only photo. Thay assured us his master would look after us. That was fortunate, because just at that time India was descending into a devastating conflict between Hindus and Muslims. This was sparked by the Ayodhya temple/mosque dispute[4] in which more than 2,000 people were killed. The day we left for our travels to Calcutta and on to Thailand, Northern India exploded in riots. It was extremely tense. The train station was in chaos. Our train was canceled, and throngs of people roamed the platforms as the intensity of the situation increased. Finally a kind stationmaster helped us board an overnight train that was already crammed full. As we inched along the corridor, suddenly a couple of men jumped up from their berths, saying, "These are for you." When we arrived in Calcutta, friends from Camellia Tea Company met us. They had helped support our visit to India. We managed to get to their lodgings just before the whole of Calcutta was put under curfew.

Eventually, we returned to Bodhgaya with Thay's passport photo and a beautiful portrait of his master. We also brought some Buddha relics[5] and offered them to his temple. The pilgrimage to India deepened our commitment to our devotional practices, which helped carry us through so many uncertain, and sometimes miraculous, circumstances. By the time we started our work in South Africa, we had incorporated a daily practice of chanting the Great Compassion Mantra. This mantra is very well known in Chinese Buddhism and is the focus of the Dharani Sutra. The mantra has eighty-seven lines, which embody Kuan Yin's "forty-two hands and eyes." They hold gentle and fierce symbols of perfect compassionate response, such as a vase of nectar to soothe, a willow branch to heal, an arrow to pierce the heart, a mirror to reflect truth, a whisk to brush away obstructive karma, a shield to protect, an axe to cut through obstructions, and so on. It is said that chanting the mantra activates the energy of Kuan Yin.

In our tiny hermitage, nestled on the slopes of Bamboo Mountain near the border between Lesotho and South Africa, we began practicing and teaching a synthesis of Theravada, Pure Land Buddhism, and Chan (Zen) during one-to-three-month retreats. The first three-month retreat was in the year 2000. We were five participants living in a few huts and a tepee. The retreat started well, but it ended with a series of increasingly dramatic events. After two and a half months, we were beset by hurricane-force winds that whipped down the mountain plateau of Lesotho. We had just finished a Chan sesshin,[6] which focuses on "turning the mind back" through inner listening and inquiry. This is the essence of Kuan Yin practice. We were drinking a hot cup of tea in our kitchen shack, listening to the howling wind, when Mike, one of the practitioners, burst open the kitchen door and shouted, "Kittisaro, your hut has disappeared." Because we'd been in silence for a few months, and were in a bit of a strange state, we just looked at him, and carried on with our tea. "YOUR HUT IS GONE!!"

The wind had picked up the hut as if it were a matchbox, and thrown it fifteen yards away. Everything was smashed. A beautiful and delicate statue of Kuan Yin, however, survived in one piece. We gathered up what we could as the wind screamed around us, careful to put our two beloved pictures of Kuan Yin and Mother Mary in a safe drawer in the most stable building. Shortly after that, the tepee flew apart, and by afternoon a distant fire sweeping down from Lesotho was racing through the dry African veldt toward us. Within a very short space of time it was jumping the human-made protective firebreaks, and igniting trees and buildings as it went. We saw a river of fire coming right at us. It was time to leave. We grabbed our beloved dog Jack, bundled into a car, and sped down the road.

Just at the point when the local town was about to evacuate, the wind dropped down, and the fire was contained. When we got back to the Dharmagiri, we were worried the whole site would be burned to the ground. But hopefully our firebreak had held. Every year before the dry winter season, each property is required by law to burn a firebreak around its boundary, for its own safety and that of its neighbors. We had created a particularly wide one on our vulnerable western side, exposed to the powerful Berg winds coming down from the mountains. There was no way our thatched meditation room could survive without that break holding. The fire had jumped over our 300-meter break! Yet, the meditation room was still standing, with burning debris and flaming logs within a yard of it.

During the cleanup, we checked on the picture of Kuan Yin we'd placed in the drawer. Mother Mary was still there, but Kuan Yin had mysteriously disappeared. Two days later she reappeared, lying face-up on a patch of burned land just outside our kitchen shack, which we had walked over dozens of times. When the fire officer came out to inspect the local area, he couldn't believe the thatched meditation room was still standing. "There's been a miracle here," he said. Throughout the retreat we had been contemplating a phrase from a Kuan Yin practice: *The response and the Way are intertwined inconceivably.* These were not empty words!

RETURN THE HEARING

In the Shurangama Sutra, an important text at the heart of Chinese Buddhism, we find Avalokitesvara (Kuan Yin)[7] explaining her method of awakening, which is *returning the hearing* or *listening into the self-nature.* Avalokitesvara is known as the one who "Contemplates the Sounds of the World at Ease." The Buddha praised her method as the most efficacious for the times we are living in. In this practice, the mind returns to its source. This teaching in the Shurangama Sutta arose in response to a tricky situation for venerable Ananda. Ananda, the Buddha's cousin and attendant, was waylaid on alms round by a beautiful woman whom we simply know as Matangi's daughter. Matangi ran a house of prostitution. The daughter saw Ananda and fell madly in love with him on first sight. She told her mother she had to have him. "Don't mess with the Buddha's disciples," she warned her daughter. But Matangi's daughter was insistent and pleaded with her mother to put a spell on him. And so the spell was enacted, and against his better judgment, Ananda was ensnared by the spell.

Back in the gathering of monks, the Buddha saw with his divine eye that Ananda was on the verge of transgressing his precepts. He recited the great protection of the Shurangama Mantra to break the spell, and sent Manjushri to invite Ananda and Matangi's daughter to come together before him. When they arrived, the Buddha asked all of the gathered bodhisattvas and enlightened disciples, twenty-five in all, to share their method of awakening so Manjushri could choose which would be most effective for helping Ananda. The Buddha said to Manjushri: "I now wish to cause Ananda to become enlightened, and so I ask which of these twenty-five practices is appropriate to his faculties, and which will be, after my demise, the easiest expedient door for beings of this realm to enter, in order to accomplish the Bodhisattva vehicle and seek the unsurpassed Way."[8] After hearing all twenty-five methods, the last being Kuan Yin's, we get Manjushri's response:

I now evaluate, Tathagata,
What the Contemplator of Sounds (Kuan Yin) has explained:
It is like someone in a quiet place,
When drums are rolled throughout the ten directions,
Hearing at once the sounds from all ten places. . . .

The eyes cannot see through solid forms.
The mouth and the nose are much the same.
The body registers awareness only through contact.
The mind, tangled in thoughts, lacks clear connections.
Sounds can be heard even through solid walls.
The ears can listen to things both near and far.
None of the other five organs can match this.[9]

In this passage the efficacy of hearing is laid out. Manjushri explains that sound has a vibratory dimension, and that hearing surpasses taste, touch, sight, and smell. Thought, as a sense, is also not so limited, but it entangles the mind and eclipses its natural luminosity. When sound is used as a meditation object, it has several different effects. It enables a more open and global awareness, and connects to the deep intimacy of the hearing nature.

The nature of sounds is based in motion and stillness.
One hears according to whether there is sound.
With no sound, there is said to be no hearing.
But this does not mean that the hearing nature is gone.
In the absence of sound, the nature is not ended;
Nor does it arise in the presence of sound.
Entirely beyond arising and ceasing,
It is, then, truly everlasting.[10]

In this passage we are introduced to the idea that the essence of hearing is beyond sound. The contemplation of sound leads the practitioner, through listening, into the realization of "that which never dies." Whether sound is there, or not, listening remains. Here we see one of the main principles of Chan, or Zen meditation. Rather than "chase" the objects of our senses, the practice is to turn the mind around on itself. *Who is the one chasing, seeing, and listening?* The one who contemplates sound does not follow sound. She does not get lost in the appearance of things, but rather allows sound to reveal the listening nature itself, which the sutra names as everlasting. Words like "everlasting" or "eternal" can be problematic as they conjure up an endless span of time, when in fact Manjushri is pointing to a leap beyond time. Perhaps a better term is "ever-present."[11]

Ever-present, even in dream-thinking,
It [the hearing nature] does not disappear when conditions and thought are gone.
Enlightened, this contemplation transcends cognition,
Reaching beyond both the body and the mind.
Now, in the Saha World [samsara], the theory of sounds
Has been proclaimed and understood.

Yet beings are confused about the source of hearing.
They follow sounds and so turn and flow [in samsara]. . . .
. . .
Ananda, you should listen attentively:
. . . Why don't you listen to your own hearing?
Hearing does not arise spontaneously;
It gets its name due to sounds.
But when hearing returns and is free of sound,
What does one call that which is set free?

Finally Manjushri exhorts the "great assembly" to practice Kuan Yin's method:

Ananda, and everyone in the great assembly,
Turn back your hearing.
Return the hearing to hear your own nature.
The nature will become the supreme Way.
This is what perfect insight really means.
This is the gateway entered by Buddhas as many as dust motes.
This is the one path leading to Nirvana.
Tathagatas of the past perfected this method.
Bodhisattvas now merge with this total brightness.
People of the future who study and practice
Will also rely on this Dharma. . . .
For those who seek to escape the mundane world,
And perfect the mind of Nirvana,
The best way is to contemplate the sounds of the world.[12]

Manjushri announces that not only is Kuan Yin's method the best for Ananda, but also those "floundering in the final age."[13] "It is the way to the true mind." As the Buddha questions and instructs Matangi's daughter and Ananda further, the daughter is enlightened, even before Ananda. It is said, in the commentary of Master Hua, that they had been together for five hundred lifetimes, which is why they had a strong affinity with each other.

On the awakening of Matangi's daughter, the commentary continues: "The river of desire dried up in her. Love is like a torrential river, which flows on ceaselessly, swirling around you on all sides. But when Matangi's daughter heard the Buddha speak dharma, for her . . . the fire of love and desire was transformed into an indestructible vajra body."[14]

This spell-breaking teaching isn't focused on the objects of experience, but on "who or what" is experiencing. The practice of *returning the hearing* begins with the simple exercise of contemplating sounds we hear. Each sound, whether it is pleasant or unpleasant, dissolves into silence. Both sound and silence are rooted in deep listening or pure hearing. When hearing is freed from "chasing sounds" it rests in its own nature. Similarly, when the mind stops chasing, it returns to its own inherent peace.

This is where we truly meet the Buddha and Kuan Yin, not in historical time or in mythological stories. We meet them right here and now, in the depth of the listening heart. There is only one heart. A friend talked about the deep anguish she felt whenever she thought about her child, who had died suddenly. When the thoughts came, grief would engulf her. Being a practitioner, she contemplated this. One day she realized that when she listened into the silence of the heart, her child was right there listening too.

KUAN YIN'S ENLIGHTENMENT

In the Shurangama Sutra, Kuan Yin reveals her enlightenment through contemplating sound, and returning the hearing until all distinctions dissolve:

"Suddenly I transcended the mundane and transcendental worlds, and throughout the ten directions a perfect brightness prevailed. I obtained two supreme states. First I was united with the fundamental, wonderfully enlightened mind of all the Buddhas of the ten directions, and I gained a strength of compassion equal to that of all the Buddhas. Second, I was united below with all living beings in the six paths, and I gained a kind regard for all living beings equally."[15]

Kuan Yin reveals the secret, from which springs her inconceivable powers of response. Who exactly is Kuan Yin? Kuan Yin is not Eastern or Western, male or female. The accomplishments of bodhisattvas and realized beings represent our deepest nature, our true heart. They are not beings of the past, but beings of the future, who demonstrate our potential.

Master Hua, who introduced us to the Kuan Yin Dharmas, used a lot of humor in his teaching. There is a practice that is popular with devotees of Kuan Yin: reciting her name over and over, *namo kuan shr yin pu sa*. This means, "I return my life to the one who listens to the sounds of the world at ease." This mantra is a concentration practice, which protects the mind. It is also a faith-based practice, calling on Kuan Yin's merciful response. To help doubting Westerners, who are skeptical by nature, Master Hua said, "If you can't say Kuan Yin's name, say your own name. When you know who you truly are, you will meet Kuan Yin!" Master Hua's teaching often followed in the paradoxical style of the *prajnaparamita* texts, which at every turn both postulate the true wonderful nature of reality, and then set about deconstructing the very premise they propose. In the end it really leaves us nowhere to stand, other than in simple awe of the indescribable mystery.

True Emptiness does not obstruct Wonderful Existence.
Wonderful Existence does not obstruct True Emptiness.
True Emptiness isn't empty; Wonderful Existence doesn't exist.
Because True emptiness isn't empty, it is therefore called Wonderful Existence;
Wonderful Existence doesn't exist, and so it's called True Emptiness.

—Master Hua

CHAPTER ELEVEN

Radical Reflection

Kittisaro

When Bodhisattva Avalokiteshvara[1] *was practicing the profound* prajna paramita, *she illuminated the five* skandhas *and saw that they are all empty, and she crossed beyond all suffering and difficulty.*

—The Heart Sutra

When Thanissara and I first arrived in South Africa in 1994 the atmosphere was laced with the threat of violence, fear, and suspicion. It was a society that was still very segregated in spite of the tremendous victory over apartheid. During our first teaching engagement in Johannesburg, a member of a small meditation group showed us around. At one point she opened her bag and showed us her gun as nonchalantly as if she were pointing out her lipstick. Clearly we weren't in the monastery anymore! Over the next few years we heard numerous stories of hijackings, murder, and rape. We visited affluent white people who lived within barred windows, high electrified walls, and alarmed houses, while in contrast we saw that the rural black African communities were extremely impoverished, under-resourced, and marginalized. Basically we had arrived into a deeply traumatized situation, the shock of which was strangely muted by the accepted "normalcy" of it all. Offsetting the societal dissonance were stunning landscapes, sweeping mountain ranges, pristine beaches, and evocative game parks.

Over our initial years of teaching Dharma, it became clear that in spite of the truly heroic act of overcoming apartheid, the psychological wounds would be much harder to overcome. Early on at Dharmagiri, not long after the land was acquired in January 1995, a Zulu family—a mother called Angel and her three sons—who were refugees of political violence, took up residence in the empty gatehouse. They stayed for eight years. We supported each of the children through schooling and various trainings. However, each was overwhelmed by the challenges of a deeply unequal society. Staying in school and finding jobs in an area that has 80 percent unemployment was a never-ending impossibility. The youngest son, Nkululekho, who liked to use his English name, Sydney, had patiently met one challenge after another until he managed to secure a coveted position in the police force. It was his dream come true.

Sydney threw himself into his training. He was strong, principled, and full of the ideals of youth. On his home visits (by then he considered us as white parental figures) he talked of being trained in the use of guns and of harrowing car chases on the tail of hijacked cars. The last time we spoke to Sydney, he was full of self-respect and hope. We had helped him build his own small house, and he was ready to fully enter the responsibilities of manhood. However, it was not to be. At the age of twenty-four he was shot in the head while in the line of duty, chasing a gang of robbers in a local township.

The loss of Sydney hit us hard. Unfortunately, his murder was only part of the daily toll of early death, AIDS, racism, denial, and fractured relationships that we encountered in South Africa. It has never been an easy environment within which to plant the seeds of the Dharma. We met one challenging crisis after another. Eventually, however, when the abusive and racially divisive behavior of someone we trusted embroiled us in a highly conflicted situation, we suddenly found ourselves isolated. It was time to take a breather. A friend, who was a close disciple of Master Hua, advised, "When it was too dangerous for the ancients to practice in a new place, they withdrew and went into long retreat."

As Thanissara and I reflected on our situation in South Africa, we made the decision to take some time out from teaching and the various administrative duties of running a meditation hermitage. We were exhausted and had both been profoundly impacted by our experience of the discordant relational field of South Africa. I recharge and gain strength from solitude and meditation. So in 2006, about fifteen years after my first yearlong silent retreat in the forest of Chithurst Monastery, I entered a second year of silence, this time on Dharmagiri's ancient sacred mountain. Conversely, Thanissara knew she would benefit from being part of a healthy, supportive community of friends and colleagues. She went back to England to study for a masters degree in Mindfulness-Based Psychotherapy at the Karuna Institute. Her decision to do this coincided with her wish to work around the themes of healing the effects of spiritual bypassing.[2]

We were grateful for this precious sabbatical, and happy to offer each other the freedom to choose how best to use the time. We closed Dharmagiri, Thanissara began her MA course overseas, and I savored the silence and solitude. I was very fortunate that a dear friend and former monastic, Marlene Matheson, offered me logistical support. Marlene kept the basic running of the hermitage intact and supplied me with daily simple meals. It was time to turn inward.

Delighting in meditation, I was grateful to just be: listening to my body and energy levels, receiving the emotional residue in the heart, following my own schedule, free from having to teach and explain things. I must admit, though, I wasn't really alone. I had the loving company of an elite personal trainer and fearless Dharma protector, our dear four-legged friend Jack. My only daily duty, one that I enjoyed immensely, was to feed Jack and go on walks with him on the road, and into the mountains. When I was meditating in stillness, he was my ever-faithful guardian. His unabashed enthusiasm for life helped me recognize the heavy burdens I was carrying. I knew I needed to turn the mind to letting go. I memorized a verse from the Dhammapada,[3] which became the touchstone of my practice.

Akase padam natthi, samano natthi bahire,
Papancabhirata paja, nippapanca tathagata.

There are no footprints in the sky;
You won't find the sage out there.
The world delights in conceptual proliferation (*papanca*).
Buddhas delight in the ending of that (*nippapanca*).

Akase padam natthi, samano natthi bahire,
Sankhara sassata natthi, natthi buddhanam injitam.

There are no footprints in the sky;
You won't find the sage out there.
There are no eternal conditioned things.
Buddhas never waver.[4]

The Buddha taught that the generation of suffering is intimately connected to the process of perception, particularly the way in which we relate to thinking. When concepts and thoughts are entertained without wisdom, then the world becomes fragmented and filled with complexity. The Buddha called this tendency *papanca*, or "conceptual proliferation."[5] A simple thought like "me" gives rise to a "you." A "this" necessitates a "that." As conditions change, the notion of time is created. The actual flow of sense experience is ever-changing and ungraspable, but the nature of language imparts apparent solidity and "thingness" to the world. When thought and concept is thus conjoined with ignorance, it leads to grasping, proliferation, increasing complexity, and the suffering of endless "birth and death." We think we've attained something, like "my happiness," and we're left with perpetual frustration, bound by the mercurial, discriminating mind.

Our true nature is like the infinite sky, unmarked by whatever drama temporarily appears in its vast space. Climbing the mountain behind our cottage, patiently returning to the simplicity of one step at a time, the heart remembers its essential spaciousness. On retreat, in all activities, I practiced letting thoughts subside into the stillness, observing the way heedless thinking complicates, entangles, and traps the sense of "me" into sticky webs of suffering. Mindful of a thought, like the momentary glimpse of a colorful sunbird flashing through the light, the heart remains undisturbed, serene in its sky-like presence. Whatever the circumstance, bodily movement or stillness, feeling well or distressed, with good concentration or scattered attention, I brought everything back to awareness.

The ending of *papanca—nippapanca*—reveals the true, undivided nature of this mysterious dharma realm. When the proliferating tendency of the mind ceases, even for a moment, the ever-peaceful radiant heart is recognized. *Papanca* means "to spread out," and the word conveys the dynamic web of thoughts and concepts that create our sense of reality. Rather than illuminating reality, *papanca* actually eclipses the direct seeing of what is really true. *Papanca* endlessly separates, and *nippapanca* means the cessation of that. It is a profound practice, to see through thinking and its activity of concretizing the self and the world. This is done, not by hating thought, but by mindfully noticing a thought, particularly its beginning and ending.

On my retreat, having space and not being in a hurry, I used thought consciously to explore the nature of thought. This was a transformative technique that Ajahn Sumedho taught us in our early monastic retreats, decades ago. He instructed us to take any thought, like "My name is . . ." and slow it down. In those moments, rather than heedlessly thinking about this and that, there is a conscious reflection on thought itself, and its origin. For a moment it is possible to see thought as just thought, a vibrating perception that arises out of silence and returns to silence. Usually thought is part of a phrase, a sentence, a paragraph, and a story, a whole enchanting framing of reality.

Ajahn Sumedho would encourage us to notice the gaps between the thoughts. "Mind the gap," he would say, playing off the loudspeaker warnings in the London Underground. In this radical reflection, we were invited to plunge into the gap, returning to the source, the gateway to the mystery. As we realize the true empty nature of thought, we begin to experience the whole, undivided wonder of the moment, undistorted by *papanca*. I knew what to do. This is how I used my time on silent retreat at Dharmagiri—calming the proliferating, ever-complicating, crazy-making mind. Whether feeding Jack, bowing, chanting, walking, or lying down, I kept returning to the source, letting each thought and its cessation take me back home.

What is the quality of presence when there is no thought? This is a powerful contemplation. Try it! While the narratives and descriptive processes of thought have their place, they are endless. *Papanca* is described in the Lotus Sutra as "a yak being enamored with its tail." We feel we can capture something by thinking about it. In reality, when we grasp at thoughts, the very process of trying to possess a piece of life ensures that it continually eludes us. We can never hold on, so the thoughts go round and round.

The transformative power of a conscious, mindful thought is that it reveals its own transiency. For example, the thought "Who is thinking?" is an invitation to make contact with the present moment. In doing so, the thinking process is recognized for what it is. When we're not so enchanted by our thoughts, we notice something else, something quite simple. We notice that all thoughts manifest and dissolve back into silent listening. This is a great relief. We don't have to become shaped by our thinking. We can be liberated from its bondage. In seeing thought as "just thought," the sky of the heart is revealed, with no footprints. "You won't find the sage out there." When there is wisdom, the endless searching for happiness "somewhere else" vanishes. Where is there to go? Beautiful thoughts and ugly thoughts, all arise and cease in awareness, and yet awareness remains unmoved.

Awakening means a fundamental shift takes place. It is a shift from looking for ourselves outside in the ten thousand things to recognizing that our true nature is beyond definition. That transformation of understanding is the work of wisdom, the essential quality of heart that carries us across the turbulent sea of suffering to safety and ease. The Buddha refers to this liberating activity with the phrase *Yoniso manasikara*. It is often translated as "wisely reflecting." *Yoni* means "womb" and *manas* refers to the mind. Taken as a whole we can interpret the phrase as "placing the mind and its activities in the womb of awareness." Wise reflection does not stop at the superficial cognition of the world, but it plumbs the depths of awareness, exploring the unmoving ground of "knowing" within which all the apparent differences of life manifest. I like the English translation "radical reflection" for this significant term, since it echoes the "re-membering" of all phenomena to its source, the matrix of awareness that makes all experience possible. The word "radical" has its etymological connection to "root." Radical reflection contemplates the root, the origin, the place where all things merge. It is another way of talking about Kuan Yin's method of meditation, returning the hearing and listening into the true nature.

Every morning of my retreat, while I was walking with Jack, I recited the Heart Sutra and contemplated its meaning. In this teaching Avalokitesvara (Kuan Yin) urges Shariputra[6] to look ever more deeply into the nature of the five skandhas of forms, feelings, perceptions, conditioning tendencies, and sensory consciousness. In doing so, the Sutra introduces us to emptiness. On one level the discourse seems like nonsense: "form is not different from emptiness, emptiness is not different from form. . . . Shariputra, all dharmas are empty . . . therefore in emptiness there are no eyes, ears, nose, tongue, body, or mind. . . ."[7] The myriad distinctions in our experience of the world seem so obviously real, but that is only the apparent reality. This teaching of radical reflection points to the ultimate principle, the true heart, which can be realized if we deeply reflect on phenomena. Form and emptiness seem different, but they are actually "not two," the differentiation melting into the serene gaze of nondual suchness.

Avalokitesvara declares that the *skandhas* are empty, and on perceiving them as such, again and again, one gradually "crosses beyond all suffering and difficulty." Actually, as I discovered, this is not easy to accomplish, which is why dedicated ongoing meditation practice is key in the unfolding and maturing of insight. The most profound form of meditation is the direct reflection on the mind itself. When I bring attention to the immediacy of my sensory experience, I notice how transitory it actually is. Everything I think, feel, my inner narratives, even my cognition of the world, is so utterly porous. As I contemplate the reality of the *skandhas, everything I take to be me,* I realize how insubstantial my objective experience is. The seemingly solid world, therefore, is an illusion fabricated and sustained by *papanca*, conceptual proliferation. As I listen profoundly into my experience, it's obvious that words cannot define reality. So what is real? The teaching on emptiness shatters our whole habitual operating system, all our assumptions. It leads us to a quality of naked, open awe and interest, a childlike gaze, which is precisely the "eye of dharma" needed for deeper inquiry.

Once Ajahn Chah was walking with his disciples when he pointed to a very large boulder and said, "Is it heavy?" Looking over at the huge rock, the monks said, "Yes, it's really heavy." Ajahn Chah smiled and said, "It's not heavy if you don't pick it up." Right where it's heavy, we discover release. In this way Ajahn Chah showed us how suffering and the ending of suffering are found in the same place.

> We extinguish fire at the place at which it appears. Wherever it is hot, that's where we can make it cool. And so it is with Enlightenment. Nibbana is found in *Samsara*. Enlightenment and delusion exist in the same place, just as do hot and cold. It's hot where it was cold and cold where it was hot. When heat arises, the coolness disappears, and when there is coolness, there's no more heat. In this way Nibbana and *Samsara* are the same.[8]

"Where is the suffering?" I would hear Ajahn Chah ask me in my mind. "Is it heavy?" Again and again during my silent year of meditation on the mountain, I would notice the stress, the burden, the sense that something was difficult, and question where the problem really lay. For example, when I found myself feeling betrayed, worrying how to make Dharmagiri work, or overwhelmed by the innumerable scary possibilities of what might happen, I asked the question, "Is it heavy?" Not if you don't lift it! In a moment of letting anxiety, or out-of-control worry, be just what it is—not fighting or getting swept away by it—the heaviness disappears. Right where there was suffering, peace appears. Sometimes in those moments, painful sensations were still experienced in my body, but the added distress of believing "it shouldn't be this way" had vanished. Putting down the burden.

The insight into emptiness, pointed to in the Heart Sutra, encourages us to investigate how we make things real and separate through our misunderstanding of the mind and the nature of concepts, how we create burdens. Through the practice of radical reflection, we recognize when we are carrying something unnecessarily, and we learn to let go. We also get a feeling for not picking things up in the first place. The Sutra even encourages us not to cling to the Buddhist teachings themselves. Instead, it exhorts a radical trust in awakening. The only method, which isn't a method, is to dwell *such,* in awareness itself, to trust that. We don't have to let go if we haven't picked something up. It takes a lot of energy to carry around the burdens of our life, all the things that weigh us down. This is not to deny that we have responsibilities, but all too often we take them on in a way that misses the true effortless empty nature of this moment.

In the Heart Sutra, Avalokitesvara points out that both phenomena and the self are empty. Laboring under the illusion of a self is the heaviest burden of all. This is a challenging teaching, one that is difficult to comprehend. And so another doorway into this understanding is to consider the illusion of ownership. We say we own things, we even feel we own our body and our life. But as Ajahn Chah pointed out frequently, if we owned this body we could tell it not to get sick or old, and it would obey. Or, if we owned our feelings, we could tell ourselves never to get angry! We may have possessions, but we don't really "own" them. Everything goes its own way according to its nature. Similarly, our very dear "self," and all that we take to be me and mine, is also destined to fade. So why do we have such attachment to the self? The Buddha compared the sense of self, conjured up by consciousness, to a mesmerizing magic show. Radical reflection bursts the bubble of enchantment. Deep questioning dispels the illusion.

The initial work of *vipassana,* or insight meditation, is to reflect on the objects of mind. We study them closely, both in their wholesome and unwholesome qualities. Discerning the difference between wholesome and unwholesome intention and mind states is important. It establishes the foundation for awakening. However, being a good person and a good meditator, while praiseworthy, doesn't necessarily free us. As good meditators we can still get hung up on trying to get the mind more peaceful and the body just right. In Zen they call this "polishing a brick to make a mirror." It's an endless and futile occupation. We have just transferred our desire to make the world perfect to an attempt to make the conditions of body and mind perfect. We are still under the sway of delusion. We are still wrestling with boulders, albeit more refined ones.

During my long silent retreat on the mountain, I reflected frequently on the persistent desire for more profound states of *samadhi* and success in spiritual accomplishment. Naturally, as I got deeper into the retreat, the accumulated effects of sustained practice and many hours of formal meditation gave rise to some unusual experiences. Sometimes the subtle vibration and energetic currents of my body were so powerful I thought I was going to levitate. Excited, I wanted more. I also enjoyed doing recitation practice, sometimes all night long, and seeing what special states would appear. But there was always this sense that no matter how much practice I did, it was not enough. I noticed that elusive uncomfortable feeling, and knew it was important to contemplate. The first ennobling truth, *dukkha* needs to be understood.

A significant memory helped me reflect on the mind that always wants another special state. I was bedridden for many years as a monk, afflicted with debilitating exhaustion and intestinal inflammation that followed my bout with typhoid fever. I often felt that I was letting the community down. During that period I couldn't go to meetings or work externally in the monastery as other monks did. Lying down all the time was hard to accept, as I had always been active and was used to achieving so much in my life. One night, however, I had a dream of Ajahn Chah. All the monks were able to sit up while Ajahn Chah went around offering honey to them, like a special treat. I felt ashamed that I was lying down, but I was looking forward to having some of the honey. As Ajahn Chah got closer,

I struggled to sit up and he stopped me. "Don't worry about it," he said. "You don't have to get up." But he didn't give me a spoonful of honey. He just reached with his hand and grabbed this uncomfortable place right inside my throat and said, "All you need to do is keep looking at that sense of self."

The dream was a powerful reminder. Getting caught in wanting the next treat, the next special state, I kept missing the perfection of *here and now*. Becoming a good meditator is a heavy boulder to carry. I hadn't emptied the sense of self that still had something to achieve. Ajahn Chah was always encouraging us to inquire, "Who does this belong to?" When I asked that question, "Me, dumbo!" often appeared in the heart. Who is this me? As I reflected on that transitory and seductive voice, I marveled at how unquestioningly we believe our thoughts to be "me." As soon as I saw the clinging, I let go and there was peace. But one insight is not the end; we need to do this again and again and again, because we forget.

During my retreat, in every activity, I kept laying down the burden, deepening my capacity to abide in that place of non-possession. I used several skillful means that I'd practiced extensively over the years to support this radical reflection— returning to the mind ground, the matrix, and the root.

SKILLFUL MEANS: RETURNING TO THE SOURCE

I Am

An important breakthrough occurred early in my monastic life when I received some tips from Sri Nisagardatta, whose teachings are recorded in a wonderful book called *I Am That*. My dear friend Ajahn Anando sent this book to me when I was a young monk at Ajahn Jun's monastery in Thailand. It had a revolutionary effect on my practice. Up until then I had been the one "polishing a brick to make a mirror." I kept trying to get my meditation right, my states of mind peaceful, and my body compliant with my will. None of that was working particularly well. Instead it led me into despair. In retrospect the despair was important, because it helped me give up. It helped me to recognize the perpetual burden of trying to get somewhere. When the book *I Am That* arrived, I was ready to hear what Sri Nisagardatta had to say.

> Awareness is primordial; it is the original state, beginning-less, endless, uncaused, unsupported, without parts, without change. Consciousness is on contact, a reflection against a surface, a state of duality. There can be no consciousness without awareness, but there can be awareness without consciousness, as in deep sleep. Awareness is absolute, consciousness is relative to its content; consciousness is always of something. Consciousness is partial and changeful, awareness is total, changeless, calm and silent. And it is the common matrix of every experience. . . . Interest in your stream of consciousness takes you to awareness.[9]

He encourages practitioners to continually return to the thought "I am," to reflect on the transitory nature of the thought itself, and give attention to the ever-present background of awareness where all thoughts, good and bad, dissolve. The "I am" habitually attaches to an object, a *this* or *that,* but do we ever reflect on the awareness itself?

For the first time I shifted my attention from the objects of consciousness to awareness. I practiced with the "I am," noticing its ephemeral bubble-like nature, letting it dissolve, resting in the effortless ground of knowing. I started welcoming into the heart all the thoughts I was afraid of, and those I habitually cherished, observing them rise and cease back into unmoving presence. This was my first taste of radical reflection, returning to the source. I was set on a new course, which resonated perfectly with the ongoing teachings I received in the monastery around suffering and the end of suffering. Throughout my sabbatical retreat at Dharmagiri, the words of Sri Nisargadatta were a great inspiration, always pointing me back from the endless complexity of the world to the unifying field of awareness.

Hua Tou: *Turning the Mind to the Deathless*

My interest in the methods of radical reflection opened further through the teachings of Master Hsuan Hua and Master Hsu Yun. In Chinese

Chan Buddhism, the most direct approach is Kuan Yin's method, the practice of "turning the mind back to its source." This is done through the use of a question that has no particular answer. Actually, Master Hsu Yun taught that the ancients had no need for the method of asking unanswerable questions, such as koans.[10] Initial instructions given to disciples were simple: "Stop," or "Lay everything down." This is similar to Ajahn Chah's "Don't pick up the boulder," or "Let go." Apparently, in the old days, such an instruction could enlighten just on the spot.

There have always been those who have awakened on hearing a snippet of Dharma, right from the time of the Buddha. However, over the centuries, as Hsu Yun records, the minds of disciples became dull, so the Chan masters had to devise other methods: the most favored being the *hua tou*, a question that directs the mind to the source, the fundamental principle. For example, "Who is mindful?" The question gives rise to doubt. Where is this me that thinks it's running the show? Whatever answer the mind throws up, is not the answer. The Chan masters called this method "fighting poison with poison" or "fighting fire with fire." The aim of this skillful means is to use a single thought to reveal, oppose, and arrest the multitude of thoughts. The question stops the thinking mind, momentarily, and the silent doubt ponders deeply into the suchness of things. The *hua tou* subdues conceptual proliferation and reveals that which never dies.

I like the analogy of fighting fire with fire, as it resonates with the burning of firebreaks, which we need to do every year at Dharmagiri. Dharmagiri is situated in vast grasslands that are bone-dry in winter. This makes the whole area susceptible to fires that can sweep through on the back of intense winds. High winds and fires are a frightening feature of wintertime in the Drakensberg Mountains. Every year we have to burn firebreaks to protect the hermitage and our neighbors. Sometimes, to stop a fire before it destroys life and property, you have to set fire to the grass in front of the runaway fire. This small fire is designed to burn back against the wind, to take away the fuel. It's called a "back-burn." The *hua tou* is like a back-burn. You place a question in the mind, which extinguishes the fuel needed for the mind to wander and proliferate, the fuel being thought.

Hua tou literally means the "head of thought" or the "origin of a thought." It is the place before thought, before creation—the place from which thought arises and into which it dissolves. It is also the place that Ajahn Chah pointed to in my dream. Although only a dream, it was completely in the style of Ajahn Chah. He had taken me by the throat and told me to keep looking at my sense of self. This was a powerful teaching. During my period of severe sickness, I was always trying to get off the ground, thinking I had to be out there doing something. Getting off the ground became synonymous with existence, with being a good monk or someone that was contributing and successful. Each thought defined my identity and evaluated how I was doing. Each thought arises from the "ground" of the mind. Using a *hua tou*—a thought like Who is thinking?—exposes the emptiness of thought. The question turns the mind back on itself. It consumes the sense of a solid separate me who thinks. It reveals the timeless background of the mind—the underlying, cool, listening presence. The deathless.

The question "who" empties the self that is constructed by thought, like a pin pops a balloon. The *hua tou* directs attention to the place before thought, the uncreated, so it is important when using this method to listen carefully to the silence before the thought, and after the thought, to intimately know that thinking is a transitory guest passing through the mind. To empty the sense of external phenomena, we can use the question "What is it?" The contemplation collapses any assumption that something "out there" has permanence. Alternatively, the question "What is really happening right now?" reveals and empties any fixed perceptions and constructed narratives we might have about ourselves, or the world. In contact with the world, immediately we tend to make judgments about our experience. "I am like this" or "She is like that." However, using the *hua tou*—whichever one seems right for us—will unveil the insubstantiality of thought, and shatter the artificially constructed walls of the mind. Nothing is fixed. Knowing that, letting go of grasping, the heart recognizes the essential luminous stillness that, as Nisargadatta says, "is the common matrix of every experience."

During the retreat my favorite *hua tous* were "What remains?" and

"What never dies?" I placed these questions in the heart and patiently listened to the inner silence, noticing the unshakable suchness right in the midst of change. Over the years I have cultivated an appreciation for this inquiry. It reveals a peaceful silent and present abiding that is not disturbed by the flickering thoughts moving through the heart. I like the directness of this practice. It points right to the root cause of suffering. Eventually there comes a time when we look straight at "birth and death." In this context I don't mean being born as a baby and dying as an old person. For one who meditates, birth is the identification with thoughts and the apparent thingness they imply. Birth identifies with becoming someone, acquiring stuff, doing the next thing, or taking on the roles we play. Consequently, death is the experience of wavering and loss felt when something we're leaning on (identified with) changes or ends.

All conditions are impermanent. As Ajahn Chah said frequently, "If you look for certainty in that which is uncertain, you are bound to suffer." Letting go, there is peace. That's why Buddhas never waver. Not being born into conditions, there is no aging and no death.

THE SHURANGAMA *SAMADHI*

The Shurangama Sutra[11] discusses "two fundamental roots"[12] that need to be thoroughly understood for awakening. According to the Buddha, if spiritual practitioners do not understand these principles, they are like someone "who cooks sand in the hope of creating a savory delicacy. They may pass through as many eons as there are motes of dust, but in the end they will not obtain what they want." The first is the root of endless birth and death: the mind that seizes upon conditions and mistakes its identity with the world of phenomena. The outcome of this ignorance is *samsara*, perpetual cycles of suffering, loss, and anxiety. The second fundamental root of the mind is called the "original brightness," or " beginning-less bodhi nirvana," the "primal bright essence of consciousness that brings forth all conditions." During the forty-five years that the Buddha taught, he described the liberated mind in many ways, such as the *bodhi* (awakened) mind, the unconditioned, the peaceful, the secure, the wonderful, the deathless, the destination, or nirvana.

The problem with giving a name to the ultimate principle is that it sounds like another thing we have to look for and try to attain. Whatever we call it, is not it. As is said in the Tao Te Ching, "The name that can be named is not the eternal name." The true nature is empty of all designations, empty of "marks." The Buddha used words and spoke out of compassion, endeavoring to communicate his subtle understanding for the welfare of all. Recognizing the limitation of language, however, he exclaimed, "This dharma cannot be described. Words fall silent before it." The ever-present original brightness is only realized when the grasping mind is relinquished.

Shurangama means "durable." The Shurangama *samadhi* is unwavering, for it takes *nibbana* as its object. The skillful means I have been discussing—wise reflection, stopping the proliferating mind, the I am, the *hua tou*—all return the mind to its root. Radical reflection is the function of wisdom. In Mahayana Buddhism wisdom is considered feminine, because its primordial depth is womblike. It gives birth to the awakened ones, and guides wise and compassionate response within the world. Considered the Mother of all the Buddhas, *prajna paramita*—the spiritual perfection of intuitive wisdom—carries the seeker across the sea of suffering to safety. The Buddha names wisdom as foremost among the spiritual faculties, because without it one is trapped in the duality of self and other, and never transcends birth and death. Lost in the proliferating tendencies of the mind, the heart does not recognize its own pure undivided substance.

During my sabbatical year on retreat I had the precious opportunity to continually empty the heart of subtle splits. Many times a day I would reflect on a phrase from the Heart Sutra: "All dharmas are empty of characteristics." I noticed that habitually my thoughts would label, define, and concretize whatever was happening, making that activity seem real. While walking, I ordinarily gave reality to the "characteristic" of movement. Emptying the heart of that perception, letting that thought dissolve, I noticed the essential stillness within walking. I practiced walking while perceiving the unmoving suchness that is always here and now. While sitting and feeling peaceful, when the heart attached to the perception of stillness, I noticed the movement within stillness—the breath flowing, the sensations vibrating, the sounds flickering. I reflected on stillness within movement and movement within stillness, emptying the rigid distinctions I make unconsciously, all the time. Movement and stillness, each is just a way of talking. Letting thoughts subside, the true Dharma is not moving and not still.

Similarly, there is a tendency to create a difference between good states and bad states, mindful moments and heedless moments, enlightened and deluded, in here and out there, feeling peaceful and suffering, meditating and not meditating, being on retreat and being back in the world. Every time I noticed the heart making a mark, creating a split, I practiced letting that thought go, revealing its essential emptiness. This beautiful and peaceful practice is sometimes called cultivating patience with the non-production of dharmas. Everything is as it is, not getting bigger or smaller, better or worse.

As the self-created walls of my mind dissolved, through the persistent practice of nonproliferation, everything appeared within awareness. Nothing was far away. I didn't feel lonely, for it was clear that all of creation arises and ceases within this one heart. Every morning I enjoyed bowing slowly and mindfully one hundred and eight times, counting one bead with each bow, remembering the Buddhas of each direction, bodhisattvas, teachers, family, loved ones, friends, fellow beings, the various categories of creatures, all the great saints and sages from other religions, the universe, and all the galaxies, even those I dislike, all beings without exception. In this practice I bring all the dimensions of my life together into harmony. Finding the body and thought, gathering them into the heart of awareness, feeling the sensation of the bead in my fingers, touching my head to the ground, surrendering to the silence, I give everything back to the mystery. Every impression dissolves perfectly into the vast boundless field of awareness, just as every flash of lightning returns to the immensity of the night sky.

At the end of each day, I consciously shared the blessings of my practice with all beings. Letting the marks of self and other disappear, I experienced a tangible force releasing through my body, emanating powerfully in all directions, blessing the land and all her creatures. What grace to have the opportunity to spend a silent year in prayer and contemplation on an ancient sacred mountain. What a gift to know that quiet contemplation blesses everything around it. Although it might look passive, when the apartheid of the heart—the insidious separations created by the mind—is overcome in silence, the wounds of the world are healed. We are all brothers and sisters in birth and death, refugees from the Promised Land. One family. One home.

My retreat was coming to a close. I felt restored, profoundly grateful, humbled, and encouraged. Even though my extended time for contemplation had shown me clearly the many ways I still suffer—the myriad desires, aversions, and delusions of the heart—at least I had a trustworthy path of practice, a way to return to profound peace. I knew that heedless thinking—*papanca*—was the main source of my suffering, and I determined to continue the practice of stopping the proliferating mind in my daily life. I was already emptying the distinction between meditation and ordinary activity, so I was looking forward to the challenge of testing my contemplative skills again in the midst of daily life. I felt ready to return to the responsibilities of teaching and running a meditation hermitage.

My retreat reaffirmed that daily devotional practice—like bowing and the recitation of mantras and chants—is an indispensable support. First, these practices connect me regularly to the boundless blessings of the enlightened heart, and dissolve the contracted places where the sense of self gets stuck. They help me overcome anxiety and return to a place of trust. Second, they offer an opportunity to put the cognitive faculty in perspective. Every morning I chanted the Great Compassion Mantra, the Shurangama Mantra, and recited various sutras. I've done this every day for many years, on retreat or off. During this year of retreat, however, I realized how vitally important devotional practice is for deepening wisdom. In recitation, the flow of the mantra happens automatically, since one has memorized the text. In order to recite, one uses the thinking faculty. As the mantra flows through the awareness, however, I hold the cognitive faculty lightly, mindfully letting each phrase dissolve into silence. The steady movement of the mantra is like a swiftly revolving blade that shatters every concept. Although devotional practices might appear dualistic, I've found they are excellent ways to destroy the walls of the mind and reveal the open, trusting background of awareness.

Our true nature, the heart of hearts, which is profoundly wise, lies hidden within the depths of our being—that is, until we begin to awaken. Our task is then to bring this primordial wisdom to the fore so it informs our understanding, our perspectives, and our activity. When everything returns to the depth of knowing, we enter the great unknown, the sacred mystery. The Heart Sutra offers no methods, except the immediate and radical reliance on the truth of our original nature. To recognize our bright, primordially intelligent nature, here and now, is called "The Great Return."

> *Try to be mindful and let things take their natural course. Then your mind will become still in any surroundings, like a clear forest pool. All kinds of wonderful, rare animals will come to drink at the pool, and you will clearly see the nature of all things. You will see many strange and wonderful things come and go, but you will be still. This is the happiness of the Buddha.*[13]
>
> –Ajahn Chah

CHAPTER TWELVE

The Wounded Warrior

Thanissara

Only the wounded understand the agonies of the wounded.

—Mirabai[1]

Awakening is to return to our natural state. While our agendas complicate life, in contrast our natural state is simple; it isn't planning or anxious. It just is. There is no fear of loss and no big accomplishment to gain. Awakening, said the Buddha, is "here and now, timeless and ever inviting us inward." It is not a special experience we can capture. Although I have experienced awakenings, they are now memories, like fading butterflies. Awakening isn't an experience; it is the end of experience. We don't need a unique experience to notice the truest thing we can say about ourselves: that we simply are.

While the presence of our natural state is innate, the maturing and integration of awakening is a gradual process. Zen master Huang Po said, "We cannot know what we have always been. We can only become intuitively aware of our original state, previously hidden by the clouds of illusion." Dispelling "the clouds of illusion" is a patient process. Awakening is not a static state we reach where we never experience conflict, pain, or suffering. This is a childish idea of enlightenment. A trap in meditation is aiming for a special experience, hoping it will remove us from life's challenges and transform us into a super spiritual, Teflon-like power person who has all the answers. Instead, awakening is humbling, because we have to concede our fundamental state of "unknowing," and understand our deepest nature is a mystery.

As the awakening process integrates into our life, we are not lifted *up and out* of our challenges; instead it takes us *down and through* the layers of our personal and collective unconscious. As we become more aware, what is held in the shadow is illuminated. Inevitably we meet wounds related to themes of belonging, acceptance, safety, self-love, and self-expression. There is a quality of love in Buddhist practice, called *metta,* which can help us navigate these tender and sometimes devastating places. *Metta* means to keep the heart "softened." It is a quality of universal love that is kind, even if what is around us is conflicted and unkind. For *metta* to mature beyond an inner meditation practice, it has to be tested in the flesh and blood of relationship. This is the acid test of our practice.

Often what blocks our ability to feel kindness toward others is that we haven't developed it around those parts in ourselves that have been prematurely dismissed, shamed, or judged. As we come to terms with our own deeper wounds, we begin to understand others better. Some of our deepest wounds occur in early developmental processes that weren't negotiated well. Even with the best parenting and schooling, we inevitably carry some psychological wounding. In response, the self-structure becomes shaped to defend against the original pain felt when needs were not met, or were thwarted in insensitive or harsh ways.

Some wounds are passed on through our national, ancestral, and karmic inheritance. Some can also be inflicted through social pressures that arise due to prejudice, for example around race, class, gender, or sexual orientation. When such wounds aren't resolved, the self struggles to maintain its inner integrity. This can impede our ability to negotiate the world well. We can find ourselves overwhelmed by the smallest challenge, and susceptible to feelings of futility. However, it is also the case that our wounds are the catalyst for spiritual and psychological maturation. For this to happen we need to take care not to use spiritual teachings to prematurely avoid the pain of our underlying hurt. The term for this is "spiritual bypassing." This is when we displace unacceptable feelings by projecting them onto others. For example, to compensate for feeling worthless, we develop a superior spiritual persona, project our self-aversion onto others, and then become intolerant of them. In doing so, we fail to reclaim the fullness of our own energy.

It's not always easy to see ourselves, and when we do it can be humbling to see the projections of our mind! One day I was on a silent retreat when someone I didn't know walked into the dining area where I was eating my meal. I looked up at them and thought, "That person doesn't like me." At the same moment I saw that actually I really didn't like myself. The mind had just projected its self-aversion onto someone else. When we do this, we abdicate responsibility for our own negativity, which in this case was unfair for the poor unsuspecting person trying to get their lunch! As we become aware of the mind's projections we can unmask tendencies, like self-aversion, and stop perpetuating deeply held beliefs, like about our intrinsic "badness." A common tendency in spiritual life is to repress these unsettling feelings and compensate by idealizing the self as spiritual. When this happens, usually those around us have to hold our shadow.

Spiritual bypassing means we don't see our effect on others. We can use the idea of spiritual transcendence like a shield, dismissing feedback and putting down others, saying, "They don't really understand emptiness or the true teachings. If they did they wouldn't be complaining!" Sometimes in spiritual circles abusive practices are justified in the name of "higher teachings," so shadow dynamics can be conveniently dismissed in the name of spiritual ideology. However, a true understanding of emptiness brings depth of intimacy with life; we feel with others, are responsive and have ethics, humor, joy, and compassion. On the other hand, ideological emptiness is usually colored by avoidance, disdain, dismissal, and aversion. It can also mask a laziness and inability to engage in relationships authentically. It's important to know the difference between true emptiness and false emptiness. The first liberates, is joyful, and can transfer blessings, while the second disguises an immaturity and tends to be abusive. When this happens there is a loss of humility, receptivity to feedback, sensitivity, and kindness. Unfortunately, teachings like "emptiness" and "nonattachment" can be used to dismiss the self and its unhealed wounds, which in turn bury those hurts deeper into the unconscious.

Buddhism emphasizes a creed of "nonattachment," so the word "attachment" usually has negative connotations for practitioners. In Buddhist thought attachment is basically seen as the primary cause of suffering. However, it has a very different meaning in psychology, where the importance of positive attachment in early developmental processes is emphasized. Babies and children need a consistent, loving, and safe "attached" relationship with at least one primary caregiver for healthy social and emotional development. This early bonding sets the pattern for further relationships. When there are ruptures in this process, it tends to lead to various forms of psychological suffering later in life. Therefore, spiritual work will inevitably touch wounds that have come about due to a disruption within this vital aspect of nurturing.

If we don't understand this territory, spiritual practices will most likely be used to prematurely dismiss these painful wounds in the name of a perceived ideal of enlightenment. The energetic pain of our wounds is then pushed beneath our conscious awareness. It becomes part of the shadow. What is held in the unconscious will have great power to direct our lives and influence our behavior. This is how it is possible for spiritual practitioners to have great lucidity and clarity, yet still be emotionally immature and sometimes even destructive. When this happens what is held in the shadow is projected out. The symptoms of this are many, but in essence we split the world into "friends" and "enemies," and we find ourselves intolerant of others when they diverge from our narcissistic need for affirmation. We also become particularly angry and judgmental of those who express our own shadow issues. This dynamic shows up as those who denounce homosexuality and then have secret gay sex, or religious moralists who curb-crawl for the services of prostitutes, putting down others for doing or saying the very things they do. If we are very split, we will need others to be receptacles for our shadow and will harshly condemn those we project onto. This is why puritanical and fascist movements, which in their rigidity are unable to accept their own hatred, fear, and lust, are prone to violently attack marginalized groups, and at the extreme, commit genocide.

Unfortunately, idealized spirituality, while seductive, is dangerous; it can obscure our vision and sabotage the real work that needs to happen. Coming to terms with our shadow is a challenging and humble process, but it is vital territory to negotiate if our awakening is to integrate all aspects of our personal and collective lives. It will often require that we enter into early childhood psychological material, which is tender, sometimes embarrassing, and usually messy. However, if we are not willing to do so we can become inwardly split and outwardly damaging, so at the very least some rudimentary understanding of this subject is important for those who are committed to awakening.

On the whole, we are not that aware of the wounds held within the unconscious. We experience their symptoms as depression, obsessive anxiety, paranoia, or inappropriate and addictive behaviors, but we don't really know what fuels these effects. It can be hard to access and see the causes of early wounds solely through meditation. Sometimes we become "good meditators," but in the process use meditation techniques to repress what we don't want to deal with. We can push things away as a temporary strategy, but it won't lead to a healthy result. Generally speaking, for deep wounds we need help to go beneath our defenses. We develop sophisticated psychological defenses that keep us from conflicted and chaotic feelings that threaten our sense of cohesive self. Our defenses have their part to play; they help us negotiate the world. However, they can also undermine our well-being and deplete our life energy. In meditation we feel the effects of our psychological wounds, and can contemplate them as sensation and feeling tone, but not necessarily be able to access their cause or resolve them. In many ways meditation practice is less concerned with the content of mind, or the reasons for our emotional and psychological experience, and more concerned with the construct of the mind. Meditation practice tends to focus more on the impermanence of phenomena and less on why it appears in the way it does.

Meditation and psycho-spiritual work, however, can support each other. The awareness training of meditation enhances therapeutic practices by tapping into the present-moment appearance of the mind's process in order to access what is held in the unconscious. There is then the possibility of healing wounds, or conversely, recognizing latent positive tendencies that have been suppressed. The causes of our wounds may not be altogether clear, but dysfunctional beliefs such as low self-esteem, and the pain that goes with that, can be seen and released. Feeling the original wounds to our sensitivity can be overwhelming, which is why we develop such sophisticated defenses to shield from their intolerable effect. Meditation can offer the focus and containment needed to sustain attention when we touch these areas. It also brings compassion into the therapeutic process. Through the kind, safe, and careful inquiry of another—the therapist—healing can be quickened. As these deep wounds happened within relationship, the optimum situation for their healing is also within relationship.

While Kittisaro used his sabbatical to deepen his meditation practice, I undertook a period of therapeutic training and healing. I entered a two-year MA program in Mindfulness-Based Psychotherapy Practice at the Karuna Institute[2] in England. Their style of psycho-spiritual work, called Core Process Psychotherapy, is rooted in Buddhist teaching and practice. It focuses on the use of awareness as the main medium for transformation and healing. Its central practice, which is deceptively simple, uses two direct and non-invasive questions, to which the recipient chooses the extent to which they wish to respond. These questions—"What is happening now?" and "How is that?"—are effective, but the real power of this approach is the quality of awareness with which the process is held. The potency of awareness is heightened when working with others who share a commitment to present-moment inquiry, loving-kindness, and safety. Safety is enabled in therapeutic work through ethical sensitivity, the appropriate holding of boundaries, and confidentiality. Applying the work of relational awareness with these intentions in place allows for a fulcrum around which hidden truths can emerge.

Psychotherapeutic work focuses on healing personal wounds and encouraging personal health. However, we don't just operate as an individual; when someone walks into a therapy room they energetically bring their family, culture, and society. In fact, they arrive with the world and its history. We may think the past has gone, but the residue of huge historical forces ripple on and shape both the personal and collective self. The impact of wars, economic emigration, slavery, famine, and persecution generate deep intergenerational issues around belonging, lack, and security. This in turn can condition abusive, addictive, and pathological types of behavior. The larger causes of psychological wounding are also coupled with the unpredictable effects of our unique personal karmic inheritance. No wonder we want to use teachings such as "non-self," "nonattachment," and "emptiness" to catapult ourselves beyond this matrix of pain and complexity. However, deep unconscious and unhealed patterns tend to repeat themselves, which is why those who are victimized sometimes go on to exploit others. With increased awareness, however, there is the possibility of resolving our wounds so we don't repeat patterns of abuse.

We live in an interdependent world, which influences our personal experience; therefore, healing the personal engages the collective. A powerful aspect of our collective and ancestral inheritance is the influence of patriarchy, which has shaped human consciousness for millennia. The effects of patriarchy influence everyone, regardless of gender. The classical definition of patriarchy is "social, political, and economic systems where the role of the male assumes primary authority." However, we can widen that to power assumed due to entitlements claimed, not only through gender, but also through race, caste, class, geography, or economic advantage. Patriarchy can have benevolent, protective, and philanthropic dimensions, but its shadow claims entitlement through the subordination and marginalization of others, which can even extend to a sense of ownership of them. This historical inheritance has, in particular, generated an imbalance between masculine and feminine. The essential dynamic of the shadow patriarch, whether operating within a man or woman, is the unrelenting drive to power, dominance, and control. In many ways this attempts to compensate for the loss of connection, love, and belonging, and ultimately for the loss of an ability to feel intimacy with life. When not caught in their own shadow of passivity and manipulation, these nurturing qualities, which generate an inclusive and cohesive relational field, are the natural domain of the healthy feminine.

The impact of patriarchal wounding and the corresponding loss of ground for the feminine play out within the Buddhist transmission. Unfortunately, Buddhist teachings have been used, and sometimes distorted, to justify gender discrimination. I encountered the impact of this as a Buddhist nun. For centuries women have been considered illegitimate within the monastic Sangha. For legitimacy there has to be full ordination, which has been vigorously obstructed, even though the Buddha set the precedent for it.[3] As a result, nuns do not receive the same level of economic support or respect, and are often seen as second-class citizens or failed women, in contrast to men, who are lionized when they take the robes. I was shocked when I first saw that many women from Buddhist cultures made offerings to monks, hoping the merit they gained would help them be reborn as men. This internalized misogyny is insidious, and instead of being openly challenged, it's often colluded with, and even encouraged. Ultimate teachings, which rightly point beyond identity, are wrongly applied when they are used to dismiss the effects of discrimination. Using transcendent teachings like this is sometimes called "upleveling." This is when teachings on nonattachment or emptiness are used to dismiss careful consideration of abusive practices, erroneous religious views, and unhealthy relationship dynamics.

Institutionalized patriarchy is also embedded in colonial practices, which pretty much shape the whole globe, but perhaps nowhere more than Africa. When Kittisaro and I first went to South Africa in 1994, we stepped into a country formed by centuries of colonialism, decades of apartheid, and a deeply ingrained African patriarchy. The Buddhist Retreat Center in Ixopo, KwaZulu Natal, where we first landed, is set in the Midlands, an area of languid hills that span from the Indian Ocean to the mighty Drakensberg Mountains. Alan Paton opened his renowned novel *Cry the Beloved Country* with the lines, "There is a lovely road that runs from Ixopo into the hills. These hills are grass-covered and rolling, and they are lovely beyond any singing of it." Here, in the 1980s, the vision of its founders and guides, the Van Loons, became the flagship for Buddhism in South Africa. The center makes a significant offering as a place of peace, safety, and inner reflection. Surrounded by a stunning landscape, it has a diverse and uplifting program. As resident guiding teachers, Kittisaro and I taught dozens of retreats and workshops, and helped develop the center's resources, over a period of about seven years. A large Zulu staff work in the kitchens, on the land, and in maintenance. This was very different from our monastic experience, where monks, nuns, and lay residents did manual work. Basically, the center operated within a feudal system. This reflected the surrounding conservative farming culture, and the deeply systemic system of white entitlement and black servitude woven into the matrix of South African society at that time.

It was a culture shock to arrive into rural South Africa. Although apartheid had officially ended, it still rolled on, affecting most every aspect of daily life. Black and white people lived closely entwined, but a million miles apart. What I experienced as discordant was accepted as the norm. African workers were "boys" and "girls," and while we lived in comfort and ate well, a fifteen-minute walk away the local Zulu population lived in abject poverty. I didn't have the inbred defenses to filter out this disturbing dynamic or the complex feelings it entailed. I felt guilty about my white privilege, distressed about the poverty of our local community, and aware of a constant undertow of dislocation. I was out of place. While the local African community was deeply rooted in their land and culture, I felt that as whites we were rootless. Basically, I was overwhelmed by the dissonance of trauma held within the "relational field."

We arrived at a time when the country was swept by the euphoria of liberation after its first free elections—but also by a wave of violence. Systems founded in violence, legislating against people to control and diminish them, plant the seeds of fear, paranoia, and vengeance. People would come on our retreats and talk of hijackings, rapes, and murder. The fear of "them" and what "they" might do was pervasive. "Never go into a township!" "Make sure your house and car are locked securely!" "Put bars on your windows!" "Be careful if you go out after dark!"

The underlying tenor of fear and anxiety was overwhelming. One night, Kittisaro and I were driving through a rural area, trying to do something pretty normal, go to a movie. A young African man, who careened off the freeway without braking, slammed into our car. *That's it,* I thought, *we're toast.* However, as we looked at the cars' crumpled fenders, the shocked man couldn't have been friendlier. After this incident, I became aware of how rapidly I was internalizing fear. Every time I heard the common white refrain "Africa is not for sissies," my innate "sissieness" would do a wobble and pirouette. However, I knew if we were to work in South Africa, I needed to accept the possibility of being caught in a violent incident. Making that conscious helped me decide that I wanted to work against living from a fear-based dynamic.

We psychologically internalize the impact of patriarchal systems. To undo that conditioning is a big journey for all of us, both personally and collectively. First, we have to acknowledge how our natural state of sensitivity closes down. Social and state systems that promote apartheid-type dynamics create societies that desensitize people. In many ways our global society is increasingly an apartheid dynamic, where those with wealth and entitlement distance themselves from those caught in cycles of servitude and poverty. The karma of this is that we feel fear and paranoia. When will "they" come over the border to take what we have? We disconnect from our heart, which in reality knows we are all a part of one another. This is what the heart naturally feels. It feels its connection to life; it knows itself as life. Yet we fear that radical intimacy, and so obsess about our differences.

When we divide against others, we also divide against the natural sensitivity of our heart, which is an intolerable and insidious pain. It's a pain that's hard to own and to feel. Usually it's easier to project onto those around. When there is a lot of damage to the fabric of self, family, and society, there is a constant shifting of pain onto others. However, those "others" have to stay invisible or defined in lesser ways to support the rationale for such dehumanizing treatment. When we have privilege, it blinds us. Generally speaking, those without power will know far more about their "masters" than the other way around. A patriarchal dynamic makes "the other" invisible to itself. It then fears and condemns those who challenge the system, or who threaten its power base. These systems are maintained through a million small daily ways that break real and authentic contact. But in moments of opening to the inner psychological pain of this dynamic, we begin a journey of reclamation. If you've noticed, it's hard to sustain division if really look into another's eyes. Instead you will see the same vulnerability we all share. In the moment of truly seeing another, apartheid collapses. We are then only looking at ourselves.

It's easy to criticize apartheid systems, and harder to see how we internalize and perpetuate aspects of patriarchy, apartheid, and colonialism in our collective and personal lives. If we can't confront our blind spots, however, sometimes life will do it for us.

We had been living right next to the Zulu community, divided as if by a wall of glass. That glass was about to crack open with the advent of HIV and AIDS. The smiling, yet dour, workers, whose lives were mostly invisible to us, were about to become much more visible. It was a cruel twist of fate that after the elation of deposing Apartheid Rule, the country was beset by the devastating pandemic of AIDS. The wildfire spread of the virus was enabled through a potent mix of governmental denial, tribal stigma, a cultural entitlement that allowed men to have unprotected sex with multiple partners, erroneous myths, lethargy, and a chronic lack of resources and education. The AIDS pandemic has taken millions to their deaths and created a legacy of child-headed households. It devastated already fragmented communities, and heavily impacted the most vulnerable: women and children. As the glass wall fractured under the pressure of the tsunami of AIDS, the "enlightenment journey" was no longer a personal luxury.

In those days, many young people we knew became infected, and many died from AIDS. No antiretroviral medicine was available, and fear, despair, and shame were rife. Soon, we became engaged in our local rural communities, as we all entered the sharp learning curve of living with AIDS. I remember our first educational workshop. A group of young Zulu activists came into the rural community next to the Buddhist Center. The induna, or headman of the village, divided the group between men and women, who sat in different classrooms. The activists stood up and told the community they were HIV-positive, which was true. No one believed them. The community didn't believe the cause of the deaths of their young people was AIDS. They thought it was something bad sprinkled on them by white people from airplanes, or it was a curse put on them by someone in the village. The activists then went on to talk about using condoms. One old, bent-over granny, taking forever to get out of her chair, tried to stand upright to object. She was dumbfounded. How can this thing (a condom) stop you dying in ten years' time? In a community that had low literacy, no access to the Internet, and no education about how HIV worked, this unfamiliar thing called a condom seemed an unlikely way to stop a new strange and terrible disease.

With financial backing from overseas Buddhist groups, particularly San Francisco Insight, London Insight, and Buddhist Global Relief, we cofounded and supported several outreach programs that focused on training care workers and community development. Our efforts were part of a larger movement of nonprofit grassroots responses that emerged all over the country. Many groups simply transitioned from anti-apartheid work to AIDS response initiatives. Within ten to fifteen years, activists had forced the South African government and pharmaceutical companies to provide free and low-cost antiretroviral medicine. Rural communities, where mention of sex was previously taboo, became proficient in learning the ins and outs of protective sexual practices. Positive Living support groups mushroomed, gender rights became an issue, and as AIDS highlighted the lack of resources in communities, development projects and literacy programs increased. While much good work continues to be done, it doesn't diminish the huge amount still needed.

Sister Abegail Ntleko, a great ally and dear friend, engaged the AIDS crisis in our local area with great energy and fearlessness. She is a remarkable woman who was finally recognized for her fifty years of community service as recipient of the "Wise Giving Unsung Hero Award," given by His Holiness the Dalai Lama. In her recent book *Empty Hands*,[4] she tells of how she negotiated her way through a patriarchal father and tribe, and an apartheid regime, to become well-loved within all communities, as a guide, elder, and advocate for the vulnerable. Through it all, she emerged with her remarkable spirit intact. Sister Abe now runs a home for her children and teenagers, all twenty of them! Sister Abe, or Gogo as she is affectionately called, like Mr. Mandela, is one of South Africa's luminaries forged from ground zero of patriarchal colonialism and apartheid. She emerged victorious through the power of her spiritual faith and love of humanity.

Our journey into South Africa was a far cry from our introspective monastic lifestyle. Instead, our path became one of innovation, overwhelm, frustration, but also hope. For fifteen years we fund-raised, guided, and helped. We met great and generous people, those who were on the AIDS industry bandwagon, cranks with crazy theories, those who were dedicated and selfless, and those who had dubious motives. It was heartbreaking and inspiring. A kid who always stays with me is Mhlonishwa. He was about eleven when I met him in his grandmother's broken-down hut. She was surrounded by twelve orphans and just a bag of old potatoes. He had some sort of complication from TB, and had been lying on the floor wrapped up in a blanket for about three years. He was very bright, and his aspiration was to attend school, but he couldn't get there. The day his wheelchair arrived, his community built a pathway and ramp to the classroom. Even though, very sadly, he died shortly after starting school, his radiant smile, surrounded by school friends, continues to uplift me.

Working in any activist situation is challenging. It's impossible to enter a traumatized relational field and come away unscathed. What starts as a simple, honest intention to help can become an intricate maze of relational complexity, where power dynamics and peoples' sense of ownership fractures the goodness of the work. Here the shadow dwells, slamming us to the ground yet also inviting us to part the clouds of illusion that eclipse our innate awakened nature. In the midst of challenge, our practice is to keep moving beyond the projections and splits of the mind. To draw it all back into the listening, quiet, spacious heart; to lay down our grasping and hurts, and offer it all back into the mystery of life.

One night, about a year into our new life in South Africa, I had a powerful dream. It was so vivid that it woke me up with a start. I was sure the person I'd dreamed of was in my room. In the dream I was walking down a dusty road hand in hand with Kittisaro. A powerful African woman, who exuded strength, health, vitality, and fertility, stood in our way. She caught me by the arm and pulled me to one side. Suddenly milk poured from her breasts into my mouth. It kept pouring and pouring until I was suffocating. I couldn't breathe and I started to panic. She told me to relax. As her milk overflowed and poured over Kittisaro, the panic shifted to a deep feeling of letting go and trust. She gave me a mantra and let me know that Kittisaro would be healed. Suddenly I was pulled out of the dream and was wide awake. I felt we had been welcomed. It was like Mother Africa was allowing us to be there, and do our work. I knew we received her blessing, and that it was okay to be in this land, that there would be protection in the face of all we would meet.

Whatever happens in life, our practice is to meet it. Ajahn Chah encouraged his disciples to practice like an earthworm, rather than to try and be a Buddha. An earthworm goes down through the mud, rather than catapulting its way into the light. In the same way, we have to work through the shadow to reclaim and heal our deeper heart. It's also like a butterfly. In the process of its transformation, a caterpillar digests itself and becomes mush before reemerging into a beautiful, delicate, winged butterfly.

These days it seems the world it getting more chaotic and dangerous, but there is also potential here. As the shadows are drawn into the light of our awareness, there's the opportunity to free human consciousness from old dysfunctional beliefs. Rather than using spirituality to push away what is held in the shadow, the invitation is to touch our wounds with loving awareness so we can move beyond them. As a global consciousness, we are in an evolutionary process; it is painful, confused, and fraught with danger. However, as each of us awakens beyond the apartheid of the mind, as we choose to live beyond the energy of fear and oppression, we will birth the winged butterfly of our future.

So don't be frightened, dear friend, if a sadness confronts you larger than any you have ever known, casting its shadow over all you do. You must think that something is happening within you, and remember that life has not forgotten you; it holds you in its hand and will not let you fall. Why would you want to exclude from your life any uneasiness, any pain, any depression, since you don't know what work they are accomplishing within you?

–Rainer Maria Rilke

CHAPTER THIRTEEN

Through the Night Door

Thanissara

You, darkness that I come from, I love you more than all the fires that fence in the world, for the fire makes a circle of light for everyone and then no one outside learns of you. But the darkness pulls in everything, shapes and fires, animals and myself, how easily it gathers them! Powers and people– And it is possible a great presence is moving near me. I have faith in nights.

–Rainer Maria Rilke

The collective is always personal, and that is where we must start. As the Buddha encouraged, we begin with the body. In this fathom long body, this perceptive form, I make known the world, its arising, its ceasing and the path leading to its cessation.[1] When I entered monastic life, I wasn't so identified with gender, but with my desire to enter a lifestyle that inspired me. However, Buddhist monasticism, which shapes the transmission of the Dharma, has a 2,560 year patriachal imperative which mostly sees women as lesser and as a problem. As I entered the monastic relational field, inevitably this potent history had a personal impact. As nuns we oscillated in a perpetually ambivalent dynamic which I found increasingly painful. Daily teachings encouraged "letting go" of all self-identification, including gender. In spite of my spiritual ideal to live those teachings, my body knew otherwise.

I developed a cough that wouldn't go away no matter what I tried to do to cure it. Eventually I realized that it was a symptom of having no voice. Decisions were made about us, as nuns, that didn't include us. However much the status of nuns was rationalized as irrelevant to enlightenment, and however much I tried to accord with that, my body wouldn't comply.

As the first development of mindfulness, the Buddha directs us to establish mindfulness of the body. If we understand mindfulness as a purely clinical observation of sensations, it can distance us from a meaningful relationship with the body's intelligence. If we just see the body as a bundle of pleasant and unpleasant sensations, which we dismiss, we overlook the information within feeling. Holding mindfulness, or loving awareness, to body sensation helps us receive the messages energetically held within the body. Deeply held beliefs that shape the whole matrix of the self can be accessed through their surface appearance as sensation and feeling tone. In this process what is revealed, beneath the presenting "felt sense" experience, is the personal, familial, ancestral, and collective history that is held within the body as cellular memory.

Mindfulness of embodied experience enables a tapping into the energetic impressions of what has gone before. These manifest as feeling tones, states of mind, beliefs, moods, and an overall energetic patterning that constitutes the shaping of self. In the awakening process, a decrease in identification with the body can paradoxically deepen our experience of embodiment. Taking the body less personally lessens constriction around the body and increases sensitivity to it. As we become more aware, we see the symbiotic relationship of body and mind. This enabled me to explore the impact of patriarchy as it is held in my own emotional and physical body.

I wasn't able to explore this therapeutically as a monastic, but I had the opportunity to do so after I disrobed. In one session, in a small therapy-training group, I became aware of a tight sensation around my head. I had the sense of a tight cap being placed on my head. Connecting with the physical sensation revealed a "felt sense" experience of fear. The "felt sense" is a term coined by Eugene Gendlin in relationship to his Focusing Work.[2] It means having a global sense of something. The felt sense is composed of sensations, emotional tones, feelings and intuitive sensing, and can include imagery or words. It is a way of accessing information that is usually unconscious. Focusing is also a process of finding meaning and placement for material retrieved through the felt sense.

I had been placed in the "client role" in the group after I voiced my upset that one of the men in the group was always taking central place, and getting more attention. That wasn't necessarily the case, but in that moment, that was how I experienced it. As the session began, applying sustained awareness to physical sensations as an access point, I tracked the felt sense. In doing so, layers of material became conscious. The sensation of fear was linked to a lack of self-esteem. An internal narrative of sabotaging inner voices became conscious: "Who do you think you are? You shouldn't take central place, you can't do this, you're not worth it." The corresponding energetic movement was to curl up and disappear.

I felt shame. I was too "demanding." Being "demanding" was often a criticism leveled at women, or at nuns, when concerns were raised about the impact of gender inequity in the monastery. As I continued to track the feeling tones, there was anxiety that I would be judged for not conforming to some internalized belief about how I should be. "I need to be small in order to belong, so I can be accepted and safe." Suddenly this feeling felt ancient. I became aware that the shadow side of "conforming" was a less "pretty" me that was resentful and uncooperative. As I tracked the process, guided by the person leading the inquiry, I plunged into a feeling of loss of power, at the core of which was the life statement *I have no right to be here.*

As the session continued, the felt sense of another inherited layer came into focus. Historically, in Britain, working-class people did not move beyond their station in life. Statements like "Who does she think she is?" kept you firmly in place. This put-down inevitably becomes internalized. My father and his family had moved from Dublin to England around the time of the Second World War. Being Irish in England was difficult. In spite of most of the family leaving their home city of Dublin, my grandfather, whom I never met, stayed behind in Ireland.

Immigration brings dislocation, and sometimes shame. It's quite common for immigrants to maintain silence about the conditions and circumstances that led to their decision to relocate to another country. This is a complex legacy for the children of immigrants, as it leaves a vacuum of shadowy territories, stories and connections with relatives that are lost, language and accents that are changed, customs and geographical areas that are severed, and family secrets that are hidden.

On the English side, my mother and her parents went through two brutal world wars, including the London Blitz, where they spent hours in their shack of a shelter in the garden, while bombs fell around them. The First World War of 1914 was a "legitimate" slaughter of millions across European battlefields, in the name of colonial goliaths gone mad. A war my English grandfather couldn't speak of without tears coming to his eyes. In the female line of both British and Irish families, many have stories of distant aunts being put in mental institutions or taking their lives, or undergoing botched abortions. These are lives that recede into invisibility: those devastated, falling to the wayside in poor and unforgiving global, social, and religious systems, shaped by a colonial imperative.

In this session I "touched" an old place where compliance and invisibility meant survival. As the inquiry continued, the feeling of pressure around my head became more pronounced. It was if a tight cap pushed down my life force. I had never seen that sensation as an "object" of attention, because it was so woven into the sense of "me." I glimpsed the fear of being "outspoken" from a collective female inheritance. The sensation of being "capped" was a much more subtle version of foot binding in China, which was a way of controlling the movement of women. Though internalized oppression, felt as a lack of worth, is invisible from the outside, it can be just as crippling. As I tracked the process, I saw the belief, though irrational, that "taking central place" was life-threatening. The fear was there to keep me "safe" and "in line." However, it had the effect of generating a subtle sense of depression, which I had often felt in my life.

The inner voice of "not good enough" sabotages and generates endless self-doubt, especially when it came to maturing into individual and collective confidence as a group of nuns. The easier default is to enable others, even at one's own expense. That is female conditioning within patriarchy, but often it leaves no clear sense of one's own authority, belonging, or voice. Certainly that was a pervasive feeling I had within a monastic system that was heavily gender-biased. In my therapeutic inquiry, I was surprised how much sadness I felt about the loss of potential due to a power dynamic that seemed to continually distort the possibility of a healthy relational field.

The choices we make, and the lives we lead, are influenced by the subliminal, ancestral messaging we inherit on a cellular level. The past haunts us in ways we sometimes don't see, passing on unresolved disturbances to future generations. I once heard that Khoisan ("bushman") art, when depicting traumatic events, was sometimes painted on sacred spots like ancient rock faces, as a way of helping absorb the shock. I don't know if that's true, but it's interesting how art helps heal trauma, but also how trauma can be a catalyst for some of our most potent expressions of creativity, which find their conception in the cauldron of the wounded soul.

I like to think that our wounds, just like the classical five hindrances, are not shameful things, but catalysts for personal and collective transformation, social justice movements, literary and artistic expression, and a more compassionate world. The wounding of the "soul" is something we all inherit, and yet with the power of wise reflection and loving awareness we can extricate our life force from redundant and dysfunctional beliefs.

The inner scripts we live, which are conditioned from long past, are not particularly appropriate for our present reality, but nevertheless they have power over us. They permeate the self-structure. In Buddhist understanding, perception, feeling, our beliefs, and underlying tendencies generate patterns that form the sense of self. The "shaping of self" is called *sankhara*. *Sankhara* literally means "put together." It is conditioning from the past that determines the future. To revert to a computer analogy,

analogy, *sankhara* is made up of the layers of programming that have been downloaded onto the empty hard drive of the mind. These programs run the self and its expression in the world.

Although our tendencies feel personal, they are mostly inherited. We may think injustices like slavery, war, or genocide are things of the past, but the resonances are carried as genetic and cellular memory. If we see the world in terms of rebirth we will have a sense for the influence of "unfinished business" from previous lives. We may feel this as resonance with a piece of history, which dovetails into our current lives. Alternatively, we may find ourselves in positive relationships that are a continuum of what has gone before, or that confront us with challenges that feel ancient, and still in need of resolution. Sometimes such resolution happens through long and complex processes; sometimes it can happen in a fleeting exchange.

A friend of mine told of a significant meeting she had with a stranger when working as a receptionist in a hotel in Italy. As a child she often had recurring nightmares of Nazi storm troopers killing her family. In her waking life she felt a negative reaction when she heard the German language, so she decided to overcome this by spending time learning German, and working in Germany. One day a group of elderly Germans came to visit the hotel where she worked. A powerful feeling arose as she signed in one of the men, which perplexed her. She felt she "knew" the man, that there was some sense of uncanny recognition from her terrifying dreams. She also felt panicked by his presence. Unexpectedly, the man insisted she personally accept a large amount of money. Having an impeccable sense of ethics, my friend initially refused, but then felt intuitively prompted to accept the money. The whole transaction was short, the man walked away, and they didn't speak again. On looking at the register she saw his hometown was Dachau, the site of a notorious Nazi concentration camp. As she read it a shiver came over her; she'd always felt a strong connection with events around the holocaust in this particular area, but it was something she never spoke about. She didn't have a particular feeling for past lives, but when she told me the story she said she felt some kind of karmic debt was cleared.

In the mystical Jewish tradition of the Kabbalah there is the idea of *tikkun* or "making correction." We draw challenges to ourselves, which present an opportunity to resolve what has gone before. *Tikkun olam* is a further idea of "repairing the world." The story of Christ touches into a similar archetype, of taking on the sins of others through a great act of sacrifice and forgiveness, in order to bring about redemption. These religious themes of suffering, sacrifice, repair, redemption, and healing speak to our deepest heart. As we do this inner work and the fruits of the work are expressed in our lives, it contributes to the increase of our collective awareness. We are not isolated entities; we affect one another. Mindful and loving awareness has the power to mend old wounds and resolve ancient injustices. They clear and transform the momentum of our unconscious conditioning, and liberate our energy, both personally and collectively.

During the therapy session, when I tracked the sensation of being "capped," old erroneous and limiting beliefs were revealed. The therapeutic application of loving awareness, particularly from the group around me, enabled a movement toward my healing. In that session the natural intelligence of the body took over. It spontaneously moved from a cramped posture into a strong warrior-type pose. My arms extended out, and in my mind's eye, I saw my hands holding spears. This opened into an energetic release around the skull, bringing a fuller sense of embodiment. It was as if the energy that had been "dammed up" for ages was able to flow through the whole body, enabling me to reclaim inner authenticity and personal power. From that session on, as the therapeutic process integrated, I realized that I experienced a lessening of depression, frustration, and anxiety in my daily life.

Therapeutic process can be slow. Sometimes, however, healing can happen quickly, as the fundamental intelligence of awareness has the power to make sudden and dramatic shifts.

The documentary film *The Weeping Camel*[3] demonstrates the quantum shifts possible through the power of awareness. It tells the story of a mother camel and calf traumatized by an extremely difficult birth. It's set on the Mongolian plateau, the bleakest of environments, among a close-knit nomadic family whose lives are intertwined with the fortunes of the land and its weather patterns. It is a harsh landscape, warmed only by the care each family member extends to ensure mutual well-being and survival, of both themselves and the animals on whose lives they depend. This obvious communal cohesion conveys a belonging many of us, in our fast-moving world, probably rarely experience.

The family is concerned, during birthing season, when a camel becomes stuck during her labor. This eventually causes the herders to pull, by hooves and legs, the incapacitated calf from the mother's womb. As the newborn arrives on the earth with a thud, we notice it is a beautiful white calf. Sadly, though, the mother rejects it. Over the course of the next few days she can't be induced, by trick or pressure, to allow the abandoned calf to suckle. It is as if the unbearable pain of its birth is re-created every time the calf draws near, upsetting the mother. Each time she frets and pushes her calf away. The family tries all means, but it becomes clear that without the mother's acceptance, the calf won't survive.

As the dilemma deepens the two young sons set off to the local village to seek help. In due course, they return with an older man. He is the school music teacher, but also a shaman. After he has been welcomed, the teacher picks up his instrument, walks to the camel, and sits nearby. The family gathers around him, all looking directly at the mother camel. Not far away is the abandoned and ailing calf. As the musician begins to play his haunting tune on a simple stringed instrument, the nomadic mother gently rubs the side of the camel's body, where her heart is, while singing a melodic song, as if calling into the very soul of the camel.

Slowly, the tension in the camel softens and large tears fall from her eyes. Everyone connects in a state of empathetic presence as the music, camel, calf, woman stroking the mother camel, the landscape, and the family all merge into a unified state. Healing arises gently and naturally. That it doesn't take long is surprising and unsurprising—surprising because we assume healing takes time, and unsurprising because we intuitively recognize that we are witnessing a deeply natural process. Within a short time the calf is reintroduced to the mother camel. She accepts her baby, as it reaches up to drink deeply for the first time from her udder.

This true story evokes the power of the mysterious force that seeks healing, and more deeply, seeks to express the innate oneness of life. That such healing occurred had a lot to do with the openness and interconnectedness of the animals, and a people that recognize the need to support one another for their mutual welfare. Such an interrelated community could not tolerate an alienated individualism. In the shedding of complication, healing arose. No one "took action." Instead, induced by a caring presence into a state of unified awareness, harmony was restored. The mother camel was able to feel the enormous pain of the birth, and through her tears, she let it go.

With the right conditions in place, shifts of awareness and release of old wounds can be quick. However, the work of integration requires patience. When I think of the kind of patience needed on this path of awakening, I think of the maturity of Mr. Mandela. I remember seeing the small prison cell in which he lived for much of his twenty-seven years of wrongful imprisonment. It defies comprehension how such a large man (on so many levels) withstood this tiny space for so long. Mr. Mandela's ability to transform such a bitter experience into compassion enabled a whole country to make a relatively bloodless transition of political power. I also think of the twenty-one years of Mahatma Gandhi's preparation in South Africa, where he learned his art of nonviolent resistance, which eventually brought down the British Empire in India. I think of numerous unsung heroes who offer service to the poor, sick, and marginalized, sometimes in the face of the most appalling circumstances. I think of each of us, and have faith that the power of our presence, which connects us to the deepest intelligence of the Dharma, can transform the challenges of our times.

I planted the creeper of love, and silently watered it with my tears; now, it has grown and overspread my dwelling. You offered me a cup of poison, which I drank with joy.

–Mirabai

CHAPTER FOURTEEN

The Nectar in the Fire
Thanissara

Your task is not to seek for love, but merely to seek and find all the barriers within yourself that you have built against it.

–Rumi

Meditation and therapeutic work, by making the unconscious conscious, reveal our deeper wounds and enable healing. A small trigger can be all that's needed to dive into painful *sankhara*, our primary patterning. In my own healing, a small event triggered a process that began to turn the tide. It was a silly incident, a disagreement between Kittisaro and myself about how much to tip a waiter at a restaurant. We were at a beach resort, taking a break from a difficult dynamic in our work in South Africa. I was already under a lot of stress and susceptible to reactivity. This small incident, and the overall stress we were under, catalyzed my deeper issues around security, placement, and belonging—which in turn activated a familiar whirlpool of confusing feelings, triggering my default defense of disassociation.

One of our most primitive defense mechanisms is to freeze. When we feel under threat our instinctive reactions are to fight, flee, or freeze. These reactions pull us out of a parasympathetic nervous system, which regulates deeper rhythms of calm, digestion, rest, and relaxation. The sympathetic nervous system, on the other hand, activates in response to threat. When it does, we are pulled into survival mode. For many in our stressed world, it is becoming harder to drop out of sympathetic activation back into the parasympathetic, so it can regulate our system. When whole societies are threatened, or feel threatened—as in the ongoing "red alerts" in the height of the terrorist narrative in the U.S. and elsewhere—we are pulled into a heightened sympathetic response, which means we are in the least optimal mode for wise response. If we are reacting to an immediate life threat, instinctual response can be good; however, we don't always want to be in that mode, as it can lead to overreaction, creating more problems. Also, over time, our system will become depleted and stressed if we are always on high alert.

When we move into "freeze mode" it's hard to think coherently. Basically, our system is in shock, so we begin to disconnect from our experience. Over the years I've experienced this mechanism as a chemical reaction that affects the brain. This response, common for many people, aims to protect us by shutting down our system; it's a survival strategy. When conflict can't be managed or emotional reactions threaten the fragile cohesion of the self, the natural intelligence of the system is to disassociate. Disassociation takes us out of the body and scrambles the brain. Clarity of thought diminishes, and the capacity to respond coherently or effectively shuts down. As we become more adept at mindfulness, we can slow reactivity and turn it around to appropriate response. However, the process of psycho-spiritual transformation is just that: it's a process. We don't always catch ourselves before spiraling into reactivity.

Once activated, layers of painful feelings and discordant voices slice away at any sense of congruence, trust, and well-being. That evening at the beach resort, I knew I was in irrational territory. I was touching into the deeper matrix of the self-structure, which forms basic patterns of survival at a very young age, when we develop primitive reactions to pleasure and pain. That night my primary defenses were triggered. However,

I was at a place in my practice where I had enough mindfulness to track the process as I entered one of our deepest wounds: the belief that no one is there for us. The feeling is like the howl of a lonely wolf as it falls through thin ice into freezing and unforgiving water.

Actually it was nighttime by the Indian Ocean. It was warm and balmy, and I was with someone I loved and cherished, and certainly everything was okay. However, as I started to be consumed by this vortex of old conditioning, I felt the freeze of increasing isolation, as if moving into colder and colder water. Looking out to the pitch-dark ocean, I felt a strong pull to walk into it, even though I knew it was shark-infested. At the depth of this wound was the movement toward complete annihilation. But as I understand it, this innate intention toward death, a wish for suicide, didn't surface until I had enough mindfulness to feel its utter desolation. A desolation that offers no redemption, no mercy; nothing can get through. It is anger turned to ice. It is utter aloneness, an icy blackness, which consumes all last vestiges of warmth, hope, light, self-love, and well-being.

My training in mindful awareness enabled me to hold steady at the edge of this great darkness, into which poured all the wounds we had encountered in South Africa: the impossibility of poverty, the complexity of racism, the overwhelming consequences of AIDS, the most devastating betrayals of trust. It was if a trap door opened, letting all the "orphans" tumble in: the wounded, the marginalized, the lonely, and the abandoned. The Hungarian poet János Pilinszky, who witnessed the horror of Nazi concentration camps, wrote a haunting poem. It talks about the vulnerable "self child" hoping for love but abandoned to death. This is our own "self child," but also the hopeful "self child" of all beings who must inevitably meet the agony of *samsara*.

Once upon a time there was a lonely wolf, lonelier than the angels.
He happened to come to a village where he fell in love with the first house he saw. Already he loved its walls, the caresses of its bricklayers;
but the windows stopped him. In the room sat people.
Apart from God, nobody ever found them so beautiful as this child-like beast.

So at night he went into the house.
He stopped in the middle of the room and never moved from there anymore. He stood all through the night, with wide eyes and on into the morning.
When he was beaten to death.[1]

There are good reasons to disassociate from the harshness of life. We hope our spirituality or new age idealism can wrap us in cotton wool and protect us. But alas, awakening demands a truthful passage through life. Fortunately it's a journey we can only take with the support and love of others. My ability to stay with the process that night by the Indian Ocean was made possible by the loving presence of my dearest husband and partner, Kittisaro, as he sat beside me, holding my hand. The loving presence of another, particularly when there is no judgment, can be vital in our ability to negotiate these dark and difficult territories. Perhaps this is the deepest meaning of Sangha, or spiritual friendship: not only to inspire one another, but to be there for one another in moments of utter darkness and shine a light. When our wounds are received with loving-kindness, the possibility of redemption and healing does indeed emerge. That night by the ocean, when Kittisaro came to hold my hand, as we just sat quietly together that simple touch helped me track back from the edge of obliteration. It is here that we understand the value of what we truly offer one another as humans. The holding of a hand at times of pain and loss is worth more than a conquering army.

As we reclaim the split-off parts of ourselves, individually and collectively, we begin the journey of transforming our deepest pains into compassion and mercy. But first we need to stop projecting our pain onto others and come to terms with our feelings. Often we don't like to think of ourselves as having primitive and violent feelings of rage, resentment, or jealousy. We feel ashamed if we are depressed or have suicidal impulses. These are all deeply unacceptable emotions, which we are quick to demonize. The last thing we want is to be identified as someone who has these kinds of feelings. We like the idea of spirituality making us calm, peaceful, radiant, and loving. We are not so keen on the idea that awakening could actually trawl us through the darkest recesses of our psyche.

Ironically, the Buddhist perspective on the emptiness of self allows a clearer investigation into the shadows and wounds of the self. Although these difficult feelings and mind states feel very personal, ultimately they aren't. They start as personal, but on investigation they reveal their inherent emptiness. It's like when Ajahn Chah responded to a young woman who wanted to know how to deal with anger. Ajahn Chah asked whose anger it was. She said it was hers. He pointed out that if that was the case, she should be able to tell it to go away. "Whenever the mind is happy or sad, don't fall for it; it's all deception," he said. Ajahn Chah points to the real truth of the situation. However, there's a difference between taking an honest and humble journey through the layers of the self, and the premature transcendence of it. As we heal all that is painful, and hidden, we become more fearless and less divided or divisive. We will be able to integrate lost and damaged energies that have haunted and undermined our well-being; our "transcendence" won't be fragile, easily disturbed, and founded in the need to repress or project what is uncomfortable.

As we meditate we become more sensitive; and at times we feel the emotions of other people and misinterpret them as our own. In this regard, the teaching on non-self is helpful—it reminds us not to immediately personalize everything we feel. Sometimes what we feel is actually projected onto us. Not consciously, but we can also pick up energetic material that is floating and unowned within the "relational field."

To give an example: In the monastery we would meet formally for breakfast. We mostly sat in silence as we ate a simple meal of oatmeal. One morning the senior monk was late because he had to conduct a disrobing ceremony; the young man who had been disrobed sat at the back of the hall in lay clothes. I didn't have any particular feeling about his disrobing but as I looked at the senior monk I felt, and almost saw, a wave of energy roll across the floor toward me. I was hit by emotion that was so strong, I had to leave the room immediately and find a quiet place to weep. I didn't know the psychological term "transference" then, but it was the first time I clearly felt a dynamic I had always suspected: that we can end up processing what is unacknowledged in the "relational field." Knowing this, we can allow energies to move through our system without getting tangled in narratives and suffering.

As we perceive shadow material more clearly, we won't be so susceptible to internalizing the projections that come our way. Some projections can be overly idealized and seductive, and some are negative and even deadly. It's important to discern, as much as possible, what belongs to us and what doesn't, so we can withdraw the negativity and ideals we project, and conversely, see through what is projected onto us. If we overly depend on affirmation or become devastated by criticism, we will suffer unnecessarily and lose our balance. While the field of projection is a thick web we are all immersed in, with some awareness and inquiry there can be discernment. Therapists are trained to feel the projective material, and hand it back to the client as skillfully as possible. This is a great service.

Ajahn Chah was a great therapist. He said being a teacher is like being like a trash can that people dump their garbage into. He also said we should make sure there is no bottom on our trash can, so garbage is able to flow through! Having "no bottom" was a metaphor for seeing the emptiness of self and conditions. It seemed nothing much would stick to Ajahn Chah. However, he was compassionate, allowing people to project their need for a wise father figure; then, when they were steadier, he would hand back their own spiritual power, encouraging people to "interview themselves" rather than have him tell them where they were at!

Meditation really helps as we navigate these territories. Sit quietly and sense what is present—the feelings, shadows, and thoughts—and then inquire, "What do I need to take responsibility for here?" Listen in to what emerges as "felt sense" within your body. This inquiry is particularly pertinent if there is conflict. Usually in the midst of conflict the shadow is highly activated, presenting us with an opportunity. There is such a strong tendency to want to shift responsibility and blame onto someone else. It can be someone we once thought was great, but now we can't find a positive thing to say about them. Maybe we were once in love with them, but now we hate them. There may be good reasons to blame, but in the process there's almost always some aspect of our own unconsciousness that is contributing to the situation. It may be our own naïveté or gullibility in overly idealizing another or a situation; or our desires and anger may have contributed to the disharmony. If we shift the blame too quickly, we won't understand how our projections operate. And if we assume we're the ones totally at fault, we won't be able to free ourselves from the projections of others.

The willingness to meet and feel the disturbance in this territory is already the movement of compassion. It helps us own and work with our displaced hope, idealization, anger, fear, or resentment. As we do so, what is not ours will fall away more easefully. The negative energy that has been projected unfairly will inevitably, at some time or another, return to the one who is responsible for it. Once, when the Buddha was severely and unfairly criticized, he responded by asking the person, "If a gift is given, and not accepted, what happens?" The person had to say, "Well, it goes back to the giver." The same with shadow energy: there is no obligation to carry what is not ours.

Transformative work is a fierce undertaking. It is the fire of purification. Rumi said "the rose's rarest essence lives in the thorn." In the cauldron of *dukkha,* the most sublime qualities of the heart are forged. Embracing the hurt, we learn to trust that there is something greater, something mysterious and full of grace. Just as the thorn and rose are of the same plant, so in the heart of pain is a doorway to the tender heart. Like the evening when Kittisaro held my hand, a kindly touch bridges all that separates and diminishes. It reassures us that suffering is temporary, and that love is always far greater.

When suffering is touched by compassionate awareness, its power to overwhelm weakens. In other words, healing is facilitated by the ability to feel the original wounding to our sensitivity. Gently, layers of patterning that generate painful self-structures can unpeel. The heart of darkness, the devastating blow to our being, this core of our wounds, can be felt and acknowledged. Through the innate and wise response of the aware heart, there can be movement toward health. Pain then is a porthole to the reclamation of the exiled pieces of our self.

Our personal wounds mirror those within the collective. The will to scorch and destroy our magnificent earth emerges from the wounded heart. Unchecked greed and hatred have left a trail of devastation through human history. But we have a choice. Do we continue our path of ruin or are we able to change course? Increasing our awareness and mindfulness means we are not destined to repeat patterns from the past. The Buddha stated, "Mindfulness is the path to the deathless, heedlessness is the path of death, those who are mindful never die, while those who are heedless are as if dead already." With the practice of mindfulness we choose life over death. We affirm our lives rather than continuing patterns of devastation. As we release identification with the particular, to enter communion with the whole, we experience ourselves as inseparable from life, from everything that breathes, everything that feels, everything that longs to be met with care, love, and empathy. This understanding encourages nurture over exploitation, consensus over dominance, and cooperation over control. It is a spirituality that honors the earth and all her sentient beings over a transcendence that is disconnected, insensitive, and uncaring. It is a shift from patriarchal ownership and empire-building, to careful stewardship and protection of the healthy masculine.

But first we need to reclaim the wounds held in the shadow, so we can decant positive, life-affirming energies from the crippled energy that manifests as suffering. The journey into maturing a love that can dissolve the deepest of pains is a long one. A wonderful friend and Dharma teacher, Godwin Samararatne,[2] used to warn against what he called "idiot compassion." We can't be too naive. Sometimes people can be very damaging, manipulative, and abusive, and so we need to be careful what we allow into our lives. If we are developed in our practice, we can meet all kinds of situations. Even so, Ajahn Chah advised, "Don't think you have a ten-wheeler truck when you have a wheelbarrow!" Holding skillful boundaries is an act of compassion for oneself, and it is with the self that we must start. There can still be kindness, forgiveness, and wise relationship, but if disquiet arises, it can be a warning. We must then discern what exactly is happening.

As we work through our own suffering, our ability to help others becomes more effective. We then begin to know fulfillment. The Buddha himself recognized the need to serve after his awakening. He realized that those who have nothing to serve live unhappily. In wondering about this, he concluded that the optimum service is to the Dharma. To live fully, we need something beyond ourselves to serve. This keeps the heart content and grateful. It helps us feel a joyful connection with the flow of life.

As we move beyond limited conditioning and become conduits for awakened activity, we enter the domain of the bodhisattva ideal, where instead of avoiding suffering, we embrace it. Devotional practice can really help widen our capacity to hold suffering. One of the joys of monastic life was the support of very dear friends in the nuns' community. A few of us ran an "underground bhakti group." The purpose was to chant, just for the joy of it. In a field in England, we invoked a wondrous range of beings of light through our heartfelt devotions. Sometimes, there's a response. The bodhisattvas come to help.

In the midst of a retreat, during which we focused on devotional practice, a dear friend from South Africa experienced a miraculous response. She had taken some time out to walk. Suddenly she found herself in a life-threatening situation:

> I was walking with a friend in a forest when we realized we were being followed, and we knew at once the man was dangerous. He caught up, stopped us, and asked me to go with him. As I refused and turned away, he grabbed my neck and pushed me to the ground. My friend threw a log at him, which gave me a chance to get on my feet, and we ran. But something told me to stop. I sensed that the chase was strengthening him, casting us as predator and prey in an ancient story with an inevitable ending. To stop that story's momentum, I stopped running, turned to face him, and shouted, "What do you want?"
>
> In that moment, everything changed in a way that is impossible to describe. For the first time in my life I was entirely without fear, knowing with utter conviction that no matter what this man did to me, he could never hurt me. As he grabbed my wrist, I was overwhelmed by a powerful love for him and for everything; the forest

around us burst into radiant, pulsating life, as if the trees were on fire with the same love. In this indescribable experience, a few sensations remain clear: everyone who had ever loved me came to mind, and I felt their presence there among the trees; my protection was beyond question and I was overcome by a joyful peace I had never known.

When the man held a knife to my throat and told me to lie down and be quiet, his sadness ached in me. A mother watching her small child hurt himself through ignorance might feel the same way. I wanted him to stop endangering himself in this way, not with any urgency or fear, but simply because I could see that his self-torment was unnecessary. I spoke words I don't remember choosing: "You're a man. You're a good man. You don't hurt people." Whether or not he understood, I felt his relief as he too realized he didn't have to do what he was doing. His grip on my wrist softened but I stayed with him, holding his hand, and repeated the words, "You're a man. A good man."

By now my friend had found a heavy branch as a weapon, and was quietly making it clear she would put up a fight. I released my hand, he lowered the knife, and my friend and I walked away.

That night, the man came to me in a dream. He wanted to show me something—a wound in the side of his back. It was a deep, fatal gash, raw and bleeding, and I knew it had been there a long, long time. With the same love I had known in the forest, I put my hand on the wound. Afterward, when I told the story to others, they commented on -our courage. My friend showed extraordinary courage, but what happened to me was something different. It was grace, and it is everyone's.[3]

Ultimately, it doesn't matter where the suffering comes from. It's just suffering. This is the perspective of the bodhisattva heart. At the place where suffering arises, so does awareness revealing a refuge that is strong, fearless, empathetic, and merciful. This is the refuge of our shared intimate heart. It is a place of grace.

Mindful awareness is the great cauldron of transformation. It is the portal through which unspeakable pain becomes transformed. It is a great relief to accept the demons and wounds we carry, both personally and collectively. They wait to be noticed, embraced, and healed. As our mindfulness and loving awareness strengthens, we will have the confidence to meet suffering, knowing it to be the catalyst for our awakening, and the means through which love and compassion mature. We will know how to extract nectar from the fire.

> *Just as the ocean's salty water taken into clouds turns sweet,*
> *The stable mind works to benefit others; turning poison into healing nectar.*
>
> –Saraha[4]

CHAPTER FIFTEEN

Until the End of Time

Kittisaro

Compassion says I'm everything, wisdom says I'm nothing.
Between these two banks, the life of an awakened one flows.

–Sri Nisargadatta

Once when a senior abbot told Ajahn Chah that he had enough of this endless *samsara*—that he was definitely "not coming back!"—Ajahn Chah responded, "What about the rest of us?" Living with suffering is hard, but it can also be a catalyst for great compassion. When your heart is open and deeply touched, you don't just abandon someone. The brilliance of the Buddha's teaching is that he focused on the experience of suffering as the key to unlock the prison we live within, the prison of the conditioned and reactive mind. When we work with the experience of suffering, we begin to find our way home. As we do so, naturally we benefit others through our understanding. The impulse to deepen our awakening in order to benefit others is called the *bodhisattva intention* or *bodhicitta*. Wisdom and compassion are not separate; one without the other is incomplete.

As our practice deepens, the Four Ennobling Truths transform into the Four Great Bodhisattva Vows. *Bodhisattva* conjures up a heroic person who is dedicated to serving others. *Bodhi* means "awakening" and *sattva* means "being." *Bodhisattva* therefore literally means a person who is intent on awakening, and who supports and is committed to the awakening of others. Bodhisattvas are not going anywhere. They have transcended the idea of time. The essential attitude of the bodhisattva is profound patience; they are willing to be with how it is and respond from there. As bodhisattvas in training, we orient ourselves around an honest here-and-now connection with how things are. The more we are rooted in the steadiness of present-moment awareness, the more leverage we have to effectively respond to every circumstance and assist others in distress.

It is one thing to know the peace of letting go: when we truly let go we experience this fundamental principle, which is the same peace the Buddha realized. The Buddha said *wherever you taste the sea, it's salty*. He used this as an analogy for the nature of *nibbana*. Wherever we let go, we taste the one taste: the taste of deliverance and peace. However, it is another thing to respond appropriately and skillfully to the myriad circumstances of life. This is the special aptitude of a fully enlightened Buddha. A fully enlightened being not only knows how to let go, but also understands how to respond to people in a way that's perfect for their needs, so that they too can leave behind suffering and enjoy well-being. Full awakening is not only about unshakable peace, but also about manifesting a wisely compassionate response within the world.

The Buddha recounted his own journey as a bodhisattva, saying that countless eons ago when he was a young Brahmin ascetic named Sumedha he met a fully awakened Buddha called Dipankara.[1] Inspired by Dipankara's peaceful presence and marvelous capacity to help countless living beings leave behind suffering, Sumedha brought forth the deep resolve to become a Buddha himself. It is said that Dipankara Buddha recognized the potential of Sumedha and gave a prophecy of his future Buddhahood. Dipankara said, "In the ages of the future, you will come to be a Buddha called Sakyamuni."

According to Buddhist mythology, Sumedha's solemn intention ripened when Prince Siddhartha became Sakyamuni Buddha. This narrative draws on an important archetypal truth, which is the power of intention. In the bodhisattva practice this development of intentionality is called *vow power*. Bodhisattvas make vows to better serve living beings throughout each of their lifetimes. The essence of this resolution is expressed in the classical Four Great Bodhisattva Vows. Actually, there are infinite possibilities for bodhisattva vows. For example, Ksitigarbha—Earth Store Bodhisattva—has vowed to stay near hellish realms in order to rescue living beings, resolving not to be a Buddha himself until everyone else has attained peace. Others like Samantabhadra (Universal Worthy) make vows to always turn the wheel of the Dharma, and constantly serve living beings. His Ten Great Vows are a blueprint for Bodhisattva conduct. Of all the vows, my favorite are those of Kuan Yin Bodhisattva, who in her immeasurable mercy forever rests in the awakened heart, listening and responding to the cries of living beings.

We could dismiss the bodhisattva intention as *desire*, which simply leads to more *becoming* and a sense of never really getting finished, especially as there are so many beings that are suffering! The desire of the bodhisattva, however, is emptied of self-identification. Little by little desire is refined and purified into an adamantine compassionate resolve rooted in unmoving *suchness*. In the classical Jataka tales, which describe the many lives of Buddha Sakyamuni in training as a Bodhisattva, we see him perfecting each of the *paramitas*, the ten spiritual perfections. These are generosity, ethics, renunciation, wisdom, great effort, patience, truthfulness, determination (vow power), loving-kindness, and equanimity. He cultivated the *paramitas* through countless lifetimes. These *paramitas* are wholesome qualities of mind; the word itself literally means "perfection" or "that which carries one across the sea of suffering to liberation." In Mahayana Buddhism the list of the *paramitas* is a little different; however, what is essential is that they are skillful qualities of heart and mind that blossom into Buddhahood.

THE FOUR BODHISATTVA VOWS

Countless beings suffer. I vow to liberate them all.
Afflictions are inexhaustible. I vow to cut through (transform) them all.
Dharma doors (skillful means) are endless. I vow to cultivate them all.
The Buddha path (full Awakening) is unsurpassed, I vow to realize it.[2]

The practice of taking the Four Great Vows aligns with the bodhisattva intention to orientate our life toward Awakening as an act of service. It is a beautiful and graceful intention. I can think of no other aspiration within the range of human endeavor that carries so much potential, power, and majesty. The vows are not meant as egoic statements but as a trustworthy compass for our life. Rather than interpret the vows from the perspective of the self, which leads to grandiose inflation or an overwhelming sense of impossibility, one generates sincere intentions that arise from the deepest understanding of emptiness. As we gradually empty the heart from the distortion of *self-serving* strategies, we tap into the innate core of the universe, whose very pulse resonates with these vows.

Compassionate response is the prompting of life itself as it unfolds into full selfless awareness. In the depth of the bodhisattva's heart there is an intimacy with all of life. There is the understanding that all sentient beings have deep kinship and are in a process of Awakening. In a Christian idiom, the self-sacrifice of Christ demonstrates perfectly the archetypal journey of the bodhisattva. However, what the practitioner ultimately sacrifices is not so much their body, but their identification with ego. In doing so, she or he arrives into the heart of "God," the oneness that ever seeks to know and express itself through creation. The language of the vows, as transmitted through several thousand years, may seem archaic, but more important than their form is their spirit. They act as a polar star to show the way for living beings through the turbulent sea of birth and death.

The First Bodhisattva Vow

The First Noble Truth and accompanying practice is: "There is suffering. Suffering needs to be understood." This motivation matures into the First

Bodhisattva Vow: "Countless beings suffer; I vow to liberate them all." This is an amazing thought. It's counter-intuitive, as our instinct is to only look to our own welfare or that of our family, tribe, and country. Instead, this vow begins to turn the mind away from an obsession around "me" and "mine" and encourages us to consider the welfare of others, regardless of their circumstance, where they live, or who they are. Because all living beings are part of our Dharma Body, the bodhisattva understands that there is no ultimate separation between helping another and helping oneself. Opening to the experience of suffering, as encouraged in the First Truth, becomes a vehicle for deepening compassion. Initially we say, "It's my suffering!" However, little by little we start to gain insight into how we perpetuate it. As we do so, we can let go of the causes and taste some peace. If we can do this, others can too.

Actually, in the aware heart there is no ultimate distinction between self and other. As we understand how the sense of "me" and "you" emerges from the discriminating mind, the distinctions dissolve. Ultimately, how is my suffering different from your suffering? It is just suffering. Our instinct is to turn away from suffering, to create distinctions like "That's not mine and I don't need to deal with it." Instead, little by little, this vow encourages a perspective that allows us to embrace suffering wherever we meet it. It encourages us to keep our hearts open and our minds agile and responsive.

We are being invited on a transformative journey, a sacred pilgrimage into the ever-deepening capacity of our heart. This movement naturally taps into the most profound level of motivation, which is the intention of the bodhisattva. Cultivating compassion is the practice of the First Great Vow. A bodhisattva is willing to feel suffering in order to investigate it. The motivation to understand suffering and to be free from it ripens our humanity, and gradually blesses us with the sensitivity, power, understanding, and desire to serve others.

Sometimes the most powerful teachers arrive in unexpected ways. A tiny flea-infested puppy mysteriously found its way down a rugged mountain, through the wilderness to our doorstep. When Thanissara immediately wanted to keep him, I was reluctant, thinking it would be trouble. Thankfully, she won out in the end, for I had no idea that this little furry fellow would touch our hearts and induct us more deeply into the sublime perfection of love. Over time he became my personal trainer, and together we walked the mountains. He guided me back to vitality and joy. When it seemed everyone else had abandoned us, our little friend Jack was ever loyal and always happy to see us—unless we wanted to give him a bath! Our hearts opened. His suffering became our suffering, his joy was our joy.

Jack was a legend on the road. Often in South Africa the white people's dogs bark at the blacks, and the black people's dogs bark at the whites. Jack, however, was a bilingual peacemaker and everybody loved him—except baboons. He had many names. The Zulus called him Numzaan—the Man—because Jack was in charge of all the work projects, and he took naps whenever he pleased. He loved to sit on the mountainside like a lion and gaze out across his territory. His Old Testament name was Jacob, because he was forever wrestling with angels, bounding into the wild to challenge intruders, and protecting us from harm. His New Testament name was Lazarus, because he came back from the dead many times after being injured, poisoned, and even kidnapped. Ajahn Sucitto dubbed him Vajrapani after the great Dharma Protector. And we just called him Jack. Vajrapani Jacob Lazarus Numzaan Jack Weinberg, the first and last! He touched people's hearts. He had many amazing, gut-wrenching adventures, for living in the rural mountains of Kwa Zulu Natal has its multitude of perils. Even so, he was faithfully and blissfully present in our shrine room for countless meditation retreats and devotional ceremonies.

Those precious moments when we feel love are important, because we sense that deep kinship with a fellow being, and begin to see beyond the lonely prison of separateness. Seeing him tremble when he was frightened, I naturally felt with him—com-passion—and wanted to help. The last few months of his fourteen-year life I nursed him day and night as the debilitating effects of his brain tumor took their toll. Even though I couldn't rest properly, I didn't mind, because sleeping next to him I could listen to his breathing and respond whenever he had a seizure or needed help to turn over.

What a beautiful, sacred impulse, to feel with another being and wish to take on their suffering, to look for ways to make another's life free of distress. Jack was like our child. When he died, surrounded by beautiful chants and oceans of loving gratitude, we all cried—even our loyal local vet. After Jack's last breath, I was amazed to hear a howl of loss rip its way through my body from the depths of my being. In so many ways he was my teacher, showing me the beauty of deeply caring for another. Can we learn to widen that feeling to include all our fellow beings? This is the vision of the bodhisattva. This is the teaching of the Buddha.

The Buddha identified loving-kindness—*metta*—as one of the essential qualities of heart that carries us to awakening. He encouraged his disciples to develop it and extend its healing blessing to all beings universally. He taught in the Metta Sutta: "Even as a mother protects with her life, her child, her only child, so with a boundless heart should one cherish all living beings." This might seem impossible, but the Buddha is showing us the direction, and revealing the boundless treasure hidden in our own heart. We cultivate this large-hearted attitude, little by little, patiently and persistently. We can notice when we are touched by someone and naturally wish them well; be interested in that feeling of kindness and expand it to include ourselves and others—those we like, the ones we're neutral about, and even beings we dislike. This takes practice, but when we remember how important loving-kindness is for healing ourselves and the world, we'll find the energy arrives. Actually, all living beings are our brothers and sisters in birth and death. We all suffer and wish to leave it behind. Reflecting like this, we don't do to others what we don't want them to do to us. An important premise for this practice is the principle: to others as to oneself.

Our teacher Ajahn Sumedho taught us that the seed of *metta* is the attitude of non-contention, non-fighting, the willingness to allow things to be as they are and welcome them into our hearts. Sometimes if we try and convince ourselves we love everyone, it just feels false, or we end up in denial about all the reactions of resentment and aversion that regularly assail the heart. On the other hand, when we practice this friendly intention with all our thoughts, sensations, and moods—pleasant and unpleasant, beautiful and ugly—we find ourselves in an openhearted abiding that is not disturbed by anything. Whatever is bothering us, we welcome that too, just as it is, with an attitude of not-fighting, not harboring ill will. I'm very grateful to have been taught a gateway into this practice that is accessible.

The mind of loving-kindness and harmlessness becomes a larger container for our life. It receives harmful impulses so they can be contemplated and transformed. Mindfulness and awareness function in the same way. They enable a larger context from which to inquire. The Buddha offered an important simile, of the salt crystal, to describe the ripening of unwholesome past actions that result in suffering. He used the image of a lump of salt in a small amount of water. That water would become unfit to drink, because it's too salty, unpleasant-tasting, and difficult to digest. However, the Buddha went on to inquire, "What if you place that salt crystal into the Ganges, a flowing river of pure water? Could you drink the water then?" If you have a larger container of purity within which to dissolve toxicity, you hardly notice it. In the same way, the Buddha taught that the cultivation of wholesome qualities like generosity, virtuous restraint, mindfulness, wise reflection, and loving-kindness generates a spacious state of mind that will dissolve obstruction and lessen suffering. To develop these activities of the path is similar to taking the salt and putting it into a large body of fresh water.

When we don't cultivate these expanded states of mind, the difficult feelings and circumstances of our lives tend to drag us off to hellish states of anguish, isolation, depression, rage, and despair. We get swept away and "turned by the state," overwhelmed by the painful feelings. Instead, the bodhisattva "turns the state around" with wisdom and compassion.

As a Buddhist monk I was also a prison chaplain in the southwest of England. On one occasion I visited a high-security prison—an old, cold-looking, grim stone building in the middle of the Moors in Devon. I had been invited to lead a Wesak meeting—the celebration of the main Buddhist holy day—for high-security prisoners who usually were not allowed to meet together as they were considered too dangerous. When I arrived in my robes, the stony-faced guards led me through the various security checks and iron gates to a small dingy classroom with about a dozen prisoners sitting around on the floor. I was a bit nervous and thought I'd break the ice by getting everyone to introduce themselves and tell me a little bit about why they were interested in meditation. As we were going around the circle, the guards waiting outside the door started to mock me, "Hare Krishna, Hare Hare. Hey, Harry, have you seen Barry? What about Larry? Harry, Harry, quite contrary." They kept up a steady flow of noisy taunts. This threw me off, and I could see my group was getting upset. I knew I couldn't pretend the disturbance wasn't happening, so I suggested we practice some loving-kindness meditation. The guy sitting next to me, Arthur, who had just told us he was in for murder, said in a tight, mean voice, "I don't have any kindness. If I had the chance I'd break his neck again!"

Well, I thought, what a start, we're really swinging along here! For a few moments I wasn't quite sure how to proceed. There was a very toxic and volatile energy in the room that was hard to bear. As I stayed with the uncomfortable feelings, I remembered the essence of the teaching. We don't have to pretend to like everything or be dishonest. I asked Arthur if he could have some kindness for the conviction "I don't have any kindness or compassion." I encouraged him just to hear that inner voice with its harsh judgment, along with the painful feelings, and see if he could allow them to be as they were, not fight them or add ill will to the situation, but to receive the whole sense of himself in a more spacious and kindly way. As we all practiced non-contention and a kind *willingness to be with* the ongoing taunts and our reactions, giving friendly space to it all, a remarkable meltdown occurred. Soon Arthur started crying and the room softened, the atmosphere transformed, and for a magical period we weren't trapped in a prison anymore. We enjoyed the measureless divine abiding of loving-kindness. We were flying, and the thick stone walls, the dingy room, and mocking voices all melted away, illumined and suffused by a boundless heart of nonresistance.

We were blown away. Arthur had never considered kindness for himself, or looked at the fiery, mean conviction that he didn't have it, which was like jagged concrete in his heart. As we all practiced allowing, befriending, and being with the feelings, everything started to soften. Just a few minutes of making space to receive the pain of the past and present with some kindness creates a larger healing container. It initiates a journey that starts to allow the deep-rooted patterns of bitterness to dissolve. The journey isn't over, of course, but it's an important beginning. Amidst the ridicule we were happy, flowing in that larger river of wakefulness. We were resting for a time in the original radiance of our hearts, sensing our common humanity and the great ocean of our collective being. Eventually the heckling by the guards petered out. Maybe they had a change of heart.

Any time we feel the wish to help others and then act on it, we are in the territory of this First Bodhisattva Vow. As we practice kindness, not pushing things away, we will naturally see more clearly. Our insight will deepen and our understanding will become increasingly subtle. We'll see the crippling limitation of the assumptions we make about ourselves, the way we're imprisoned by our opinions, and how we trap others in the same way. Ajahn Sumedho said the most compassionate thing we can do for another is not trap them with our views. Can we remember that behind all the personas of that person we dislike is a radiant heart, just waiting to be remembered? If we see the potential for awakening in another, then perhaps for a moment they are more likely to discover it themselves.

The bodhisattva—the awakened being committed to the awakening of others—understands that because of emptiness there are no ultimate distinctions between self and other; she understands that the universe is a seamless whole. At the most profound level of interconnection, the bodhisattva is other living beings, and other living beings are the bodhisattva. The bodhisattva rooted in primordial awareness transcends time and has great patience, and so can say with confidence, "Countless beings suffer. I vow to liberate them all."

The Second Bodhisattva Vow

The Second Noble Truth and accompanying practice is, "There is a cause of suffering. This cause (desire and aversion) needs to be let go of." This motivation blossoms into the second Bodhisattva Vow: "Afflictions are inexhaustible. I vow to cut through (transform) them all." We are afflicted with various difficult states of mind: the judging mind, the tyrannical mind, the pea-soup mind, the frantic monkey-mind, the rage that wants to destroy the universe mind, the helpless victim that feels like nothing's going right mind, and on and on. These afflictions are not only within, we see them all around us, manifesting as oppression, misery, exploitation, ecological devastation, and war mongering. *Afflictions are inexhaustible.* They are completely and utterly daunting and overwhelming. However, in spite of that, the bodhisattva is a warrior. She is fearless and aims to continue meeting the most intractable and appalling circumstances, however and wherever they arise. The Second Great Bodhisattva Vow is an intention that sets the mind with a sense of adamantine resolve. *I vow to stay with difficulty until I really understand and can respond in the most skillful way possible.* It's not about trying to mend and fix everything. It's about committing ourselves to stay with life as it unfolds, particularly in its suffering guises. It's a purposeful resolve that develops courage.

Ajahn Chah had a lot of sickness in his life; he had years of being with pain and discomfort. One of his beautiful and precious gifts was to inspire the courage to stay with suffering so that it could be transformed into wisdom and compassion. Ajahn Chah kept his disciples close to suffering until they understood how to end it. I remember the time when I was afraid in a Thai hospital, suffering and in pain. When Ajahn Chah came to visit and I told him I wanted to run away, he got me to laugh, and then he encouraged me to be patient. "When you are in pain, just know it. You can do this." He wasn't asking me to do something he hadn't done. His kind and knowing presence empowered me to hang in there with the seemingly unbearable circumstance. The encouragement of a wise being is a sacred transmission, reminding us that this path is possible, here and now. It sounds simple and essentially it is. In any moment we just know, "It's like this"—whether pleasant, painful, conflicted, or easeful. We know it without adding more suffering on top.

When the Buddha laid out the Three Refuges as trustworthy sources of inspiration, we might be surprised at the third one, Sangha. The first is Buddha, the Awakened One, which we align with internally by cultivating awareness: *the one who knows.* The second refuge, the Dharma, are those teachings from the Blessed One that guide us back into harmony with the *way things are,* the true nature that is always revealing itself moment after moment. One might think that these two refuges are enough for liberation—Buddha Dharma, awareness of how things are. Why have a third refuge, Sangha? Is the Buddha just padding out the numbers to get to a mystical three? No, the Buddha realized we cannot do this work alone, because we get lost, overwhelmed, confused, trapped, discouraged, etc. Our association with people of integrity—wise and compassionate beings—reminds us of the Way, inspires us to begin again, and encourages us to persevere. Once, when the Buddha's beloved attendant enthusiastically praised friendship with admirable beings as "half of the holy life," the Buddha reproved him. "Say not so, Ananda, say not so! Friendship with admirable beings is the whole of the holy life." Through association with the wise, we hear the teachings that liberate us, we see the examples that remind us of our potential, and, as the Buddha taught, we *abandon what is unskillful and develop what is skillful.*

Even if we are alone, we can remember the life and example of someone who inspires us to develop their admirable qualities in our own heart. For instance, when I remember the life of Aung San Suu Kyi, I am motivated to face my fears and allow my heart to consider, "What is for the welfare of my fellow beings?" She endured fifteen years of house arrest, constant threats to her life, and the sacrifice of precious opportunities to be with her family, all to stand up for justice against a tyrannical regime in her beloved land of Burma. Her awesome example demonstrates the power of a graceful, peaceful, courageous, nonviolent freedom fighter. She's a true bodhisattva, and remembering her can bless us with a fresh start:

> *If you are feeling helpless, help someone. . . .*
> *You should never let your fears prevent you from doing what is right.*
>
> —Aung San Suu Kyi

In South Africa we have the inspiring example of Nelson Mandela, who endured twenty-seven years of brutal imprisonment, and yet emerged free from bitterness to lead a nation into healing. He realized anger and resentment were never-ending, that they would destroy him and his vision for a peaceful land of equal opportunity. So he turned his prison into a university, shared his inspiration with fellow inmates, learned the language and poetry of his captors, and forged in the crucible of his own suffering a noble way forward, of truth and reconciliation.

The training of the bodhisattva is to be interested in our present circumstances, even if we think they are a complete write-off. Right here and now we can awaken, we can meet stress and suffering, we can overcome it through skillful negotiation with what obstructs us. We cannot help others if we have not liberated the various afflicted tendencies in our own nature. As we learn to cross over the suffering beings in our own heart, cutting through the misguided identification that keeps us bound to the wheel of birth and death, we develop the strength and groundedness in truth that will enable us to meet the afflictions of the world.

The regular practice of meditation is an indispensable tool for the aspiring bodhisattva. Meditation enables depth. Another word for meditation is "contemplation." The heart of this word is "template" or "temple." Meditation is the art of placing ourselves within a limitation, within the boundaries of a temple, so to speak, in order to gain insight into the unlimited. The words "yoga" (to yoke) and "religion" (to bind) originally implied this same paradoxical practice. By consciously surrendering to a sacred boundary, we can free ourselves from delusion and be reunited with our true nature. Herein rests the secret of the cross and the mysterious transformation of crucifixion into resurrection, the same ennobling mystical journey from suffering to its cessation that is revealed to every spiritual seeker upon Awakening.

In formal meditation we can't follow our normal patterns of distraction. When we sit still and take our attention inward we are confronted by tendencies of the mind. Ajahn Sumedho coined a great phrase for those tendencies. He called them "orphans of consciousness." He taught the importance of welcoming these orphans in order to release them. As we do so we become starkly aware of a range of difficult states of mind that we usually avoid: resistance, heaviness, anxiety, sadness, confusion. These are afflictions; they are refugees of the heart, "orphans of consciousness." They all become revealed. They parade before us and grab our attention. We need to acknowledge them rather than distract ourselves. It is like they come up for air and instead of meeting them with kindness and awareness we press them back down into the dungeon and lock the door. This solidifies negativity. We energize what we resist, creating the conditions to be overwhelmed and caught in the whirlpool of negative emotion or unskillful action at a later time. Sometimes we need to resist unwholesome impulse, but this is really only a temporary measure. In the light of awareness, afflictions are made conscious so they can be transformed with the power of *samadhi,* mindfulness, inquiry, and most important, kindness. Without kindness we get impatient and averse, often reinforcing the very tendencies we despise.

One evening as a monk, I was feeling a lot of despair. Looking out into the darkness of the night, I saw a shooting star. Suddenly it was there, blazing and streaking across the sky. Then it disappeared without a trace, leaving only the vastness. Seeing this helped me understand the need to be patient with things as they flare up. Eventually everything burns away, just like that shooting star, leaving the timeless, spacious, serene, loving, and responsive heart. In the Second Great Vow, the bodhisattva contemplates all afflictions and has confidence that she can overcome them through insight into their essential emptiness.

The Third Bodhisattva Vow

The Third Bodhisattva Vow emerges out of the Fourth Noble Truth. "There is a path out of suffering. This path should be cultivated." This becomes the Third Bodhisattva Vow, which is: "Dharma doors are endless; I vow to cultivate them all." This vow is about our intention to practice and to cultivate skillful means. This means that not only do we practice in the way we are comfortable with, but we maintain an open mind to other styles, perspectives, and approaches to the Dharma. The third Bodhisattva Vow is a commitment to be open and interested in "all Dharma doors." Dharma teachings are relative. They arise in response to the human predicament. The Buddha was able to respond appropriately to the particular needs and temperaments of those he encountered. There are many gateways into truth. Each of us has a contemplative practice that is closest to our heart, one that suits our tendencies. That can naturally change over time. Some people respond to the teaching on kindness, others the steadying power of mindfulness. Some enter the Path by studying the discourses of the Buddha, and others enter through the training rules that govern behavior. The Dharma is mutable, fluid, and not fixed. Truth transcends all traditions, methods, teachers, and even Buddhism itself. Therefore, we should maintain an open and inquiring mind, and not use the teachings in a way that makes us dogmatic.

The most immediate teaching of the Dharma is life itself. Everything is always revealing the truth of impermanence and insubstantiality. If we pay attention to this truth, it will lead us inward to the source. There is no secret transmission or attainment needed. The Dharma is always speaking to us, inviting us into our own deeper nature. If we want to help others, just imposing our own preferences on them will not work. We need to be receptive, agile, flexible, and steadily gain skill in different practices. In this way we gradually fulfill the bodhisattva path.

Pure Land Dharma Door

> *The mysterious sound of Kuan Yin's name is holy like the ocean's thunder, no other like it in the world. Therefore the mind should be constantly fixed upon her.*
>
> —The Lotus Sutra

One of my favorite Dharma doors is the Pure Land School. This is probably the least popular and most poorly understood practice in the West, though it has the largest following of all Buddhist schools in Asia. The Pure Land is a realm free of all pain, an abode of bliss and peace that is a metaphor for our deepest heart. There is a beautiful saying by Ananada Mayi Ma, one of the greatest contemporary saints of India: "The world is yours, of yourself, but you perceive it as separate. To know it as your own gives happiness, but the notion that it is apart from you causes sorrow. Either melt by devotion the sense of separateness, or burn it away by knowledge, then you will come to know yourself." Pure Land practice is the path of bhakti or devotion. It is the burning away of our sense of separation through the recitation of a holy name, and through devotional practices that open the heart. The recitation of a holy name is said to dissolve afflictions while at the same time generating a field of blessings. It connects to a larger sense of holding, presence, and a deeper sense of faith. It is a form of prayer.

Prayer isn't about asking for things, but about listening more deeply into the mystery of silence. We need to recognize that our ability to figure everything out is limited. In prayer, we accept our limitation and call on the mystery, which is also listening. One way I connect to this larger holding is through the reciting of mantras. *Mantra* means "to guide and protect the mind." There are many different mantras, which have myriad effects and resonances. Sometimes mantra is done as a concentration practice, to help steady and focus mental energy, like *Bud-dho*. It's particularly powerful when we align it with the breath. Mantra can also connect us with the deeper intention of the heart, which yearns to return home. The repetition of mantras aligns us with a current of ancient intention that has been carried by countless beings. This is similar to the Jesus prayer, the repetition of "Lord Jesus Christ, Son of God, have mercy on me, a sinner." This is a practice that links to the deeper heart of the mystery and the compassionate vow power of Jesus, while enabling the supplicant to gain mastery over the passions of body and mind. However, the most profound power of mantra and prayer is that as the words dissolve, they carry us into the depths of silence.

The most ancient Buddhist mantra that reveres the Buddha is *Namo Tassa Bhagavato Arahato Sammasambuddhasa*. "I pay homage to the

Blessed One, who is Purified and Fully Awake." We say this to honor the historical Buddha, but also to honor our own innate awakened potential. Another mantra, *Om Mani Padme Hum,* Kuan Yin's heart mantra, is a phrase that praises the indestructible, "jewel-like" enlightened nature within all manifestation.

Although I like to work with many different mantras, my favorite is holding the name of Kuan Yin—*Namo Kuan Shr Yin Pu Sa,* which translates as "I return my life to the One Who Listens at Ease to the Sounds of the World." As I say the mantra or chant it, I merge with the intention of Kuan Yin, which is profound listening and compassionate response. Kuan Yin represents an archetypal dimension of merciful compassion, quick to respond and ever committed to staying close to living beings. In the Twenty Fifth Chapter of the Lotus Sutra, the Universal Door, the Buddha teaches that those who constantly and reverently hold the name of Kuan Yin will gradually be freed from their greed, hatred, and delusion.

Kuan Yin is sometimes depicted having a thousand hands and eyes, which represent her many different efficacious responses within the world. When we're locked into a state of confusion, fear, or anxiety, when our cup is full of salt and is bitter, we could use the mantra "I'm a hopeless case, I'm a hopeless case, I'm a hopeless case." But that probably wouldn't get us very far. However, what happens if we call on the deepest wisdom and compassion in the universe? A phrase like *Om Mani Padme Hum* or *Namo Kuan Shr Yin Pu Sa* connects us to the immeasurable heart of listening and the mysterious power of compassion. We are not alone. The heart of the universe is not dead, unfeeling space. If we as practitioners can feel a little bit of compassion and a modicum of capacity to help others, can we imagine great compassion? Compassion at its depth is recognition of our most intimate connection with all of life; it has no limitation. Evoking the mantra and its underlying energetic resonance, we connect with a vastness that is rooted in unfathomable listening. Within that all the bitterness can dissolve.

Calling on the bodhisattvas is ultimately calling on our deepest nature. We are not apart from the profound intention of compassion within life itself. Mantra practice, infused with this intention, expands and uplifts the heart. Each turn of the mantra weaves us into the seamlessness of life. We get a sense of context, an ocean of loving awareness within which all suffering is dispelled. This is very different from being caught as an isolated *self*, struggling like mad. When we're really despairing, we're in a narrow, painful, and lonely place. In such times, when our sword of wisdom is blunt, when all the mindfulness we can muster just doesn't do it, and when we find ourselves in a swirl that pulls us down, this prayerful practice comes to the rescue. It connects to faith. It steadies the mind on the heart. Actually the heart never has the problem, just the mind. The heart already has within it the faith to trust.

The practice of prayerfulness is one of the most ancient and universal methods for plumbing the depths of our being, and reconnecting with inner quietude. Part of prayer life also includes others by extending good energy and support. It can range from a religious form, like intercessory prayer dedicated for the healing of another, to just wishing someone good luck. To wish and actively work for the alleviation of suffering and the welfare of others is at the heart of this bodhisattva intention. While this intention is innate to the heart, it is also cultivated as a practice. Prayer as a deliberate practice invokes a greater sense of holding than is possible when the mind is caught up in *me trying to get somewhere*. It takes us to the place where everything is okay, even if it's not okay.

A beautiful Buddhist practice is to continually share the blessing of our lives for the welfare of all beings without distinction: good and bad, powerful and weak, known and unknown. This profound spirit of universal offering underlies every activity and remembers that ultimately we are all in this together. It is a way of aligning with and calling on the force of compassion. To hold a prayerful intention with regard to the world has power. We are tapping into the deepest aspect of awareness, which is alive, responsive, and intelligent.

Sometimes we get caught in trying to figure out the immensity of it all with our brain, and the brain can't do it. It can't factor in all the eventualities, possibilities, and optimum outcomes. We can meet the problem in a different way. As Einstein said, "We can't solve the problem with the same consciousness that created it." A dualistic consciousness divides the world into "me" doing something about "the problem." Whereas holding "the problem" and the sense of "me struggling" in a prayerful way is holistic. We offer the situation into a unified field of listening that doesn't split the universe into separate pieces but holds it all. It includes loved ones as well as enemies, our hopes as well as our fears, our deepest pains and our greatest challenges. By listening in a prayerful, humble, and open way, we are guided by the undivided heart. It is from such a heart that optimum solutions and intuitive insights can arise in support of the greater welfare of the whole.

The Fourth Bodhisattva Vow

The Fourth Bodhisattva Vow emerges from the Third Noble Truth: "There is an ending of suffering. The ending of suffering needs to be realized." This motivation transforms into the Fourth Great Bodhisattva Vow: "The Buddha path is unsurpassed. I vow to fully realize it."

The Fourth Vow emerges from the realization of *nibbana*. As we deepen into the Third Noble Truth our heart is peaceful and spacious. It's delicious to taste our naturally free state. It is also very tempting to park there, and just enjoy that peace for ourselves. The Buddha was tempted to do that. He was very reluctant to teach, because he understood how difficult it would be to wake up a sleeping world and communicate the subtlety of what he had understood. Perceiving his reluctance, the great Brahma god Sahampati appeared before the Buddha and appealed to him to turn the wheel of the Dharma. He exhorted the Buddha to "go forth for the welfare of the many folk and for those who have a little dust in their eyes." In response, the Buddha did just that. For forty-five years he walked the land, teaching and enlightening others. The extraordinary efforts made by the Buddha and his disciples allowed his enlightenment to become one of the great contributions to humanity. Imagine if the Buddha simply decided to go off to a cave in the Himalayas and not say a word, thinking, "Oh, it's all too difficult. People are too ungrateful, and the world's going to the dogs anyhow. Might as well enjoy it while I can!"

The Dharma wheel continues to turn today because millions of disciples over the last two and a half thousand years have helped it turn through time and space. This is the great effort of a bodhisattva. What about us? This Fourth Vow encourages us to support the awakening of others in the same way the Buddha did. Awakening is not an end; in many ways it is a beginning. Actually, this vow understands that there is no beginning point and therefore no end. In other words, there is nowhere really to go. We're not trying to "get out," as if there's some other place that's free from all problems. We "get out" by being more fully here. When we are more fully here, deeply inquiring into the true nature of conditions, we arrive at emptiness. The Fourth Bodhisattva Vow is about the cultivation of enlightened activity that emerges from emptiness.

The paradox within the Bodhisattva Vows is that it sounds like we are going somewhere, moving onward, but in reality this kaleidoscope of the present moment forever unfolds within the immovable heart. The practice deepens our refuge in reality, and takes us to where we've always already been. The word the Buddha most frequently used to describe himself is *Tathagata*. *Tatha* means "such." which has the sense of stillness. *Gata* means both "coming" and "going." So *Tathagata* is the Thus Come One who has arrived at "suchness," and gone beyond birth and death. It implies that Awakening is both movement within stillness and stillness within movement, a state beyond all description. Timelessly present, dwelling in emptiness, the bodhisattva responds to the conditions of the world. This is the encouragement of the Fourth Bodhisattva Vow, which is articulated perfectly in the Diamond Sutra: "Those who set forth on this path should give birth to this thought, 'Whatever living beings there are, in whatever realms, I shall liberate them all.' And though I thus liberate countless beings, not a single being is liberated. And why not? No one can be called a bodhisattva who creates the perception of a self, other, living being, or lifespan."[3]

Teachings like this aren't to be grasped intellectually but felt intuitively. If we think about it, it all seems impossible. We just do the best that we can, moment after moment, emptying each action into the silence. I remember a time when I was very ill as a monk at Chithurst monastery. I spent virtually all of my time lying down in a small attic room, exhausted and in pain. I would often feel a bit useless because I couldn't join in any of the usual monastic activities. One cold and bleak winter afternoon, I happened to look out of my attic window and see one of the monastery guests with a rope in his hand, heading out toward the forest. He had just been released from prison and was suffering from resentment and self-hatred. I knew he was planning to take his own life. Although I was sick, I had to get up. I didn't want to take the time to put on something warmer than my thin robe. Hurrying down the deserted misty lane, I prayerfully held the name of Kuan Yin and practiced listening into my anxiety and concern.

Eventually I caught up with him underneath a tree, where he was getting his rope ready. I tried to talk him out of it, but he didn't want to listen. He was drowning in a dark, isolated vortex of despair, absolutely convinced that death was the only escape. As we stood there talking, I got colder and colder, and my teeth were chattering so much it was hard to speak. Suddenly he looked at me and exclaimed, "Your teeth are chattering!" He took off his heavy black leather jacket and put it over my shoulders. Immediately his dark state of mind shifted. I was able to give him a hug and together we walked back to the monastery. Until that moment the man had been so totally consumed in his despair, he couldn't see anything worth living for. Obviously this action didn't totally solve his problems, but his simple gesture of generosity lifted him miraculously out of a deeply isolated state, and showed him a path. He was able to make a connection with me and, from there, regain his own sense of humanity.

Generosity is the foundation of the Buddhist path of practice and the first *paramita*. Giving frees us from contraction, leads to happiness, contributes to the well-being of others, and naturally restores our sense of belonging within the larger web of life. My sickness, his pain, my concern, his gift—it all dissolved and merged back into the living silence, the great compassion heart that neither comes nor goes, and belongs to no one and everyone.

Who would have imagined that the unfolding of a mighty oak tree is hidden in a tiny acorn? In the Lotus Sutra the Buddha tells all his disciples: "Have no further doubts, let your hearts be filled with great joy, you know that you will realize Buddhahood." This Fourth Bodhisattva Vow affirms our true inheritance as a human being. The magnificent treasure of the Buddha mind is already here within the heart. We don't attain it, say the wise ones, but rather we recognize the jewel that has been here all along.

All living beings are my family.
The universe is my body.
All of space is my university.
My nature is empty and formless.
Kindness, compassion, joy, and equanimity are my function.

—Master Hua

CHAPTER SIXTEEN

An Intimate World

Kittisaro and Thanissara

There is no war, hunger, or "them" in our hearts. In our hearts we're all "us." All of us should manifest our true hearts, then we will have a world of one, as our hearts are one.

—Ram Dass

Whatever journey we undertake, it inevitably brings us back to ourselves. Finally we return to the inner silence that is present beyond the kaleidoscope of the mind. Here we meet what we longed for, our own intimate heart. When we touch our true heart, the world is transformed and the search for what we lost ends. We no longer endlessly consume the Earth to fill up our inner desolation. Instead we know our true worth. We enter our authentic self, poised within the reality of being "nothing" and "everything." Uniting earth and heaven, form and formlessness, the mindful self balances the art of letting go and the imperative to engage.

This balance is expressed in the Zen saying: *Returning from the mountaintop to the marketplace with bliss-bestowing hands.* The journey to the "mountaintop," to get perspective and gain insight and wisdom, is ever balanced by the return to the "marketplace," where we live with the intimacy of all things. This rhythm is as timeless and inevitable as the flow of the tides of the great ocean. The wave pulls inward and connects with depth, and then inexorably rushes forward to dissolve into the earth. There is a constant flow between the practice of wisdom, which requires "letting go," and the practice of compassion, which encourages "embracing." While at first wisdom and compassion seem like two distinct movements, in actuality, just like the in and out breath, they are part of a totality.

When we look out at the ocean we sometimes see huge waves with amazing crests, and sometimes we see millions of little waves with beautiful light rippling on the surface. One can look at gentle swells, or ferocious, dangerous waves. Language identifies variance. It can point our attention to different kinds of waves. We can designate them, compare them, and even surf on them. We are thrilled by them, but we don't identify with them. We don't burst into tears when a wave hits the rocks. "Oh, God, that magnificent wave, brutally shattered! It's too horrible to think about." We don't react like this because we know that a wave is not actually separate from the ocean. Language makes them appear like two things, but actually they are one. The waves and the ocean are of one substance. In reality, the big wave and the small wave are both rooted in the depth of the ocean. In the depth there's nothing happening, so to speak; it is still. Every single thing that dies, like each wave crashing on the shore, is actually returning to its source.

The waves are like the assumptions we make about our independent existence. We are a big wave, a small wave, an impressive wave, or just an insignificant ripple, and then we crash. If we think we are only a wave, we will get upset when we lose our form. "I was here, and now I'm gone." As long as we think we are a wave, we experience birth and death. The self is happy or sad, successful or failing, always being born into an identity. But as soon as the mood or circumstances change, we feel loss, which is death. Yet, just as each wave merges back into the ocean, the "sense of self," and all living things, rise and fall back into the aware heart. Knowing this, we enter a seamless universe and are satisfied.

Unfortunately, we are not satisfied. Humanity's perpetual dissatisfaction has led us into calamity. Our inability to acknowledge the deep interconnectedness of all things has precipitated enormous Earth changes. To quote from the Buddhist Declaration on Climate Change:

> Today we live in a time of great crisis, confronted by the gravest challenge that humanity has ever faced: the ecological consequences of our own collective karma. The scientific consensus is overwhelming: human activity is triggering environmental breakdown on a planetary scale. Global warming, in particular, is happening much faster than previously predicted. . . . Eminent biologists and U.N. reports concur that "business-as-usual" will drive half of all species on Earth to extinction within this century. Many scientists have concluded that the survival of human civilization is at stake. We have reached a critical juncture in our biological and social evolution.

We are hurtling toward the collapse of sustainable environments and into a world of increased scarcity, floods, fires, earthquakes, tornadoes, and droughts. Bill McKibben,[1] a leading U.S. environmentalist, has changed the name of our planet to Eaarth in order to drive home that we have irrevocably changed the planet we inhabit.

As a young prince, Siddhartha, the "Buddha-to-be," was jolted into his quest by the visitation of four heavenly messengers. These messengers are called "heavenly" because they served the purpose of waking him up. They left him in no doubt as to the fragility of his body and the human predicament. These four messengers were a sick person, an aged and decrepit person, a corpse, and a peaceful seeker. At the shock of these sobering sights, his denial of death and intoxication with youth fell away. At that moment, as the reality of impermanence penetrated deeply into his heart, the direction of Siddhartha's life utterly changed. From then on he was no longer so susceptible to enchantment. The messengers were not all bad news, however. The last messenger, the peaceful seeker, symbolized the possibility and hope of a different path.

The Buddha's story is a metaphor for our times. It reflects our current situation. We can no longer live under the delusion of creating an enchanted world into which we can escape. We cannot live independent from the results of our collective karma. Instead we are now confronted by an environment that is beset with the symptoms of death and decay. Every day more species become extinct, whole ecosystems are overwhelmed; our climate is becoming dangerously unstable. We are being faced with the same realization the Buddha had about his personal body, except now we are undergoing a collective awakening about our Earth body. In response, we can no longer hide out in denial. We have to let ourselves feel the shock of what is happening so we too can take a different path.

Underlying this critical juncture in our biological and social evolution is a crisis of conscience and consciousness. Having traveled the great oceans, conquered all the lands, extracted wealth from the Earth, and dominated her species, we now have one journey left to make. This is the most important journey we could ever undertake, because everything depends on it. The evolutionary imperative of our times demands we evolve from seeing the world "out there," separate and alien from us, to directly knowing our intimacy with all things. This is the shift from a dualistic consciousness to an *awake awareness* that recognizes nothing is apart from anything else, or from our deeper nature. If we harm someone, we harm ourselves. If we destroy and pollute, we do likewise to ourselves. If we drop bombs on other countries, we rip out a piece of our own soul. And unlike in any other time in human history, if we only look out for "our own" at the expense of everyone else, we will further precipitate the catastrophe of our collective demise.

It's understandable that we might feel overwhelmed and just give up. But if those who have increased awareness abdicate responsibility due to their preference for personal peace, then we have lost perspective. Awakening finds its completion through the spirit and activity of compassion. The Buddha was initially tempted to abdicate from teaching after his enlightenment. He could only fulfill his destiny, however, once he accepted the path of service. He understood that of all things to serve, the best was Dharma, or truth. As it turned out, that service was long and hard.

Sometimes we imagine life should get easier the more aware we are, but even great saints face challenges. Ajahn Chah was one of the greatest spiritual masters of our time, but the last ten years of his life were spent in a semi-paralyzed state in which he was unable to speak or tend to his most basic needs. Another great saint we met in India, Swami Premananda, was falsely charged and imprisoned. Swami had all sorts of magical powers; we witnessed them ourselves. As he was moved from prison to prison, he turned each one into an ashram and the guards into devotees. However, Swami died prematurely due to terrible prison conditions. Gandhi, an extraordinary spiritual and political activist, died with the name of Ram on his lips when assassinated by a fellow Hindu. We can also consider the Dalai Lama and his piercing clarity and tremendous compassion in the face of the brutal repression of Tibet. Each of these individuals met unbearable circumstances. They faced fear, hatred, and betrayal but overcame through the power of spiritual practice. These great luminaries and leaders didn't flee from the daunting tasks before them, and so were ultimately victorious. As our denial lifts, and the shock of our dangerous times crashes into our comfortable lives, we can take courage from those who have shown a different path.

As climate change deepens, it is clear that we are facing an enormous challenge. For this we need the attitude of a warrior. A warrior transforms fear, despair, and anger into clear and effective action. This requires an alertness to assess what is needed to best overcome obstacles. In ancient traditions warriors were trained to be mindful of their own death so as to keep a truly informed perspective. With this perspective, they evaluate what battles should be fought and what to leave be. It's not always easy to know how to proceed, but if we know how to hone the heart with the right attitude then we can prevail.

To meet the harsh use of power with violence is nearly always counterproductive. Even if force is needed, a spiritual warrior relinquishes hatred. Ajahn Anando, our good friend in the monastery, volunteered to go to Vietnam when he was young. He was a tough street kid who became a tough Marine. During his tour of duty he was shot and nearly died. Later, as a monk with a shaved head, his wound was visible as a large dent in the back of his skull. Anando's brush with death totally transformed his life. It took him out of the military and on to Asia and Ajahn Chah's monastery, where he became a Buddhist monk. Ajahn Anando was a very diligent and disciplined monk, and was warrior-like in his approach to spiritual practice.

After about a decade in the robes, when he was abbot of Chithurst Monastery he got into an altercation with a fellow monk. Anando lost his cool and invited the monk outside to sort it out. As they squared off, Anando, his Marine conditioning fully activated, clenched his fists, ready to strike his nemesis on the jaw. At the last moment, his monastic training came to the fore, and rather than punching his fellow monk, he got down on the ground and bowed to him. You can imagine how that gesture blew them both away—or more precisely, blew away their anger. For a moment they were able to meet in a more heartfelt space. Anando was someone who purified the warrior, from unconscious brute to courageous guardian. It takes inner strength to bow through the heat of anger. To be humble and empty enough to start again helps us bear the reality of any situation.

When we face difficulty, it's good to be well-equipped. The best protection is an ethical and mindful heart. The two Buddhist terms *hiri* and *ottappa* refer to internal ethics rather than externally imposed religious or social morals. Traditionally they are considered guardians of the world. *Ottappa* means the healthy fear that arises at the thought of wrongdoing, and *hiri* refers to a healthy sense of remorse at harm done to self or another. This kind of remorse, or conscience, is different from guilt. Guilt is an unwholesome state of mind that should be abandoned. It is a complex psychological conditioning that generates a "bad self" that can never be redeemed. A healthy sense of remorse, however, is the ability to feel the pain that results from unskillful action. That disquiet quickens our ability to be more self-aware, to make amends, or to better inform our response. The ability to be sensitive is the difference between a destructive warrior, and one who has the skill to transform negative energies into positive effect.

As we witness the dying of so much on our planet—her great oceans, her waterways, her many exquisite species—we are awakened to an unbearable reality. It's not easy to stay awake! To feel the consequences of our lifestyles is to have our heart broken again and again.

Artist Chris Jordan[2] uses his work to connect us to our sensitivity. He depicts the relationship of our consumerism to its impact on the natural world. His *Midway* Project takes us to the heart of a devastating environmental tragedy now unfolding on one of the most remote islands on Earth. Here tens of thousands of baby albatrosses lie dead on the ground, their tiny bodies filled with plastic from the Pacific Garbage Patch.[3] As our awareness increases, we connect the dots between the plastic we use every day, to the political promotion of oil companies, to the marginalization of organic material—such as hemp, which can be used as biodegradable plastic—and finally to a mother feeding her chick plastic bottle tops.

To witness a young albatross open wide
its translucent, newborn throat,
open the soft, pink shell to its mother,
to the contents of the sea she carried
in her body for thousands of miles,
for over twenty million years–to watch,
today, the chick wholly embrace
the amber-colored squid oil
and cloaked shards of plastic,
to see it all slip down in an act
of ancient swallowing–is to witness
eons of trust absorbed into nature's gut.
And for our own trusting throats
defended by lips, teeth and taste buds,
we evolved to sweeten what poisons us.[4]

When our natural human sensitivity is dulled and our ability to feel remorse falters, there is breakdown. Internally, it creates the causes for a lack of psychological well-being; externally, the ethical glue that maintains social cohesion comes undone, and the conditions for environmental destruction go unchecked. An inner ethic is an evolutionary step beyond social pressure and religious morals. Once awakened, this sense of conscience will inevitably put us at odds with the exploitative paradigm of our culture. In addition, we'll be faced with our own inner tendencies to skim over the damaging consequences of our heedlessness. The development of an internal ethic is a demanding spiritual practice. Its basic premise is to do as little harm as possible.

Based in ethical intention and attuned to human sensitivity, the spiritual warrior also trains in mindfulness. Amidst increasing intensity, instead of being distracted or overwhelmed, mindful attention creates a vital space that affords considered response rather than conditioned reactivity. It gives the possibility of being a conduit of an intuitive and universally wise solution. If we stay open, mindful, and inquiring in our engagement, ways forward become possible. The Pali word for mindfulness, *sati,* suggests a "re-membering" of what has been split apart. Holding a still point of presence allows the fragmented, the abandoned and torn, to regroup and heal. This practice of presence also deepens our ability to tolerate uncertainty. The process of stripping away the layers of our usual strategies brings us into the naked and open vulnerability of the heart. Here we listen anew into the promptings of *wise knowing* that can guide us with true intelligence.

The listening, intelligent, and aware heart includes everything. Nothing is outside or split away. We contemplate it all, destructive and merciless shadow energies, as well as beauty, courage, and inspiration. The Shurangama Sutra states that while we imagine the mind to be separate from phenomena, in reality all phenomena, including the great Earth, appear within the mind. This understanding illuminates the profound indivisibility of all things. The tiniest ants to the furthest stars, all that we know, and the one knowing, are the interwoven tapestry of consciousness. Recognizing this, the heart knows its intimacy with all things. The pain and fear of our separateness and the devastation of our alienation can thaw. We find our ability to steward and protect our precious Earth. After all, even though we are temporary visitors, this marvelous planet is the only home we have.

The Heart Sutra also gives some clues; this extraordinary text is like programming code for the glaring simplicity of enlightenment. The world is increasingly complex, but we only know that world because of our presence. The quality of our presence is important. We can hold "the world" in loving awareness rather than divide it into a thousand pieces. In our bedazzled state we have bowed down before our industrial and technological accomplishments. We have put our scientific scalpel to the objective world and have extracted an unbelievable river of information and accomplishment. All of this is truly amazing, and yet there is something we still haven't understood. We have conquered the objective world, but we still haven't realized who the subject is.

The Sutra encourages that "subject," our aware, present heart, to "leave dream thinking far behind, and live without walls of the mind." This is a radical invitation. The Sutra then finishes with a proclamation of absolute certainty, stating that the bodhisattva relies on a "magical mantra, an unequaled mantra, it dispels all suffering. It is true and not false." This sacred mantra, *Gate, gate, paragate, parasamgate, bodhi svaha,* exclaims, "Gone, gone, gone beyond, beyond the beyond, Awakening—So be it!" The only possibility left is to wake up!

In the Heart Sutra, Kuan Yin points beyond the dualistic mind, ever caught in trapping everything in a web of desire, fear, and complexity. Instead she reveals the true radiance at the heart of everything. On waking from our dream thinking, however, we are not soothed and mollified, but burnt down and shattered. The armor over our heart is stripped away, and what is revealed is our raw, human sensitivity.

In the midst of a crucible of destruction, the evolutionary awakening of our times is birthing a new humanity: one that feels deeply, has the crystal intelligence of primordial awareness, is infused with the divine impulse of the bodhisattva mind, and does not fear its oneness with all things. This understanding offers a new way to move within the world. But we begin with the moment, emptying inwardly, so that a deeper knowing can arise and guide us, informed by the inherent intelligence of life.

Ajahn Chah taught us not to fear emptiness. His own authentic and remarkable responses emerged from a lifetime of profound relinquishment.

He said being empty is like a round bell. It might look useless, just sitting there full of empty space. But if we cram it full of stuff, even important and significant things, it won't resonate when touched. *Clonk!* We might be afraid that an empty heart is dead, lifeless, like an enlightened stone! But the empty heart is actually filled with presence and ease. Then when something touches us, we can resonate like the clear sound of the bell, and respond appropriately.

Sometimes, though, it all just seems like too much. *Save the world? For heaven's sake, I can't even get out of bed!* What do we do when it's overwhelming? Our little dog Jack told us the secret when he was alive, again and again, dear soul: "Let's go for a walk!" He knew the way back to a good time. So often we fall into confusion and despair, not knowing what to do next about the endless torrent of upsetting scenarios racing through the heart. "Should I . . . shouldn't I? Can I . . . can't I? Will they, won't they, how could they?" We all know the feeling. So many times, encouraged by our four-legged furry friend, we would manage to walk out the door, open our eyes and ears, and set off up the mountain. Yes, the troubling swirl of thoughts and feelings was still there, but in walking we had to come into contact with our body, following each step carefully in between the boulders, alert to the terrain, aware of the breath, the weight, and the formidable force of gravity.

One step at a time up the mountain, slowly, our fractured being is remembered—the body, the feelings, the whirlpool of thoughts—all held within the healing embrace of awareness, that magic wand that reveals the sacred ground. When we do this, simply practicing presence, a mysterious alchemy takes place. We start to see things more clearly. Turning around, we look down the valley and see the tiny boxes we inhabit. Entangled inside the myriad complexities of good and bad, this and that, we lose perspective on our essential spaciousness of spirit. Somehow in the process of simply climbing up the mountain, we get realigned and connected to the reality of the moment, rather than lost in perpetual judgments about how it is or should be. We understand, and stand upright again, on that blessed, trustworthy, sacred ground that is always here and now. The compelling stories that tripped us up below still appear, but somehow they are seen in perspective for what they are. When we're in touch with the true nature of a moment, we see the Dharma and experience the essential beauty of life.

Taking the time to walk outside, we'll notice the evening dusk settling over the land, and perhaps catch the remnants of a glorious burgundy sunset lingering in the clouds. And suddenly we'll see them hidden in the growing shadows, two eland—the sacred animal of the Khoisan—standing majestic and unconcerned. In the silence, as the darkness falls and the subtle illumination of a clear moon casts a silver blessing over the world, we watch them slowly disappear into the unmoving mountain. The wonder of it all!

We're standing on a sacred mountain, wherever we are. What makes a mountain sacred? Is it the miracles that seem to happen there, the special experiences and the blessings that she bestows on all who come into her presence? Perhaps a place is sacred when it helps us trust that it's okay and important to be here, to be fully here so that we can discover again our inherent peacefulness and sanity. They say these Drakensberg Mountains are 220 million years old. That's a long time. And yet the thought of tomorrow can sometimes send us into a spin. As we open our eyes and sense how fleeting our human presence is here, reflecting on the immensity and timelessness of this ancient Mother Earth, we find again a moment of humility. What arrogance and delusion to really imagine that *I own this body, this land, these things.*

All the major events of the Buddha's life happened outside, in the midst of Mother Nature: his birth, the Awakening, the first discourse, and his death. Again and again the Buddha encouraged his disciples to go to the forest and get things in perspective. Accessing measureless states of mind dissolves the toxic contractions that shape the sense of self. In nature we rejoice in undivided beauty that cannot be captured in words. Our hearts open to the majesty of nature and resonate with sympathetic joy. We don't get jealous of a sunset, competitive with a tree, or set our self up against a spacious landscape. Amid the flowing lines of the natural world, the boundaries tend to disappear and we are restored.

All the great spiritual leaders, prophets, and saints had life-changing experiences in the midst of the natural world: the Buddha under the Bodhi Tree, Christ in the desert, Mohammed in the cave, Moses on the mountain, and Ram in the wilderness. Mother Nature is a sacred gateway to the holy ground of *nibbana,* the kingdom, the beloved, liberation, that Promised Land that has been right here under our feet all along.

In the Buddhist monastic tradition, walking on *tudong*[5](walk-about) is a liberating practice that monks and nuns undertake from time to time. Leaving the cozy confines of their monasteries, they set out in faith and walk across the land, shaking off attachments, learning again to be simple and appreciate the blessing of what is offered—a simple meal, a humble shelter, the welcome shade of a tree.

Even if we are not monks and nuns, we can still find time to go for a walk outside, and honor our beloved Mother Earth. Let her mysterious magic work on our wounded spirit. One step at a time, listening and remembering, we enter again that sacred gate to the heart. And before we know it, we'll be standing in the splendor, abiding in the majesty. Restored, we'll know what to do.

Notes

Chapter One: An Invitation

1. In this context I don't mean taking birth as a baby and dying as an old person. For one who meditates, birth is the identification with thoughts and the apparent thing-ness they imply. Birth identifies with becoming someone, acquiring stuff, doing the next thing, or taking on the roles we play. Consequently, death is the experience of wavering and loss felt when something we're leaning on (identified with) changes or ends.
2. Ajahn Sumedho is an American-born monk who at that time was the senior Western disciple of Ajahn Chah. Under his leadership, many branch monasteries in the Ajahn Chah tradition were established in the West.
3. Ajahn Munindo (born 1951 in New Zealand) is a Theravada monk and teacher in the Thai Forest School. He is abbot of Aruna Ratanagiri Monastery in the UK and has been ordained since 1974. He has written a number of books, including *Unexpected Freedom* and a contemporary translation of the Dhammapada.
4. *Ajahn* is the Thai word for teacher.
5. *Luang Por,* "Venerable Father," is a term of endearment and respect reserved for one's teacher.
6. *Dok* is the Thai word for "fall down."
7. Ajahn Pasanno was born in Canada and has been a monk for more than thirty

years in the Forest School of Ajahn Chah. He is currently abbot of Abhayagiri Monastery in California and is known for his work preserving forests in the northeast of Thailand. He has written a number of books, including coauthoring *The Island* with Ajahn Amaro.

8. In Thailand nuns traditionally wear the white robes of novices, however increasingly nuns are taking the ochre robe of higher ordination.

Chapter Two: A Stab to the Heart

1. Mahaparinibbana Sutta translation adapted from Rhys Davids, *Dialogues of the Buddha* (London: Pali Text Society, 1910), Volume Two.
2. "The Pali Canon is a vast body scriptures recorded in the ancient Indian language Pali, regarded by the Theravada school and generally considered by Scholars, to be our most reliable source of the teachings of the historical Buddha Gotama." —Bhikkhu Bodhi.
3. Maharaji passed into *mahasamadhi* in 1973 (devotees consider his presence still accessible, although his form is no longer incarnate). He is part of the tradition of saints of the Kumaon Hills of North India. In his early life he was married with three children, leaving his household life to wander as a sadhu when his youngest child was eleven. There is no biography of him; he seems to be known by different names in different areas of India, appearing and disappearing through the years. His is known in the West as Neem Karoli Baba.
4. Ram Dass, *Be Love Now* (New York: HarperCollins, 2010).
5. Jiddu Krishnamurti (1895–1986) was an Indian writer and speaker on philosophical and spiritual subjects.
6. Douglas Edison Harding (1909–2007) was an English mystic, philosopher, author, and spiritual teacher.
7. Don Juan Matus, a Yaqui Indian shaman whose teachings are recorded in a series of books written by his student Carlos Castaneda.
8. The Sutta (Pali) or Sutra (Sanskrit) is a collection of the Buddha's teachings. These teachings were first memorized and then written down several hundred years after the Buddha's death.
9. *Samsara* literally means "continuous flow" and has the sense of endless wandering through the cycles of birth, death, and rebirth, which is part of the worldview of Buddhism, Hinduism, Jainism, and other Indian-based religions.
10. Ajahn Anando was one of the first Western monks to accompany Ajahn Chah on his first visit to the UK. Anando, a.k.a. Greg Klein from Buffalo, New York (1946–1994), served in Vietnam and was awarded the Purple Heart and Stars,

Good Conduct Medal, Vietnamese Service Medal, Vietnamese Campaign Medal, and National Service Medal. He ordained in 1974 with Ajahn Chah and was abbot of Chithurst monastery from 1985–92. Anando was known as an impeccable monk and warrior practitioner who was devoted to the practice of loving-kindness. A former U.S. Vietnam vet, he was a monk for twenty years before leaving the order to marry. Two years after his disrobing, he died from a brain tumor due to a head injury sustained while on his tour of duty in Vietnam.

11. Sri Sudhir Mukerjee (1913–1997) was known by the familiar name Dadaji, while his wife Kamala was known as Didiji. Dadaji was a professor of economics. After Neem Karoli's death Dadaji wrote two books about him, *By His Grace: A Devotee's Story* and *The Near and the Dear: Stories of Neem Karoli Baba and His Devotees.*

Chapter Three: A Steady Mind

1. The words "mind" and "heart" are interchangeable translations of the Pali word *citta*. The *citta* is aware and responsive. The cognitive faculty, thinking, is only one dimension of the *citta*. For there to be *samadhi,* the body and thought need to be gathered and unified within the mind or heart of awareness. When we use the phrase "steady mind" as a translation of *samadhi,* we are talking about the training of awareness. That includes the training of the thinking mind, but is not limited by it.
2. Venerable Ajahn Tate is one of the most highly respected Buddhist monks of the Theravada School in Thailand and is internationally renowned as a master of meditation. Born in 1902, he spent over seventy years as a monk, and was a disciple in the lineage of the contemporary "forest monk" tradition of Northeast Thailand, inspired by the Venerable Ajahn Mun. In addition to his large following in Thailand, Ajahn Tate has trained many Western disciples. He died in 1994, aged 92.
3. Ajahn Lee Dhammadharo (1907–1961) was one of the foremost teachers in the Thai forest ascetic tradition of meditation, founded by Ajahn Sao and Ajahn Mun.
4. *A Dhammapada for Contemplation,* Ajahn Munindo, trans. (Belsay, England: Aruno Publications, 2006), 3: 33–34. The Dhammapada is an anthology of 423 verses and is considered one of the most popular pieces of Theravada literature. It is a succinct expression of the Buddha's teachings and is ascribed to utterances he made in response to a multitude of circumstances.
5. From Ajahn Chah's talk "Living with the Cobra," first published in Ajahn

Chah, *Bodhinyana: A Collection of Dhamma Talks* (Ubon Ratchathani, Thailand: Sangha, Bung Wai Forest Monastery 1982).

6. The Buddha tried to stop a conflict after the King of Kosala, Vidudabha, declared war on Kapilavastu. Twice he tried to stop the advancing Kosalan army. Each time, due to the Buddha's intervention King Vidudabha ordered his army to retreat. The third time, however, the Buddha was not there, and King Vidudabha army marched straight toward Kapilavastu and slaughtered the Buddha's tribe, the Sakyans.
7. Master Hsuan Hua (1918–1995) was a Chan (Zen) Buddhist master and an instrumental figure in bringing Chinese Buddhism to the U.S. He founded the City of 10,000 Buddhas, several Buddhist monasteries, Dharma Realm Buddhist Association, and a range of educational opportunities. In 1976 he founded the Dharma Realm Buddhist University, with campuses at The City of 10,000 Buddhas in Ukiah and the Institute of World Religions in Berkeley. He also established the Instilling Goodness Elementary School and the Developing Virtue Secondary School. He was responsible for translations of numerous sutras, and extensive commentaries and publications, which have been translated into numerous languages.
8. Kuan Yin is considered a great bodhisattva in Buddhism, one who is ever dedicated to the merciful response to suffering. She is a mystical/mythical being and archetypal presence that encapsulates the power of merciful response and profound wisdom. Kuan Yin is also known as Avalokitesvara in Sanskrit, the "'One Who Listens to the Sounds of the World."
9. Master Hua said he was quoting verses of Master Yung Jya in his Song of Enlightenment. Master Jung Jya was an eighth-century Chan master.
10. This conversation between Master Hua and Bhikkhu Kittisaro took place at Amaravati Buddhist Monastery on October 7, 1990. Dharma Master Heng Sure translated.
11. *Sangha* in this sense refers to the spiritual community, particularly the monastic Sangha of ordained monks and nuns. It is the third aspect of the Triple Jewel, the Three Refuges: Buddha, Dharma, and Sangha.
12. Abhidhamma Buddhist texts are "the Compilation of Philosophy, a collection of seven treatises which subject the Buddha's teachings to rigorous philosophical systematization," as defined by Bhikkhu Bodhi, a contemporary Buddhist monk, practitioner, and scholar. According to tradition, shortly after his Awakening, the Buddha spent several days in meditation, during which he formulated the Abhidhamma. Later, he traveled to the heavenly realms and taught the

Abhidhamma to the divine beings that dwelled there, including his deceased mother, Queen Maha.

Chapter Four: The Practice of Presence

1. The five hindrances are: 1. sensual desire *(kamacchanda)*; 2. aversion and ill will *(vyapada)*; 3. dullness and boredom *(thīna-middha)*; 4. restlessness, worry, and anxiety *(uddhacca-kukkucca)*; and 5. sabotaging doubt (excessive mental speculation; *vicikiccha)*.
2. This is a reference to the eight worldly winds, a common theme in Buddhist teaching. They are: gain and loss, praise and blame, fame and disrepute, pleasure and sorrow.
3. Ajahn Sucitto (born 1949) is a British-born Theravada Buddhist monk. He is, since 1992, the abbot of Cittaviveka Monastery in the UK. He ordained in Thailand in 1976. He has published numerous books, including *Turning the Wheel of Truth* and *Rude Awakenings.* He has been out to South Africa and Dharmagiri. In 2004, with Ajahn Sucitto and a small group, we made a pilgrimage to Mount Kailash in Tibet together.
4. Viveka Sutta: "Seclusion" (SN 9.1), Thanissaro Bhikkhu, trans., Access to Insight (Legacy Edition), November 30, 2013, www.accesstoinsight.org/tipitaka/sn/sn09/sn09.001.than.html .
5. Anguttara Nikaya, Thanissaro Bhikkhu, trans., in *The Wings to Awakening: An Anthology from the Pali Canon* (Barre, MA: Dhamma Dana Publications, Barre Center for Buddhist Studies, 1996), page 234.

Chapter Five: Two Kinds of Peace

1. Chithurst Monastery, when first brought by the English Sangha Trust in 1978, was a semi-derelict Victorian mansion. For the first five years, as a young and energetic monastic community, we rebuilt it and created the foundations for the beautiful monastery it is today.
2. Sri Nisargadatta Maharaj (1897–1981), was an Indian spiritual teacher and philosopher of Advaita (Nondualism). It is difficult to find out much about his personal history, since, when questioned, he'd reply "I was never born." Sri Nisargadatta, with his direct and uncompromising explanation of nondualism, is considered the most famous teacher of Advaita in modern times. In 1973, the publication of his most famous and widely translated book, *I Am That,* brought him worldwide recognition and followers.

Chapter Seven: Desire: The Core of the Matrix

1. The Sutta Nipata contains some of oldest recordings of conversations with the Buddha. This conversation with Jatukanni is recorded as the final chapter, which is called "The Way to the Beyond." It is one of sixteen conversations that the Buddha had with young Brahmin students that came to question him. The teaching that the Buddha gave Jatukanni is the essence of the Second and Third Noble Truth. The Second Truth points to the cause of stress and suffering, which is desire, and the Third Truth points to the realization of non-suffering. This excerpt adapted from H. Saddhatissa, The Sutta-Nipāta (London: Curzon, 1985).
2. Dhammapada, Nanamoli Thera, trans., in *The Life of the Buddha, as It Appears in the Pali Canon, the Oldest Authentic Record* (Kandy, Sri Lanka: Buddhist Publication Society, 1972), 153–154.

Chapter Eight: Dew Drops and a Lightning Flash

1. Jack Kornfield and Paul Breiter, *A Still Forest Pool: The Insight Meditation of Achaan Chah* (Wheaton, IL: Theosophical Publishing House, 1985), Chapter VII (Realization).
2. Totnes is currently the fulcrum of a worldwide environmental movement for sustainable towns and cities called Transition Town. The Transition Town Network supports community-led responses to climate change and shrinking supplies of cheap energy, through building resilience and happiness.
3. Master Hsu Yun, whose name means "Empty Cloud" (1840–1959), was a renowned Zen Buddhist master and one of the most influential Buddhist teachers of the nineteenth and twentieth centuries. He is often noted for his unusually long lifespan, having lived to age 119.
4. The bodhisattva intention is to dedicate one's practice entirely to the welfare of all beings, this dedication is articulated in four vows that are discussed in Chapter 15.
5. The Buddha, Samutta Nikaya: 22.95. Adapted from *The Word of the Buddha: An Outline of the Teaching of the Buddha in the Words of the Pali Canon*, Venerable Nyanatiloka, trans., 17th ed. (Kandy, Sri Lanka: Buddhist Publication Society, 2001), page 16.
6. The Lotus Sutra is highly regarded in a number of Asian countries where Mahayana Buddhism has been traditionally practiced. This quote is slightly adapted from Burton Watson's translation. *The Lotus Sutra* (New York: Columbia University Press, 1993), Chapter Two: Expedient Means, page 24.

Chapter Nine: Nibbana: The Beautiful

1. Taken from the version of the Shurangama Sutra with a commentary and translation by Master Hsuan Hua and the monks and nuns of the City of 10,000 Buddhas. *The Shurangama Sutra* is a beloved Mahayana text that highlights the supreme efficacy of Kuan Yin's meditation method of "returning the hearing to listen into the true nature." The Shurangama Sutra, Buddhist Text Translation Society, trans., 2nd ed. (Burlingame, CA: Buddhist Text Translation Society, 2002), volume two, page 55.
2. Mula Sutta: Root Sutta Anguttara Nikaya, 10.58. "Rooted in desire are all things, born of attention are all things, arising on contact are all things, converging on feeling are all things, ruled by concentration are all things, dominated by mindfulness are all things, surmounted by wisdom are all things, yielding freedom as essence are all things, merging in the deathless are all things, and ending in nirvana are all things." Adapted from Ajahn Amaro and Ajahn Pasanno, *The Island: An Anthology of the Buddha's Teachings on Nibbāna* (Redwood Valley, CA: Abhayagiri Monastic Foundation, 2009), page 128.
3. Udana VIII 3, in *The Word of the Buddha: An Outline of the Teaching of the Buddha in the Words of the Pali Canon*, Venerable Nyanatiloka, trans.,17th ed. (Kandy, Sri Lanka: Buddhist Publication Society, 2001), Chapter III: "The Noble Truth of the Extinction of Suffering."
4. Adapted with minor alterations from *The Way to the Beyond*, H. Saddhatissa, trans. (London: Curzon, 1985), Chapter V.

Chapter Ten: Contemplative Ease

1. Adapted with minor changes from *The Shurangama Sutra*, Buddhist Text Translation Society, trans., 2nd ed. (Burlingame, CA: Buddhist Text Translation Society, 2002), Volume V, Chapter 3, "Manjushri Selects the Organ of Entry," page 221.
2. The yearly Rains Retreat, or Vassa, extends for three lunar months during the monsoon. It is traditionally a time of retreat and of "staying put." This tradition was observed by the Buddha and his disciples but is likely to have been pre-Buddhist, established to avoid wandering ascetics harming crops, insects, and possibly even themselves during the heavy rains.
3. *Thay* is an affectionate, honorific term for a Vietnamese Buddhist monk.
4. "The Ayodhya dispute is a political, historical, and socioreligious debate in India, centered on a plot of land in the city of Ayodhya, located in Faizabad district, Uttar Pradesh. The main issues revolve around access to a site

traditionally regarded as the birthplace of the Hindu deity Rama; the history and location of the Babri Mosque at the site; and whether a previous Hindu temple was demolished or modified to create the mosque. The Babri Mosque was destroyed by hardline Hindu activists during a political rally that turned into a riot on December 6, 1992." Wikipedia.

5. Relics of the Buddha and various enlightened sages are objects of veneration. When an awakened being is cremated after their death, mysteriously crystals often appear in the bones. For example, beautiful and numerous crystals were found in the ashes of Ajahn Chah and Master Hua. After the Buddha's death, his body was cremated and the relics were divided into eight portions, as is described in the Mahaparinibbana Sutta (Last Days of the Buddha), Digha Nikaya. Who knows what the relics were that we gave to Thay—which had been generously given to us—but as objects of devotion, to deepen one's faith in practice, they were beautiful reminders of our human potential to wake up.
6. A *sesshin*, literally "touching the heart-mind," is a period of intensive meditation.
7. Kuan Yin is the Chinese transliteration of the Sanskrit word *Avalokitesvara*. As Kuan Yin is beyond all forms and is transgendered, we will be referring to both Kuan Yin and Avalokitesvara as "s/he" and "his/ her" to capture the incorporation of dual gender and also transcendence of gender identity.
8. Adapted with minor changes from *The Shurangama Sutra*, Buddhist Text Translation Society, trans., 2nd ed. (Burlingame, CA: Buddhist Text Translation Society, 2002), Volume V, Chapter 3, "Manjushri Selects the Organ of Entry," page 192.
9. Excerpts adapted with minor changes from *The Shurangama Sutra*, Buddhist Text Translation Society, trans., 2nd ed. (Burlingame, CA: Buddhist Text Translation Society, 2002), Volume V, Chapter 3, "Manjushri Selects the Organ of Entry," pages 212–214.
10. Adapted with minor changes from *The Shurangama Sutra*, Buddhist Text Translation Society, trans., 2nd ed. (Burlingame, CA: Buddhist Text Translation Society, 2002), Volume V, Chapter 3, "Manjushri Selects the Organ of Entry," pages 214–215.
11. In contrast, the Theravadin texts cited in earlier chapters expressed this same transcendent principle in negative terms—e.g. *amata dhamma*, "the undying, the deathless." The danger of the positive term is it can lead to a fixed view of eternalism, whereas the negative articulation can lead to the annihilationist position. Both ways point to the unshakable realization of non-grasping.
12. Excerpts adapted with minor changes from *The Shurangama Sutra*, Buddhist

Text Translation Society, trans., 2nd ed. (Burlingame, CA: Buddhist Text Translation Society, 2002), Volume V, Chapter 3, "Manjushri Selects the Organ of Entry," pages 215–230.

13. Although the Dharma is timeless, the existence in the world of its understanding and teaching is conditioned. The Buddha predicted that his own teachings would flourish and eventually fade away in the "Dharma Ending Age," to be rediscovered by the next Buddha.
14. Master Hua's commentary, *The Shurangama Sutra*, Buddhist Text Translation Society, trans., 2nd ed. (Burlingame, CA: Buddhist Text Translation Society, 2002), Volume IV, Chapter 3, "Ananda Attaches to Causes and Conditions," page 128. The Sanskrit word *vajra* usually is defined as "diamond" or "adamantine." It signifies enlightenment, or the absolute unshakable reality of emptiness.
15. Excerpts adapted with minor changes from *The Shurangama Sutra*, Buddhist Text Translation Society, trans., 2nd ed. (Burlingame, CA: Buddhist Text Translation Society, 2002), Volume V, Chapter 2, "Twenty-five Means to Enlightenment," The Ear Organ, page 139.

Chapter Eleven: Radical Reflection

1. In Mahayana Buddhism, the bodhisattva Avalokitesvara is considered one of the greatest of all the bodhisattvas. This is because s/he (in Chinese Buddhism she often appears in a favored female form as Kuan Yin) represents the perfect fusion of deep wisdom and boundless compassion.
2. Spiritual bypassing is the use of spiritual practices and beliefs to avoid psycho-emotional issues in the name of an idealized spirituality. Instead of owning and working through uncomfortable emotions—like anger, resentment, grief and despair—we dissasociate from them. When this happens, we tend to project unwanted feelings onto others. This can lead to harshly judging others for the very same issues which we have repressed. This also leads to an inner splitting which disconnects access to the fullness of our life force, stunting a true mature spirituality.
3. The Dhammapada is a popular Buddhist text with a collection of succinct sayings from the Buddha.
4. The Dhammapada, verse 254/55. Kittisaro's own translation of the text.
5. A wonderful study of the significance of *papanca* in the Pali text is presented in Bhikkhu Nanananda, *Concept and Reality* (Kandy, Sri Lanka: Buddhist Publication Society, 1971).

6. Shariputra (Sariputta in Pali), foremost in wisdom, was one of the chief disciples of the Buddha.
7. Our understanding and translation of the Heart Sutra is guided and inspired by Master Hsuan Hua, *The Heart of Prajna Paramita Sutra*, 2nd ed. (Burlingame, CA: Dharma Realm Buddhist Association, 2003).
8. Ajahn Chah, *Bodhinyāna: A Collection of Dhamma Talks* (Ubon Ratchathani, Thailand: Sangha, Bung Wai Forest Monastery, 1982). "Living With the Cobra" is also included in *Food for the Heart: The Collected Teachings of Ajahn Chah*. See Bibliography.
9. Chapter 11: "Awareness and Consciousness," in *I Am That: Talks with Sri Nisargadatta Maharaj*, Maurice Frydman and Sudhakar S. Dikshit, eds. (Durham, NC: Acorn Press, 1999).
10. A koan is an important part of Zen Buddhism. It is an unanswerable question which points beyond the conceptual framework to intuitive insight.
11. *Shurangama* means "durable or indestructible *samadhi*." This is another way of talking about enlightenment. The mind is unshakable; not because there's an effort to concentrate it, as in the mundane understanding of *samadhi*, but because it recognizes its own true nature as unmoving. Our understanding of this text is guided and inspired by Master Hua and his important translation and commentary through the Buddhist Text Translation Society.
12. *The Shurangama Sutra*, Buddhist Text Translation Society, trans., 2nd ed. (Burlingame, CA: Buddhist Text Translation Society, 2002), Volume 1, page 231.
13. Jack Kornfield and Paul Breiter, *A Still Forest Pool: The Insight Meditation of Achaan Chah* (Wheaton, IL: Theosophical Publishing House, 1985).

Chapter Twelve: The Wounded Warrior

1. Mirabai was an mystical poet and singer and devotee of Lord Krishna from Rajasthan. Some thousand prayerful songs attributed to her are popular throughout India and have been published in several translations worldwide.
2. The Karuna Institute is a nonprofit organization that runs training courses in core process psychotherapy and craniosacral therapy in England. It was founded by Maura Sills and Franklyn Sills. The name *Karuna* comes from the Sanskrit word translated as "compassion." The institute offers training and professional qualifications in psychotherapy, accredited by the United Kingdom Council of Psychotherapy (one of two independent national accreditation bodies recognized for psychotherapists and used by the UK National Health Service); and masters degrees accredited by Middlesex University.
3. *Bhikkhunis* (nuns) are one of the fourfold assembly established by the Buddha;

the other members of the fourfold assembly are monks, laymen, and laywomen. Full Bhikkhuni ordination was lost for over a thousand years until recently. It is being reinstated in Sri Lanka, Thailand, and in the West.

4. *Empty Hands*, to be published August 2015 by North Atlantic Books.

Chapter Thirteen: Through the Night Door

1. The Buddha, Rohitassa Sutta, from *The Connected Discourses of the Buddha: A New Translation of the Saṃyutta Nikā Ya*, Bhikkhu Bodhi,trans. (Somerville, MA: Wisdom Publications, 2000), SN 2.26.
2. Eugene T. Gendlin (born 1926, Vienna) is an American psychotherapist and philosopher. He is best known for his work known as "*focusing*" and "*thinking at the edge.*" "Focusing" is a psychotherapeutic process. It invites a non-judgemental, open and investigative quality of mind, directed to the experience of what is felt, sensed and intuited in the moment. It is a way of moving beneath the cognitive interpretation of experience so as to access fresh and revelatory insights about ones situation or life.
3. *The Story of the Weeping Camel*, directed by Byambasuren Davaa and Luigi Falomi, starring Janchiv Ayurzana, Chimed Ohin Amgaabazar Gonson (Germany: ThinkFilm, 2003).

Chapter Fourteen: The Nectar in the Fire

1. Hilda Schiff, in *Holocaust Poetry*, Ted Hughes, trans. (New York: St. Martin's Press, 1995).
2. Acharya Godwin Samararatne (1932–2000) was one of the leading lay meditation teachers in Sri Lanka in recent times. He established and resided in a Meditation Center at Nilambe in the central hill country near Kandy. He was a beloved teacher known for his humility, humor, and profound wisdom. He used to visit South Africa every three years to teach meditation, and during those visits we got to know him well.
3. Thanks to Elizabeth Mattson of South Africa and the UK for generously sharing her story.
4. Khenchen Thrangu Rinpoche, *A Song for the King: Saraha on Mahamudra Meditation* (Boston: Wisdom Publications, 2006).

Chapter Fifteen: Until the End of Time

1. According to some Buddhist traditions, Dipankara was a Buddha who reached enlightenment eons prior to Gautama, the historical Buddha. Generally,

Buddhists believe that there has been a succession of many Buddhas in the distant past and that many more will appear in the future; Dipankara, then, would be one of numerous previous Buddhas, while Gautama was the most recent, and Maitreya will be the next Buddha in the future.

2. Similar versions of these four classical bodhisattva vows appear frequently in Mahayana Buddhist texts. Kitissaro was first introduced to these vows and their relationship to the Four Noble Truths by Master Hua.
3. Adapted from Master Hsuan Hua's translation of *The Vajra Prajna Paramita Sutra: A General Explanation*, 2nd ed. (Burlingame, CA: Buddhist Text Translation Society, 2003).

Chapter Sixteen: An Intimate World

1. Bill McKibben (born 1960) is an American environmentalist and author who writes extensively on the impact of global warming. In 2010, the *Boston Globe* called him "probably the nation's leading environmentalist." He currently leads the organization 350.org.
2. Chris Jordan is an artist based in Seattle, Washington, who is best known for his large-scale works depicting mass consumption and waste, particularly garbage. He has been called "the 'it' artist of the green movement."
3. According to the UN Environment Programme, plastic debris causes the deaths of more than a million seabirds every year, as well as more than 100,000 marine mammals. Syringes, cigarette lighters, and toothbrushes have been found inside the stomachs of dead seabirds, which mistake them for food. Plastic is believed to constitute 90 percent of all garbage floating in the ocean. The UN Environment Programme estimated in 2006 that every square mile of ocean contains 46,000 pieces of floating plastic,
4. Victoria Sloan Jordan, "Midway V Poem—On Witnessing an Albatross Feeding," published February 10, 2012. www.midwayjourney.com/2012/02/10/midway-v-poem-on-witnessing-an-albatross-feeding/
5. *Tudong* is the Thai word for the ancient practice of pilgrimage and walking undertaken by renunciant monastics stretching back into the mists of time.

Bibliography

Amaro, Ajahn, and Ajahn Pasanno. *The Island: An Anthology of the Buddha's Teachings on Nibbana*. Redwood Valley, CA: Abhayagiri Monastic Foundation, 2009.

Amaravati and Cittaviveka Buddhist Monasteries. *Freeing the Heart: Dhamma Teachings from the Nuns' Community at Amaravati & Cittaviveka Buddhist Monasteries*. Hertfordshire, England: Amaravati Publications, 2001.

Bhikkhu Bodhi, trans. *The Connected Discourses of the Buddha: A New Translation of the Samyutta Nikaya*. Somerville, MA: Wisdom Publications, 2000.

Blofeld, John. *The Zen Teaching of Huang Po: On the Transmission of Mind*. London: Rider, 1958.

Blofeld, John Eaton Calthorpe. *Bodhisattva of Compassion: The Mystical Tradition of Kuan Yin*. Boulder, CO: Shambhala, 1977.

Bodhi, Bhikkhu. *In the Buddha's words: An Anthology of Discourses from the Pali Canon*. Boston: Wisdom Publications, 2005.

Castaneda, Carlos. *Journey to Ixtlan: The Lessons of Don Juan*. New York: Simon and Schuster, 1972.

Chah, Ajahn. *Bodhinyana: A Collection of Dhamma Talks*. Ubon Ratchathani,Thailand: Sangha, Bung Wai Forest Monastery, 1982.

Chah, Ajahn. *Food for the Heart: The Collected Teachings of Ajahn Chah*. Boston: Wisdom Publications, 2002.

Dass, Ram. *Be Love Now: The Path of the Heart*. New York: HarperOne, 2010.

Dass, Ram. *Miracle of Love: Stories about Neem Karoli Baba*. New York: Dutton, 1979.

Davids, T. W. Rhys. *Dialogues of the Buddha*. London: Pali Text Society, 1910.

Frydman, Maurice, and Sudhakar S. Dikshit. *I Am That: Talks with Sri Nisargadatta Maharaj*. Durham, NC: Acorn Press, 1999.

Goldstein, Joseph. *One Dharma: the Emerging Western Buddhism*. San Francisco: HarperSanFrancisco, 2002.

Harvey, Andrew. *The Hope: A Guide to Sacred Activism*. Carlsbad, CA: Hay House, 2009.

Hua, Master Hsuan. *The Heart of Prajna Paramita Sutra*. 2nd ed. Burlingame, CA: Dharma Realm Buddhist Association, 2003.

Hua, Master Hsuan. *The Shurangama Sutra*. 2nd ed. Burlingame, CA: Buddhist Text Translation Society, 2002.

Hua, Master Hsuan. *The Vajra Prajna Paramita Sutra: A General Explanation*. 2nd ed. Burlingame, CA: Buddhist Text Translation Society, 2003.

Khenchen Thrangu, Rinpoche. *A Song for the King: Saraha on Mahamudra Meditation*. Boston: Wisdom Publications, 2006.

Kornfield, Jack. *A Path with Heart: A Guide Through the Perils and Promises of Spiritual Life*. New York: Bantam Books, 1993.

Kornfield, Jack, and Paul Breiter. *A Still Forest Pool: The Insight Meditation of Achaan Chah*. Wheaton, IL: Theosophical Publishing House, 1985.

Lessing, Doris May. *The Grass Is Singing*. New York: Crowell, 1950.

Macy, Joanna, and Molly Young Brown. *Coming Back to Life: Practices to Reconnect Our Lives, Our World*. Gabriola Island, BC, Canada: New Society Publishers, 1998.

McKibben, Bill. *Eaarth: Making a Life on a Tough New Planet*. New York: Times Books, 2010.

Michener, James A. *The Covenant*. New York: Random House, 1980.

Munindo, Ajahn. *A Dhammapada for Contemplation*. Belsay: Aruna Publications, 2006.

Nanamoli, Thera. *The Life of the Buddha, As It Appears in the Pali Canon, the Oldest Authentic Record*. Kandy, Sri Lanka: Buddhist Publication Society, 1972.

Nanananda, Bhikkhu. "Concept and Reality in Early Buddhist Thought: An Essay on *Papanca* and *Papanca-sanna-sankha*." Kandy, Sri Lanka: Buddhist Publication Society, 1971.

Nyanatiloka, Mahathera. *The Word of the Buddha: An Outline of the Teaching of the*

Buddha in the Words of the Pali Canon. 17th ed. Kandy, Sri Lanka: Buddhist Publication Society, 2001.

Paton, Alan. *Cry, the Beloved Country: A Story of Comfort in Desolation*. New York: C. Scribner's Sons, 1948.

Saddhatissa, H. *The Sutta-Nipata*. London: Curzon, 1985.

Schiff, Hilda. *Holocaust Poetry*. New York: St. Martin's Press, 1995.

Sparks, Allister Haddon. *The Mind of South Africa*. New York: Alfred A. Knopf, 1990.

Sucitto, Ajahn. *Parami: Ways to Cross Life's Floods*. Hertfordshire, England: Amaravati Publications, 2012.

Sucitto, Ajahn. *Turning the Wheel of Truth: Commentary on the Buddha's First Teaching*. Boston: Shambhala Publications, 2010.

Sumedho, Ajahn. *Cittaviveka: Teachings from the Silent Mind : With Other Narratives of the Monastic Life*. Hemel Hempstead, England: Amaravati Publications, 1992.

Sumedho, Ajahn. *Intuitive Awareness*. Hertfordshire, England: Amaravati Publications, 2004.

Sumedho, Ajahn. *Mindfulness, the Path to the Deathless: The Meditation Teaching of Venerable Ajahn Sumedho*. Hertfordshire, England: Amaravati Publications, 1987.

Sure, Heng, and Heng Ch'au. *News from True Cultivators: Letters to the Venerable Abbot Hua*. 2nd ed. Burlingame, CA: Buddhist Text Translation Society, Dharma Realm Buddhist Association, 2002.

Thanissaro, Bhikkhu. *The Wings to Awakening: An Anthology from the Pali Canon*. Barre, MA: Dhamma Dana Publications, Barre Center for Buddhist Studies, 1996.

Watson, Burton. *The Lotus Sutra*. New York: Columbia University Press, 1993.

Welwood, John. *Toward a Psychology of Awakening: Buddhism, Psychotherapy, and the Path of Personal and Spiritual Transformation*. Boston: Shambhala, 2000.

Acknowledgments

Our thanks to all who have helped us bring *Listening to the Heart* into print.

We are profoundly grateful to:

The Buddha, for his extraordinary Awakening and compassionate resolve to tirelessly set in motion the Dharma wheel, still turning to this day, 2,560 years later.

Ajahn Chah, for embodying the Buddha's teaching with fearless wisdom, deep compassion, and life-giving humor—bestowing the courage to all his disciples that "You can do this."

Ajahn Sumedho, for courageously practicing with Ajahn Chah in the Forests of Thailand, understanding the teachings, and patiently opening the "doors of the deathless" to countless Westerners who were drawn to the Forest Tradition.

Master Hsuan Hua, for embodying the majesty of the Mahayana, and introducing us to the Kuan Yin dharmas and the power of vows.

Sri Neem Karoli Baba, the great mysterious miracle-maker, for giving us faith in enlightenment and the power of love and service.

The Buddhist Elders, teachers, and monks and nuns from the Forest

School of Ajahn Chah, the City of 10,000 Buddhas, and our many fellow teachers, friends, and associates in the Insight community. Without the selfless service of those turning the Dharma wheel, our journey would not be possible.

Alison Smith from Cape Town, for patiently transcribing our talks. Thanks for invaluable editing feedback from Chantel Oosthuysen of South Africa, and Leslie Goodman from the U.S.

Andrew Harvey, for so generously opening the door for our book to be published, and for having faith in our message.

Thanks to North Atlantic Books and its fabulous team, for its commitment to publish books supporting the evolutionary shift of our times. Thanks for the kindly encouragement of Hisae Matsuda, and to Teja Watson for taking our manuscript over the finish line, and thanks to Mary Ann Casler for the beautiful cover design of *Listening to the Heart*.

Index

C

D

E

J

K

L

M

About the Authors

Kittisaro (Harry Randolph Weinberg)

Originally from Tennessee, Kittisaro graduated from Princeton as a Rhodes Scholar and went on to study at Oxford before going to Thailand to ordain with Ajahn Chah in 1976. He was a monk for fifteen years, and during that time he taught extensively, was involved in the training of monks, and helped found Chithurst Monastery and Devon Vihara in the United Kingdom. He disrobed in 1991 and since then has taught internationally in the United States, Europe, South Africa, and Israel. He has studied and practiced Chan and Pure Land Buddhism for thirty-five years, informed by the teachings of Master Hsuan Hua. Kittisaro has completed two silent yearlong self-retreats and is currently writing in between his teaching engagements.

Thanissara (Linda Mary Peacock)

Hailing from a London Anglo-Irish family, Thanissara started Buddhist practice in the Burmese tradition of Sayagyi U Ba Khin in 1975. She was inspired to ordain after meeting Ajahn Chah and spent twelve years as a Buddhist nun, during which time she was a founding member of Chithurst Monastery and Amaravati Buddhist Monastery. She was also co-initiator of events for children and families at Amaravati. Thanissara has facilitated meditation retreats internationally for the past twenty-five years and has an MA in Mindfulness-Based Psychotherapy Practice from Middlesex University and the Karuna Institute in the UK. She has written two poetry books, *Garden of the Midnight Rosary* and *The Heart of the Bitter Almond Hedge Sutra*.

Kittisaro and Thanissara have been married since 1992. They spent seven years as guiding teachers of the Buddhist Retreat Centre KwaZulu South Africa, and then went on to found Dharmagiri Hermitage on the border of Lesotho and South Africa. They cofounded several HIV/AIDS Outreach Programs and currently support Kulungile Project, a home for children left vulnerable due to HIV/AIDS, run by Sister Abegail Ntleko, winner of the Dalai Lama Unsung Hero Award. They lead retreats in Europe, Canada, the U.S., and Israel, and regularly host one- to three-month retreats at Dharmagiri Hermitage. They are guiding teachers of Chattanooga Insight and are affiliated teachers of Spirit Rock Insight Meditation Center and Insight Meditation Society USA.